P9-EEU-084

Also by the Editors of *Cook's Illustrated*

The America's Test Kitchen Family Cookbook

The Best Recipe Series:
The *Cook's Illustrated* Guide to Grilling and Barbecue
Best American Side Dishes
The New Best Recipe
Cover & Bake
Steaks, Chops, Roasts, and Ribs
Baking Illustrated
Restaurant Favorites at Home
Perfect Vegetables
The Quick Recipe
Italian Classics
American Classics
Soups & Stews

America's Test Kitchen Live!
Inside America's Test Kitchen
Here in America's Test Kitchen
The America's Test Kitchen Cookbook

The Best Kitchen Quick Tips

The Complete Book of Pasta and Noodles
The *Cook's Illustrated* Complete Book of Poultry

How to Barbecue and Roast on the Grill
How to Cook Chicken Breasts
How to Cook Chinese Favorites
How to Cook Garden Vegetables
How to Cook Shrimp and Other Shellfish
How to Grill
How to Make an American Layer Cake
How to Make Cookie Jar Favorites
How to Make Ice Cream
How to Make Muffins, Biscuits, and Scones
How to Make Pasta Sauces
How to Make Pot Pies and Casseroles
How to Make Salad
How to Make Sauces and Gravies
How to Make Simple Fruit Desserts
How to Make Soup
How to Make Stew
How to Sauté

To order any of our books, visit us at
www.cooksillustrated.com
www.americastestkitchen.com
or call us at 800-611-0759

COOKING AT HOME WITH AMERICA'S TEST KITCHEN

COOKING AT HOME WITH

America's
TEST KITCHEN

BY THE EDITORS OF
COOK'S ILLUSTRATED

ILLUSTRATIONS
John Burgoyne

PHOTOGRAPHY
Daniel J. van Ackere
Carl Tremblay

AMERICA'S TEST KITCHEN
BROOKLINE, MASSACHUSETTS

America's Test Kitchen
17 Station Street
Brookline, MA 02445

ISBN 0-936184-89-2
Library of Congress Cataloging-in-Publication Data
The Editors of *Cook's Illustrated*

Cooking at Home with America's Test Kitchen: The All-New 2006 Companion to the Public Television Series
1st Edition

ISBN 0-936184-89-2 (hardback): $34.95
1. Cooking. 1. Title
2005

Manufactured in the United States of America

10 9 8 7 6 5 4 3 2 1

Distributed by America's Test Kitchen
17 Station Street, Brookline, MA 02445

Senior Editor: Lori Galvin
Editorial Assistant: Elizabeth Wray Emery
Series and Jacket Designer: Amy Klee
Book Production Specialist: Ron Bilodeau
Photographers: Carl Tremblay (color and selected black-and-white food photography);
Daniel J. van Ackere (documentary and silhouette photography);
Front Cover Photograph: John Goodman
Illustrator: John Burgoyne
Senior Production Manager: Jessica Lindheimer Quirk
Copyeditor: Cheryl Redmond
Proofreader: Holly Hartman
Indexer: Elizabeth Parson

CONTENTS

PREFACE BY CHRISTOPHER KIMBALL ix

WELCOME TO AMERICA'S TEST KITCHEN xi

A NOTE ON CONVERSIONS 344

INDEX 348

CHAPTER 1
Eggs for Brunch 3

CHAPTER 2
Tex-Mex Favorites 15

CHAPTER 3
South-of-the-Border Soups 27

CHAPTER 4
Cooking with Squash 39

CHAPTER 5
Dinner on a Dime 49

CHAPTER 6
One-Skillet Dinners 61

CHAPTER 7
American Classics 71

CHAPTER 8
Meat and Potatoes 85

CHAPTER 9
High-Roast Chicken Dinner 95

CHAPTER 10
Let's Talk Turkey 107

CHAPTER 11
Pork Chops and Tenderloin 133

CHAPTER 12
Fish Steaks 101 147

CHAPTER 13
Seafood Classics 163

CHAPTER 14
Italian Classics 175

CHAPTER 15
Two Curry Traditions 185

CHAPTER 16
Asian Chicken Classics 201

CHAPTER 17
Paella Party 211

CHAPTER 18
Grilled Pizza 221

CHAPTER 19
Grill-Roasted Pork Loin 245

CHAPTER 20
Pulled Pork and Cornbread 259

CHAPTER 21
Rethinking Barbecued Chicken 273

CHAPTER 22
Summer Fruit Desserts 285

CHAPTER 23
Deep-Dish Apple Pie 297

CHAPTER 24
Cookies 313

CHAPTER 25
Old-Fashioned Birthday Cake 325

CHAPTER 26
German Chocolate Cake 333

PREFACE

In Memory of Dean Gaskill, Director of Photography

ONCE OR TWICE PER YEAR I AM ASKED TO PREACH AT OUR small Methodist church in Vermont. The reason is well known to the entire congregation, a group that might number a couple of dozen folks on a good Sunday. If our minister, Reverend Bort, conscripts a real preacher, it costs the church $50. Members of the congregation who are willing to stand at the pulpit and make the best of it offer their services gratis. It's simply a matter of husbanding scarce resources.

I have given a number of sermons over the years, many of them related to food and cooking, but have always steered clear of the common Sunday message, "Why Bad Things Happen to Good People." The reason is simple. I have no idea why bad things happen to the best of us.

All of this is an odd preface for a book of cookery, one that contains the recipes, equipment tests, tastings, tips, and science information found in the sixth season of our public television show, *America's Test Kitchen.* But the notion of bad things happening to good people is unfortunately apt in this case. Dean Gaskill, our director of photography, was taken seriously ill this year and died in late August. He leaves his wife, Sylvia, and son, Justin.

To appreciate Dean's contribution to *America's Test Kitchen,* you need to understand that none of us in front of the camera had the least idea what we were doing back in 2000 (our first season). Dean was the senior crew member, the guy who set the tone for the whole show, and his equanimity in the face of horrid performances made the show possible. So many times, I remember standing in front of the cameras to introduce the show when I was tired, ill at ease, or simply not communicating with the audience. Dean would smile like a warm, concerned uncle, make a quiet suggestion, and then push me forward into a better take. I came to look to Dean more than anyone else in the studio for support and advice. I could just glance at his face—checking for a mournful gaze or, more hopefully, a wry smile—to determine whether I was going to be home for dinner or not. Most nights, I arrived home well after the kids were in bed.

You can like our show or not, make our recipes or not, or prefer any number of livelier food shows on other channels, but please know that *America's Test Kitchen* is not a "show" or a "performance" as such. We are indeed a family of cooks, cameramen, editors, producers, sound guys, make-up artists, and an army of test kitchen staff who get together one month per year to cook for our television audience. The cooks are the same folks who cook in our facility every day, the kitchen is real, and what happens to us during the rest of the year matters as well. What happened this year was hard—Dean left us, but he is still part of our family, still part of the tradition of *America's Test Kitchen.*

Dean didn't boast or talk a good game about camera work or the technical trivia of television. He was a quiet, thoughtful man. But he sure knew what had to be done and how to do it. And, of course, that makes me wonder once again why bad things happen to good people. I guess that someday I am going to have to preach a sermon about it, but after the loss of Dean Gaskill, a man who meant so much to so many, I am afraid that I will be unable to find a satisfactory answer. To his family, I say that your loss is beyond words. On behalf of the staff of *America's Test Kitchen,* I say that Dean will always be part of our extended family. And to Dean, I say that each and every time I look into the blank face of a camera, I will see you looking back, in the twilight, knowing that your faith in us will not pass. It is an unexpected comfort to those of us left behind, knowing that good people endure in our hearts, in our minds, and in our undiminished hopes for the future.

Christopher Kimball
Founder and editor, *Cook's Illustrated*
Host, *America's Test Kitchen*
Brookline, Massachusetts, 2005

WELCOME TO AMERICA'S TEST KITCHEN

AMERICA'S TEST KITCHEN IS A VERY REAL 2,500-SQUARE-foot kitchen located just outside of Boston. It is the home of *Cook's Illustrated* and is the Monday through Friday destination of more than two dozen test cooks, editors, food scientists, tasters, photographers, and cookware specialists. Our mission is to test recipes over and over again until we understand how and why they work and until we arrive at the best version.

Our television show highlights the best recipes developed in the test kitchen during the past year—those recipes that our test kitchen staff makes at home time and time again. These recipes are accompanied by our most exhaustive equipment tests and our most interesting food tastings.

Christopher Kimball, the founder and editor of *Cook's Illustrated* magazine, is host of the show and asks the questions you might ask. It's the job of our two chefs, Julia Collin Davison and Bridget Lancaster, to demonstrate our recipes. And this year, two more chefs from the test kitchen, Rebecca Hays and Erika Bruce, joined the show. The chefs show Chris what works, what doesn't, and explain why. In the process, they discuss (and show us) the best and worst examples from our development process—the pizza that stuck to the grill grate, the mashed potatoes that curdled, and the cookies that overbaked.

Adam Ried, our equipment guru, shares the highlights from our detailed testing process in Equipment Corner segments. He brings with him our favorite (and least favorite) gadgets and tools. He tells you which knives performed best in a dozen kitchen tests and shows why many turkey gadgets are nearly worthless.

Jack Bishop is our ingredient expert. He has Chris taste our favorite (and least favorite) brands of common food products—everything from steak and Parmesan cheese to Dijon mustard and supermarket stuffings. Chris may not always enjoy these exercises (butter alternatives are not that much fun to taste), but he usually learns something as Jack explains what makes one brand superior to another.

Although there are just seven cooks and editors who appear on the television show, another 50 people worked to make the show a reality. Location manager Jim McCormack spent months to ensure that taping would run smoothly. Executive chefs Erin McMurrer, Dawn Yanagihara, and Sean Lawler ran the "back kitchen," where all the food that appeared on camera originated. Along with the on-air crew, Erin and Dawn also planned and organized the 26 television episodes shot in May 2005. Melissa Baldino researched the Q & A segments and historical facts, and Garth Clingingsmith organized the tasting and equipment segments.

During the actual filming, chefs Meredith Butcher, Katie Henderson, Jeremy Sauer, and Diane Unger were in the kitchen from early in the morning to late at night helping Erin, Dawn, and Sean cook all the food needed on set. Nadia Domeq was charged with the Herculean task of making sure all the ingredients we needed were on hand. Kitchen assistants Kacey Gault, Katie Barreira, Maria Elena Delgado, and Ena Guidel also worked long hours. Charles Kelsey, Rachel Toomey, Nina West, and Elizabeth Bomze

helped coordinate the efforts of the kitchen with the television set by readying props, equipment, and food.

The staff of A La Carte Communications turned our recipes, tastings, testings, and science experiments into a lively television show. Special thanks to executive producers Geoffrey Drummond and Nat Katzman; director Herb Sevush; coordinating producer Richard Dooley; director of photography Jan Maliszewski; and editor Hugh Elliot. We also appreciate the hard work of the video production team, including Stephen Hussar, Michael McEachern, Peter Dingle, Eliat B. Goldman, Gilles Morin, Brenda Coffey, Tommy Hamilton, Patrick Ruth, Jack McPhee, Aaron Frutman, Joshua Dreyfus, Mark Romanelli, Damali Hicks, and Paul Swensen.

We also would like to thank Hope Reed, who handles station relations, and the team at American Public Television that presents the show: Cynthia Fenniman, Chris Funkhauser, Judy Barlow, and Tom Davison. Thanks also for production support from DGA Productions, Boston; Paul Swensen Productions, Santa Rosa, California; and Zebra Productions, New York.

Thermador, Kohler, Vendange Wines, Viva Towels, Formula 409, Foodsaver, and Cooking.com helped underwrite the show and we thank them for their support. Fresh produce was supplied for the show by Olgo Russo at A. Russo & Sons of Watertown, Massachusetts. Equipment for the show was supplied by Mark Cutler at Mahoney's Garden Center of Brighton, Massachusetts, and DuPont Corian. Catering for the cast and crew was provided by Basil Tree Gourmet and Natural Catering of Somerville, Massachusetts.

We hope this book gives you an inside look at America's Test Kitchen. We are passionate about our work, and we hope you enjoy our recipes as well as reading about the process by which they were created. Our mission is pretty simple. We want to help make you a better cook. We believe that our television show and this book will do just that. If you have comments or questions about the show or the book, contact us at www.americastestkitchen.com. Visit www.cooksillustrated.com for information about *Cook's Illustrated* magazine.

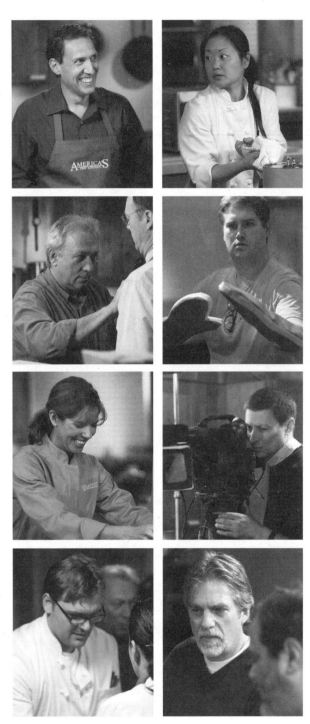

COOKING AT HOME WITH AMERICA'S TEST KITCHEN

A quick grind of pepper and our frittata mixture
is ready to be whisked and cooked.

EGGS FOR brunch

CHAPTER 1

Hosting a brunch involves much more than preparing the food—you're filling coffee mugs, passing out juice and pastries, and trying to catch up with guests. Flipping omelets to order at the stove only complicates matters. Instead, choose an egg dish that doesn't require the talents of a short-order cook. Frittatas and quiche are just the sort of hassle-free egg dishes that fit the bill.

A frittata is basically an Italian-style omelet. Most frittatas, however, are the thin sort, best served in narrow wedges to be nibbled with drinks, or are just enough to serve two as part of a meal. We wanted a heartier frittata—just as filling as a stuffed omelet, but a whole lot easier to prepare and serve—especially to a group. Thick frittatas, in our experience, aren't always foolproof—they can dry out on the edges before the interior is cooked through. We'd need to find a way to ensure a moist but cooked frittata.

Quiche is a slightly more ambitious dish because it requires a pastry crust. Quiche fillings can be problematic as well. They can sometimes be dry and rubbery or so wet that the crust underneath becomes soggy and leaden. We wanted a quiche without these drawbacks.

Whichever classic egg dish you choose for your next brunch, you can be confident that these recipes won't disappoint.

IN THIS CHAPTER

THE RECIPES

Asparagus, Ham, and Gruyère Frittata
Leek, Prosciutto, and Goat Cheese Frittata
Bacon, Potato, and Cheddar Frittata
Frittata with Broccoli Rabe, Sun-Dried Tomatoes, and Fontina

Quiche Lorraine
Crabmeat Quiche
Leek and Goat Cheese Quiche
Ham and Asparagus Quiche

Pie Dough for Prebaked Pie Shell

TASTING LAB

Supermarket Bacons

THICK AND HEARTY FRITTATA

WHAT WE WANTED: A thick, hearty frittata that's cooked through but not dried out.

A thick and hearty frittata is more challenging to cook than a regular thin frittata. When done right, a thick frittata should have a pleasing balance of egg to filling. The eggs should be cooked perfectly, firm yet moist, and be framed by a supportive browned crust. But too often, a thick frittata ends up as a lackluster, open-faced omelet lacking in height, flavor, and visual appeal. So why bother? When you're serving frittata as a main course for at least six people, a hearty frittata makes sense. No one wants to be at the stove, making thin frittatas in batches to serve a hungry crowd.

Unable to find a single cookbook version that we liked, we cobbled together a starter recipe. This required a bit of decision-making about the size of the pan and the number of eggs. Ten eggs, believe it or not, produced an insubstantial frittata if serving six hungry people. That meant an even dozen was in order, and we had to try to fit them all into a 12-inch skillet. It quickly became clear that 3 cups of cooked vegetables and meat would provide the best balance of filling to eggs, but we decided to develop a cooking method before worrying about the exact composition of the filling.

Traditional thin frittatas are cooked on the stovetop over low heat, without stirring, to allow a bottom crust to develop. When the bottom has browned and the eggs are almost set, the top is briefly cooked by flipping the frittata over in the skillet or running it under the broiler. Would one of these methods work with our decidedly un-thin frittata? After a full 15 minutes on the stovetop, the eggs in the frittata were still too runny on top. We never dared to try the flip. The broiler did a fine job on the top, but not the bottom. The eggs had spent so much time on the stovetop that the bottom had developed a thick, tough crust. Less time on the burner and more under the broiler translated to an undercooked center or, worse, a blackened, blistery top.

We reasoned that so many eggs might require more moderate heat to cook evenly. This time around, after adding the eggs to the skillet, we transferred the pan to a moderate 350-degree oven. After 15 minutes, the frittata had puffed and was cooked through. But it was very dry and had an anemic-looking surface. (We were serving this frittata top-side up; flipping it onto a serving platter was awkward.) Higher oven temperatures added some color and, in reducing the cooking time, made for a moister frittata, but the eggs were spongy, like an overcooked custard.

Frustrated, we stopped cooking to assess the situation. Of all the methods we had tried, the most promising was the traditional stovetop-to-broiler method. To reduce the time on the stovetop (the bottom of the frittata had overcooked in our earlier test), we stirred the eggs over medium heat to cook them quickly yet evenly. Then, with the eggs still on the wet side, we slid the skillet under the broiler. Nicely puffed and brown, this frittata was light, not spongy. The stirring had both cooked the eggs evenly and kept them fluffy. The broiler finished the job without overcooking them.

Repeated tries with this method did turn up a flaw. If the skillet was left under the broiler for a minute too long, the eggs crossed the line from properly cooked to overdone. Because every broiler is slightly different, we felt the need to install a failsafe step in the recipe. We decided to take the frittata out of the oven when the top had puffed and browned but the eggs in the center were still slightly wet. Then we let the frittata rest for five minutes in the skillet, allowing the residual heat to finish the cooking. This technique gave us perfectly cooked eggs every time. Now it was time to turn to the filling.

Most frittata recipes call for cheese. We tested shredded Parmesan, which tasted fine but was too dry. Gruyère, a higher-moisture cheese, was much better. We also had luck with cheddar, goat cheese, and fontina. One of the test cooks suggested cubing the cheese rather than shredding it. This was a nice touch; little pockets of melted cheese throughout

ASPARAGUS, HAM, AND GRUYÈRE FRITTATA

Makes one 12-inch frittata, serving 6 to 8

An ovensafe nonstick 12-inch skillet is a must for this recipe and the variations that follow. Because broilers vary so much in intensity, watch the frittata carefully as it cooks.

12	large eggs
3	tablespoons half-and-half
	Salt and ground black pepper
2	teaspoons olive oil
½	pound asparagus, trimmed of tough ends, spears cut on the bias into ¼-inch pieces
1	medium shallot, minced (about 3 tablespoons)
4	ounces ¼-inch-thick deli ham, cut into ½-inch cubes (about ¾ cup)
3	ounces Gruyère cheese, cut into ¼-inch cubes (about ¾ cup)

the frittata meant a more varied texture. (The goat cheese was best crumbled.) Although adding dairy other than cheese to frittatas is not traditional, we tested small amounts of heavy cream, half-and-half, and whole milk. Half-and-half was the winner, adding a touch of creaminess. (Milk turned the frittata watery, and heavy cream was too rich.)

Most any vegetable or meat can be added to a frittata, with two caveats: The food must be cut into small pieces, and it must be precooked to drive off excess moisture and fat. The latter was easy enough to do in the same skillet that would eventually hold the eggs. While many recipes claim that frittatas can be eaten cold, we prefer them on the hotter side; this keeps the cheese pleasantly gooey and the eggs from losing too much moisture.

WHAT WE LEARNED: Stirring the eggs on the stovetop hastens cooking without overbrowning the bottom and encourages a fluffy texture. To prevent overcooking, remove the frittata just before it's done and allow the residual heat of the pan to finish cooking it through.

1. Adjust an oven rack to the upper-middle position, about 5 inches from the heating element; heat the broiler. Whisk the eggs, half-and-half, ½ teaspoon salt, and ¼ teaspoon pepper in a medium bowl until well combined, about 30 seconds. Set the eggs aside.

2. Heat the oil in a 12-inch ovensafe nonstick skillet over medium heat until shimmering; add the asparagus and cook, stirring occasionally, until lightly browned and almost tender, about 3 minutes. Add the shallot and ham and cook until the shallot softens slightly, about 2 minutes. Stir the Gruyère into the eggs; add the egg mixture to the skillet and cook, using a spatula to stir and scrape the bottom of the skillet, until large curds form and the spatula begins to leave a wake but the eggs are still very wet, about 2 minutes. Shake the skillet to distribute the eggs evenly; cook without stirring for 30 seconds to let the bottom set.

3. Slide the skillet under the broiler and broil until the frittata has risen and the surface is puffed and spotty brown, 3 to 4 minutes; when cut into with a paring knife, the eggs should be slightly wet and runny. Remove the skillet from the oven and let stand 5 minutes to finish cooking; using the spatula, loosen the frittata from the skillet and slide onto a platter or cutting board. Cut into wedges and serve.

LEEK, PROSCIUTTO, AND GOAT CHEESE FRITTATA

Makes one 12-inch frittata, serving 6 to 8

The goat cheese will crumble more easily when it is chilled, straight from the refrigerator.

```
12  large eggs
 3  tablespoons half-and-half
    Salt and ground black pepper
 2  tablespoons unsalted butter
 2  small leeks, white and light green parts halved
    lengthwise, washed, and sliced thin (about
    3 cups)
 3  ounces very thinly sliced prosciutto, cut into
    ½-inch-wide strips
 ¼  cup chopped fresh basil leaves
 4  ounces goat cheese, crumbled (about 1 cup)
```

1. Adjust an oven rack to the upper-middle position, about 5 inches from the heating element; heat the broiler. Whisk the eggs, half-and-half, ½ teaspoon salt, and ¼ teaspoon pepper in a medium bowl until well combined, about 30 seconds. Set the eggs aside.

2. Heat the butter in a 12-inch ovensafe nonstick skillet over medium heat until the foaming subsides. Add the leeks and ¼ teaspoon salt; reduce the heat to low and cook covered, stirring occasionally, until softened, 8 to 10 minutes. Stir the prosciutto, basil, and half of the goat cheese into the eggs; add the egg mixture to the skillet and cook, using a spatula to stir and scrape the bottom of the skillet, until

large curds form and the spatula begins to leave a wake but the eggs are still very wet, about 2 minutes. Shake the skillet to distribute the eggs evenly; cook without stirring for 30 seconds to let the bottom set.

3. Distribute the remaining goat cheese evenly over the frittata. Slide the skillet under the broiler and broil until the frittata has risen and the surface is puffed and spotty brown, 3 to 4 minutes; when cut into with a paring knife, the eggs should be slightly wet and runny. Remove the skillet from the oven and let stand 5 minutes to finish cooking; using the spatula, loosen the frittata from the skillet and slide onto a platter or cutting board. Cut into wedges and serve.

BACON, POTATO, AND CHEDDAR FRITTATA

Makes one 12-inch frittata, serving 6 to 8

Although we like Yukon Golds best, regular baking potatoes are also good in this recipe.

```
12  large eggs
 3  tablespoons half-and-half
    Salt and ground black pepper
 8  ounces bacon (about 8 slices), cut crosswise
    into ¼-inch pieces
 1  pound Yukon Gold potatoes, peeled and cut
    into ½-inch cubes
 4  ounces cheddar cheese, cut into ¼-inch cubes
    (about ¾ cup)
 3  scallions, sliced thin on the bias (about ⅓ cup)
```

1. Adjust an oven rack to the upper-middle position, about 5 inches from the heating element; heat the broiler. Whisk the eggs, half-and-half, ½ teaspoon salt, and ¼ teaspoon pepper in a medium bowl until well combined, about 30 seconds. Set the eggs aside.

2. Fry the bacon in a 12-inch ovensafe nonstick skillet over medium heat until crisp, about 9 minutes. Using a slotted spoon, transfer the bacon to paper towel–lined plate; pour off all but 1 tablespoon of bacon fat. Add the potatoes to the skillet and cook, stirring occasionally, until golden brown and tender, 15 to 20 minutes. Stir the cheddar, scallions, and bacon into the eggs; add the egg mixture to the skillet and cook, using a spatula to stir and scrape the bottom of the skillet, until large curds form and the spatula begins to leave a wake but the eggs are still very wet, about 2 minutes. Shake the skillet to distribute the eggs evenly; cook without stirring for 30 seconds to let the bottom set.

3. Slide the skillet under the broiler and broil until the frittata has risen and the surface is puffed and spotty brown, 3 to 4 minutes; when cut into with a paring knife, the eggs should be slightly wet and runny. Remove the skillet from the oven and let stand 5 minutes to finish cooking; using the spatula, loosen the frittata from the skillet and slide onto a platter or cutting board. Cut into wedges and serve.

FRITTATA WITH BROCCOLI RABE, SUN-DRIED TOMATOES, AND FONTINA

Makes one 12-inch frittata, serving 6 to 8

Although Fontina d'Aosta is delicious served on its own, choose the more reasonably priced regular Italian fontina (about $8 per pound) for this recipe.

12	large eggs
3	tablespoons half-and-half
	Salt and ground black pepper
2	teaspoons olive oil
8	ounces broccoli rabe, washed, trimmed, and cut into 1-inch pieces (about 3 cups)
1	medium garlic clove, minced or pressed through a garlic press (about 1 teaspoon)
⅛	teaspoon red pepper flakes
3	ounces fontina cheese, cut into ¼-inch cubes (about ¾ cup)
3	ounces drained oil-packed sun-dried tomatoes, chopped coarse (about ¼ cup)

1. Adjust an oven rack to the upper-middle position, about 5 inches from the heating element; heat the broiler. Whisk the eggs, half-and-half, ½ teaspoon salt, and ¼ teaspoon pepper in a medium bowl until well combined, about 30 seconds. Set the eggs aside.

2. Heat the oil in a 12-inch ovensafe nonstick skillet over medium heat until shimmering; add the broccoli rabe and ¼ teaspoon salt and cook until beginning to brown and soften, 6 to 8 minutes. Add the garlic and pepper flakes and cook until fragrant, about 30 seconds. Stir the fontina and sun-dried tomatoes into the eggs; add the egg mixture to the skillet and cook, using a spatula to stir and scrape the bottom of the skillet, until large curds form and the spatula begins to leave a wake but the eggs are still very wet, about 2 minutes. Shake the skillet to distribute the eggs evenly; cook without stirring for 30 seconds to let the bottom set.

3. Slide the skillet under the broiler and broil until the frittata has risen and the surface is puffed and spotty brown, 3 to 4 minutes; when cut into with a paring knife, the eggs should be slightly wet and runny. Remove the skillet from the oven and let stand 5 minutes to finish cooking; using the spatula, loosen the frittata from the skillet and slide onto a platter or cutting board. Cut into wedges and serve.

TASTING LAB: Supermarket Bacons

FOOD ENTHUSIASTS AND THE MEDIA HAVE MADE A FUSS lately over the fact that retail bacon sales in the United States have risen sharply, nearly 50 percent over the last couple of years. We wondered how 10 popular national brands would stack up in a side-by-side blind tasting. We focused our tasting on the lowest common denominator—plain, regular-cut bacon—leaving aside center cut, thick and thin cut, flavored, specialty wood smoked, low salt, reduced fat, precooked, and microwave-ready. We did, however, include one nitrite-free "natural" sample because it is popular at our local natural food store.

All bacon is made from pork belly. Fresh bellies can weigh as little as 10 pounds or as much as 25 pounds. The spare ribs are removed from the belly's interior, the skin is taken off the exterior, and the remaining slab is trimmed for further processing into bacon.

The next step is curing, which is generally done in one of two ways. Many small producers of artisan (aka smokehouse or premium) bacon choose to dry-cure by rubbing the slab with a dry mixture of seasonings (which always includes salt and sugar). Large producers usually inject the slabs with a liquid brine containing salt, sugar, and sometimes liquid smoke for flavor; sodium phosphate for moisture retention during processing and cooking; sodium ascorbate or sodium erythorbate to accelerate the curing process and promote color retention; and a curing salt that includes sodium nitrite to stave off bacteria and set flavor and color characteristics. Once the cure has been applied or injected, the slabs are hung. If a dry cure has been applied, this process could stretch up to one week. Curing with an injected brine can be completed in a mere one to three hours and so is quite cost-efficient.

The final step is thermal processing, which can take as few as four to five hours or as many as 24, depending on the processor. During thermal processing, the cured pork bellies are smoked and partially cooked to an internal temperature of roughly 130 degrees, after which they finally merit the term "bacon." The bacon is chilled to approximately 24 degrees, pressed to square it off for uniform slicing, sliced, and packaged. A package of regular-cut bacon usually contains between eighteen and twenty-two slices of $\frac{1}{16}$-inch-thick slices per pound, whereas a package of thick-cut bacon, sometimes called country style, contains twelve to sixteen $\frac{1}{8}$-inch-thick slices per pound.

Of the 10 brands we tasted, only one product, the nitrite-free Applegate Farms Sunday Bacon, took tasters by surprise. Complaints arose about its unexpectedly pale color and particularly mild flavor, which led to a rating of "not recommended." A little knowledge of nitrites explains these characteristics. Sodium nitrite helps fix the red shade of the meat from its raw state by combining with the pigment myoglobin. According to Jay Wenther, director of science and technology for the American Association of Meat Processors, nitrites also contribute to bacon's characteristic cured flavor. "Nitrite-free bacon will both look and taste different from traditional bacon," he said. Having conducted hundreds of blind tastings over the years, our test kitchen has found that most folks prefer the familiar to the unfamiliar. Although Applegate received positive ratings from a couple of tasters, for most of us, nitrite-free bacon is clearly an acquired taste.

For the most part our tasters liked the other brands well enough to recommend them all, with the exception of the nitrite-free bacon. The highest-rated brand among them was Farmland, which tasters picked out as particularly meaty, full flavored, and smoky. Furthermore, neither of the two other prominent flavors in bacon—salt and sweet—dominated.

We wondered why our tasters rated Farmland the meatiest bacon in the pack. Our cadre of experts pointed out that because pork bellies are a natural product, there is no way to guarantee a perfectly consistent ratio of meat to fat from pound to pound of bacon. A simple check of many packages of the same brands of bacon confirmed that fact.

To get an accurate measure of the relative meatiness of our winning brand, Farmland, and to see how it stacked up against the least meaty brand in the group, Oscar Mayer, we sent both samples to our local food laboratory. The lab ground 3 pounds of each brand and then analyzed them for protein (lean), fat, and moisture. Sure enough, the lab confirmed our tasters' observations. Farmland had 15 percent more protein and almost 17 percent less fat than Oscar Mayer.

Smoky flavor, which is a defining characteristic of bacon, was another important factor in Farmland's success. Tasters appreciated assertive smoke, and Farmland was ranked the smokiest sample of all. Processors can give bacon smoky flavor in one (or both) of two ways: adding liquid smoke flavoring to the liquid brine or applying real smoke during thermal processing (the thermal processing "unit" is also called the smokehouse). Farmland uses the real-smoke method.

Rating Bacons

TWENTY-FOUR MEMBERS OF THE AMERICA'S TEST KITCHEN STAFF TASTED 10 BRANDS OF "REGULAR SLICED" bacon all cooked to the same degree of doneness. Bacons are listed in order of preference based on their scores in this tasting. All brands are available in supermarkets nationwide.

RECOMMENDED

Farmland Hickory Smoked Bacon

$3.99 for I pound

This "very meaty," "full-flavored" bacon (from a farm family cooperative) led the pack. Tasters noted its favorable balance of saltiness and sweetness, "good smoke flavor," and "crispy yet hearty" texture.

RECOMMENDED

Boar's Head Brand Naturally Smoked Sliced Bacon

$3.99 for I pound

Both flavor and texture were repeatedly described as "meaty." Tasters appreciated the "good balance" of flavor elements and the thick, "chewy" slices, which some claimed were "more like ham than bacon."

RECOMMENDED

Hormel Black Label Bacon, Original

$2.99 for I pound

Comments focused largely on the "hearty, balanced flavor," with a meatiness (second only to Farmland) that some likened to Serrano ham and prosciutto. A couple of tasters noted "sweet," "maple-like" flavors.

RECOMMENDED

Armour Original Premium Bacon, Hickory Smoked

$3.99 for I pound

For many, "too much sweetness" over-shadowed what some characterized as a "nice smoky flavor." This bacon had an especially low salt score, which may also have been the root of comments such as "quite bland."

RECOMMENDED

Smithfield Premium Bacon, Naturally Hickory Smoked

$3.99 for I pound

While many tasters appreciated the smokiness of this sample, some objected to it, with comments such as "chemical," "fake smoke flavor," and "like eating a campfire."

RECOMMENDED

Oscar Mayer Naturally Hardwood-Smoked Bacon

$4.99 for I pound

Nearly as expensive as some premium bacons, yet slices were considered so thin that they "disintegrate on your tongue." This sample did find fans for its "good saltiness" and "nice full flavor," yet some others found it lacking in meatiness, yawning "plain Jane."

RECOMMENDED

John Morrell Hardwood Smoked Bacon

$3.99 for I pound

Tipped the scales in perceived sweetness and fat and considered not terribly meaty. Many tasters noted a favorable balance of salt and sugar, but others felt it was "too rich," owing to a "greasy," "fatty" texture.

RECOMMENDED

Plumrose Premium Bacon, Old-Fashioned Hardwood Smoked

$3.99 for I pound

According to the label, this bacon had less sugar than most others. Salt fanciers thought it had "great flavor," but a few complained that it was "too salty" and "hammy." The slices were also too thin for many tasters.

RECOMMENDED

Jones Country Carved, Hickory Smoked Sliced Bacon

$4.49 for I pound

What some tasters considered "balanced" and "very mild" struck others as bland or "not very assertive." Thin slices cooked up "very crispy" to some, and "dry" to others.

NOT RECOMMENDED

Applegate Farms Applewood Smoked Sunday Bacon

$2.99 for I2 ounces

The only bacon in the tasting without nitrites, Applegate's "gray-green" color set it back. Though this "mild," "meaty" bacon did "taste like pork," the flavor couldn't compensate for the "muddy" color and "heavy smoke."

QUICHE

WHAT WE WANTED: A tender, buttery pastry crust filled with moist, smooth custard.

After having eaten our share of quiche with fillings so wet that they soaked the pastry, we set out to search for the ideal quiche filling formula. In our quest, we tried every probable and improbable custard combination, from whole eggs and whole milk to whole eggs with half-and-half to whole eggs with half milk and half heavy cream to eggs with several added yolks and all heavy cream.

The leanest of these mixtures tasted just that (too lean), and we rejected it as boring, with no creamy mouthfeel. The filling made with half-and-half was not as rich as one would think because half-and-half contains just 11.7 percent butterfat; it was OK but not great. The mixture containing half whole milk (which has approximately 4 percent butterfat) and half heavy cream (with 36 percent butterfat) was significantly richer; combined, the two liquids averaged 20 percent butterfat, almost twice as much as the half-and-half filling. Whole eggs, extra yolks, and all heavy cream produced a custard that was just too much of a good thing: overpoweringly rich and too creamy, even for us.

The best mixture, a medium-rich custard with good mouthfeel, fine taste, and adequate firmness, combined two whole eggs with two yolks, one cup of milk, and one cup of heavy cream. Baked in our favorite crust, it was just what we were looking for: a custard that was creamy but not cloyingly rich, its tender skin a luscious golden brown hue. It puffed slightly while baking and settled neatly as it cooled.

Of course, baking temperature is also an important factor regulating custard texture. High heat toughens egg proteins and shrinks the albumen, separating, or curdling, the mixture and squeezing out the water instead of keeping the egg in perfect suspension. Moderate heat works best.

We tested our different quiche formulas at temperatures ranging from 325 degrees to 400 degrees. Some cooks prefer to start baking at 400 degrees for 15 minutes, then reduce the heat to 350 degrees for the remaining time. We found 350 degrees slightly slow; by the time the custard set, the top, which remained a pallid yellow, had developed into a slightly rubbery, chewy skin. On the theory that warming the liquid in the custard would shorten baking time and keep the custard smoother, we tried heating the milk to 100 degrees before whisking in the eggs. Indeed, this custard set a few minutes faster, but it was otherwise unremarkable and still had a pallid color on top. We found that baking at 375 degrees was exactly right, gentle enough to preserve the custard's creamy consistency, yet hot enough to brown the top before it dried out and became rubbery.

As a test for doneness, we advise watching the oven, not the clock, looking for a light golden brown coloring on the quiche surface, which may puff up slightly as it bakes. A knife blade inserted about 1 inch from the edge should come out clean; the center may still be slightly liquid, but internal heat will finish the baking and it will solidify when cool. If your test blade comes out clean in the center, the quiche may already be slightly overbaked and should be removed from the oven at once. Be sure to set the baked quiche on a wire rack to cool, so that air circulates all around it, preventing condensation on the bottom. Allowing the quiche to cool until it is either warm or at room temperature also lets the custard settle before serving. The cooler the quiche, the more neatly it will slice.

WHAT WE LEARNED: Use a mixture of whole eggs and egg yolks along with milk and heavy cream for a silky (but not too eggy) custard. Avoid overbaking; the quiche should jiggle a bit when removed from the oven. Cool the quiche on a wire rack to prevent condensation from building up and making the crust wet.

QUICHE LORRAINE

Serves 8

Quiche Lorraine is named after the region in France in which it originated, Alsace-Lorraine. The center of the quiche will be surprisingly soft when it comes out of the oven, but the filling will continue to set (and sink somewhat) as it cools. If the pie shell has been previously baked and cooled, place it in the heating oven for about five minutes to warm it, taking care that it does not burn. Because ingredients in the variations that follow are bulkier, the amount of custard mixture has been reduced to prevent overflowing the crust.

1	recipe Pie Dough for Prebaked Pie Shell (page 12)
8	ounces (about 8 slices) bacon, cut into ½-inch pieces
2	large eggs plus 2 large egg yolks
1	cup whole milk
1	cup heavy cream
½	teaspoon salt
½	teaspoon ground white pepper
	Pinch freshly grated nutmeg
4	ounces Gruyère cheese, grated (about 1 cup)

1. Follow the directions for partially baking the pie shell until light golden brown. Remove the pie shell from the oven but do not turn off the oven.

2. Meanwhile, fry the bacon in a skillet over medium heat until crisp, about 5 minutes. Transfer the bacon with a slotted spoon to a paper towel–lined plate. Whisk together the remaining ingredients except the Gruyère in a medium bowl.

3. Spread the Gruyère and bacon evenly over the bottom of the warm pie shell and set the shell on the oven rack. Pour the custard mixture into the pie shell (it should come to about ½ inch below the crust's rim). Bake until light golden brown and a knife blade inserted about 1 inch from the edge comes out clean and the center feels set but soft like gelatin, 32 to 35 minutes. Transfer the quiche to a wire rack to cool. Serve warm or at room temperature.

VARIATIONS

CRABMEAT QUICHE

Pick through the crabmeat carefully to remove any bits of shell.

Follow the recipe for Quiche Lorraine, reducing the quantities of milk and cream to ¾ cup each. Add 2 tablespoons dry sherry and a pinch of cayenne to the custard mixture. Replace the bacon and cheese with 8 ounces (1 cup) cooked crabmeat tossed with 2 tablespoons chopped fresh chives.

LEEK AND GOAT CHEESE QUICHE

Be sure to wash the leeks thoroughly to remove any grit.

Follow the recipe for Quiche Lorraine, reducing the quantities of milk and cream to ¾ cup each. Sauté the white parts of 2 medium leeks, washed thoroughly and cut into ½-inch dice (about 2 cups), in 2 tablespoons unsalted butter over medium heat until soft, 5 to 7 minutes. Omit the bacon; substitute 4 ounces mild goat cheese, broken into ½-inch pieces, for the Gruyère. Add the leeks to the pie shell with the goat cheese.

HAM AND ASPARAGUS QUICHE

Snap the tough ends off the asparagus before cooking them.

Follow the recipe for Quiche Lorraine, reducing the quantities of milk and cream to ¾ cup each. Blanch 8 asparagus spears, cut on the bias into ½-inch pieces (about 1 cup), in 1 quart salted boiling water until crisp-tender, about 2 minutes. Drain the asparagus thoroughly. Replace the bacon and cheese with the asparagus and 4 ounces deli ham, cut into ¼-inch dice.

TECHNIQUE: Rolling and Fitting Pie Dough

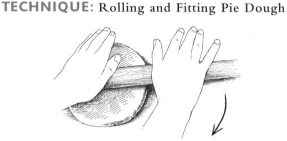

1. Using a tapered pin, roll a quarter turn, from about 2 o'clock to 5 o'clock, keeping your left hand stationary and moving the pin with your right hand.

2. Turn the dough a quarter turn and roll again as in step 1. Continue rolling until the dough is 8 or 9 inches in diameter. If necessary, lightly reflour the work surface.

3. Using a bench scraper, lift the dough onto the rolling pin, pick it up, reflour the counter, and replace the dough upside down. Keep rolling until the diameter of the dough is 3 to 4 inches wider than the pie plate.

4. Roll the dough over the pin and unroll it evenly onto the pie plate.

5. After draping the dough evenly over the pie plate, lift up the edges of the dough and ease it down into the lower creases of the pan. Press lightly to adhere the dough to the sides of the pan.

PIE DOUGH FOR PREBAKED PIE SHELL

For 1 single-crust 9-inch pie

We prefer ceramic or metal pie weights for prebaking the pie shell. If you don't own any weights, rice or dried beans can stand in, but since they're lighter than pie weights, be sure to fill up the foil-lined pie shell completely. Better yet, improvise with pennies (see page 13).

1¼	cups (6¼ ounces) unbleached all-purpose flour, plus more for rolling out the dough
1	tablespoon sugar
½	teaspoon salt
3	tablespoons vegetable shortening, chilled
4	tablespoons (½ stick) cold unsalted butter, cut into ¼-inch pieces
4–5	tablespoons ice water

1. Process the flour, sugar, and salt in a food processor until combined. Add the shortening and process until the mixture has the texture of coarse sand, about 10 seconds. Scatter the butter pieces over the flour mixture; cut the butter into the flour until the mixture is pale yellow and resembles coarse crumbs, with butter bits no larger than small peas, about ten 1-second pulses. Turn the mixture into a medium bowl.

2. Sprinkle 4 tablespoons of the ice water over the mixture. With a rubber spatula, use a folding motion to mix. Press down on the dough with the broad side of the spatula until the dough sticks together, adding up to 1 tablespoon more ice water if the dough will not come together. Flatten the dough into a 4-inch disk. Wrap in plastic and refrigerate at least 1 hour, or up to 2 days, before rolling.

3. Remove the dough from the refrigerator (if refrigerated longer than 1 hour, let stand at room temperature until malleable). Following the illustrations at left, roll the dough on a lightly floured work surface or between 2 sheets of parchment paper or plastic wrap to a 12-inch circle. Transfer the dough to a 9-inch pie plate by rolling the dough around the rolling pin and unrolling over the pan. Working around the circumference of the pie plate, ease the dough into the pan corners by gently lifting the edge of the dough with one hand while gently pressing into the pan bottom with the other hand. Trim the dough edges to extend about ½ inch beyond the rim of the pan. Fold the overhang under itself; flute the dough or press the tines of a fork against the dough to flatten it against the rim of the pie plate. Refrigerate the dough-lined pie plate until firm, about 40 minutes, then freeze until very cold, about 20 minutes.

4. Adjust an oven rack to the lower-middle position and heat the oven to 375 degrees. Remove the dough-lined pie plate from the freezer, press a doubled 12-inch piece of heavy-duty foil inside the pie shell, and fold the edges of the foil to shield the fluted edge; distribute 2 cups ceramic or metal pie weights over the foil. Bake, leaving the foil and weights in place until the dough looks dry and is light in color, 25 to 30 minutes. Carefully remove the foil and weights by gathering the corners of the foil and pulling up and out. For a partially baked crust, continue baking until light golden brown, 5 to 6 minutes; for a fully baked crust,

continue baking until deep golden brown, about 12 minutes more. Transfer to a wire rack.

TECHNIQUE: Pennies for Pie Weights

If you don't own metal or ceramic pie weights, pennies conduct heat beautifully (far better than dried beans, which are often substituted). Line the pie plate or tart pan with foil and place a couple of handfuls of pennies in the foil to hold the crust in place.

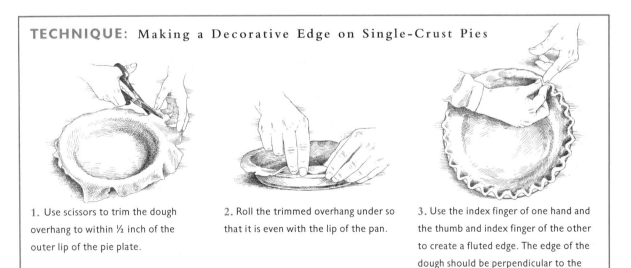

TECHNIQUE: Making a Decorative Edge on Single-Crust Pies

1. Use scissors to trim the dough overhang to within ½ inch of the outer lip of the pie plate.

2. Roll the trimmed overhang under so that it is even with the lip of the pan.

3. Use the index finger of one hand and the thumb and index finger of the other to create a fluted edge. The edge of the dough should be perpendicular to the edge of the pie plate.

In preparing quesadillas, Julia folds the tortilla around the filling, rather than stacking one tortilla on top of another, which not only makes it easier to turn and remove from the pan, but also reduces the likelihood of filling leaking out the sides.

TEX-MEX favorites

Tex-Mex food needn't be bland, greasy fare. When made right, these dishes can actually be quite fresh tasting. In this chapter, we look at a few of our favorite Tex-Mex dishes—tomato salsa, quesadillas, and beef tacos—and show just how good they can be.

Tired of watery salsa? So are we. In developing our recipe, we looked for ways to restore this classic to its fresh-from-the-garden chunky glory. Fast food chains and sports bars have corrupted the quesadilla, a simple Mexican grilled cheese sandwich, into flabby pockets overstuffed with greasy fillings. We worked to pare back the quesadilla to its humble roots. As for beef tacos, although many of us are familiar with the supermarket taco kit, complete with seasoning packet, few of us would think of eating them for dinner. Could we make a ground beef taco we'd want to eat ourselves? One thing we were sure of—our answers wouldn't be found in a taco kit.

If you've given up on eating Tex-Mex, rejecting it as second-class junk food, we urge you to give our recipes a try. We think you'll like them.

IN THIS CHAPTER

THE RECIPES

Fresh Tomato Salsa

Quesadillas
Cheddar, Bacon, and Scallion
    Quesadillas
Quesadillas with Queso Fresco
    and Roasted Peppers
Cubano Quesadillas
Corn and Black Bean Quesadillas
    with Pepper Jack Cheese

Beef Tacos

Home-Fried Taco Shells

EQUIPMENT CORNER

Quesadilla Makers

SCIENCE DESK

Why Are Some Jalapeños Spicier
    Than Others?

TASTING LAB

Flour Tortillas
Store-Bought Taco Shells

FRESH TOMATO SALSA

WHAT WE WANTED: A juicy, not watery, traditionally flavored fresh tomato salsa.

Backyard, farm-stand, and supermarket summertime tomatoes alike should be sweet, juicy, and ready for top billing in a fresh tomato salsa. But even in the midst of tomato season, some can be less than stellar. Complicating matters, salsa's popularity has opened the door to versions employing ingredients that are extravagant (smoked paprika) and extraneous (canned tomato juice), relegating fresh tomatoes to a minor role. One such recipe had us fishing around in water for minuscule pieces of tomato, while another used four different chiles but only one measly tomato.

We wanted a fresh, chunky Mexican-style salsa, or salsa cruda, that would emphasize the tomatoes; the other traditional flavors—lime, garlic, onion, chile, and cilantro—would have supporting roles. We also wanted to get the texture just right for scooping up and balancing on a tortilla chip. Simply combining salsa ingredients in one bowl for mixing and serving turned out to be a bad idea. The tomatoes exuded so much juice that the other ingredients were submerged in liquid within minutes. The first step, then, was to solve the problem of watery salsa. Peeling and seeding are often-employed techniques for removing excess moisture from tomatoes. Peeling, however, removed the structure that kept the diced pieces intact, resulting in a salsa that was too mushy. Seeding diminished the tomatoes' flavor, and tasters did not mind the presence of seeds. So much for peeling and seeding.

We recalled that here in the test kitchen we often salt tomatoes to concentrate flavor and exude liquid. This technique was promising, but because much more surface area was exposed when the tomatoes were diced, the salt penetrated too deeply and broke them down too much. We were left with mealy, mushy tomatoes, and the salsa was just as watery as before. Dicing the tomatoes larger to expose less surface area was out of the question; the tomato pieces would be too large to balance on a tortilla chip. Taking round slices of tomatoes, salting them, and then dicing them after they had drained was just too much work.

Frustrated, we diced a few whole tomatoes (skin, seeds, and all), threw them into a colander, and walked away. Thirty

minutes later, to our surprise, a few tablespoons of liquid had drained out; after a few shakes of the colander, the tomatoes were chunky and relatively dry. We found that in fewer than 30 minutes, not enough liquid drained out, whereas more time didn't produce enough additional juice to justify the wait. Overall, we found that really ripe tomatoes exude more juice than less ripe supermarket tomatoes. This simple technique, with minimal tomato prep, had accomplished a major feat: It put all tomatoes, regardless of origin, ripeness, or juiciness, on a level—and dry—playing field.

With the main technique established, we fixed the spotlight on the supporting ingredients. Red onions were preferred over white, yellow, and sweet onions for color and flavor. Jalapeño chiles were chosen over serrano, habanero, and poblano chiles because of their wide availability, slight vegetal flavor, and moderate heat. Lime juice tasted more authentic (and better) than red wine vinegar, rice vinegar, or lemon juice. Olive oil, while included at the beginning of the recipe testing process, was rejected later on when tasters found it dulled the other flavors.

We also investigated the best way to combine the ingredients and rejected all but the simplest technique. Marinating the tomatoes, onion, garlic, and chile in lime juice resulted in dull, washed-out flavors and involved extra bowls and work. We tried letting the drained tomatoes, onion, chile, garlic, and cilantro sit for a bit before adding the lime juice, sugar, and salt. Now the flavors of the chile and onion stole the show. It was much more efficient to chop the chile, onion, garlic, and cilantro and layer each ingredient on top of the tomatoes while they drained in the colander. Once the tomatoes were finished draining, the chile, onion, garlic, cilantro, and tomatoes needed just a few stirs before being finished with the lime juice, sugar, and salt, and then served.

WHAT WE LEARNED: Draining the tomatoes in a colander removes excess juices, ensuring a chunky salsa. Layering the other vegetables in the colander with the tomatoes marries the salsa's supporting flavors.

FRESH TOMATO SALSA

Makes about 3 cups

Heat varies from jalapeño to jalapeño, and because much of the heat resides in the ribs, or pale-colored, interior flesh, we suggest mincing the ribs (along with the seeds) separately from the dark green, exterior flesh, then adding the minced ribs and seeds to taste. The amount of sugar and lime juice to use depends on the ripeness of the tomatoes. The salsa can be made 2 to 3 hours in advance, but hold off adding the salt, lime juice, and sugar until just before serving. The salsa is perfect for tortilla chips, but it's also a nice accompaniment to grilled steaks, chicken, and fish.

1½ pounds firm, ripe tomatoes, cored and cut into ⅜-inch dice (about 3 cups)
1 large jalapeño chile, seeds and ribs removed and set aside (see note), exterior flesh minced (about 2 tablespoons)
½ cup minced red onion
1 small garlic clove, minced or pressed through a garlic press (about ½ teaspoon)
¼ cup chopped fresh cilantro leaves
½ teaspoon salt
   Pinch ground black pepper
2–6 teaspoons juice from 1 to 2 limes
   Sugar to taste (up to 1 teaspoon)

1. Set a large colander in a large bowl. Place the tomatoes in the colander and let them drain for 30 minutes. As the tomatoes drain, layer the jalapeño, onion, garlic, and cilantro on top. Shake the colander to drain off the excess tomato juice. Discard the juice; wipe out the bowl.

2. Transfer the contents of the colander to the now-empty bowl. Add the salt, pepper, and 2 teaspoons of the lime juice; toss to combine. Taste and add the minced jalapeño ribs and seeds, sugar, and additional lime juice to taste.

TECHNIQUE: Cutting Tomatoes for Salsa

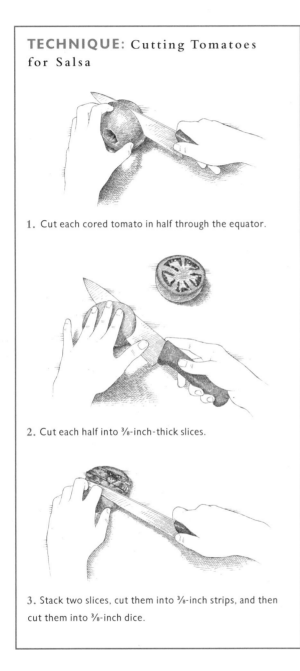

1. Cut each cored tomato in half through the equator.

2. Cut each half into ⅜-inch-thick slices.

3. Stack two slices, cut them into ⅜-inch strips, and then cut them into ⅜-inch dice.

SCIENCE DESK: Why Are Some Jalapeños Spicier Than Others?

IN THE TEST KITCHEN, WE'VE NOTICED THAT SOME jalapeños are searing hot, while others are as mild as bell peppers. We tracked down a number of theories to explain this great variation, and size kept popping up. According to this theory, a small jalapeño will be hotter than a large jalapeño, a small habanero hotter than a large one.

But when we arranged a tasting of jalapeños of various sizes, there seemed to be no correlation between size and heat. To investigate the matter further, we sent five similarly sized jalapeños to the lab, requesting levels of capsaicin and dihydrocapsaicin, the compounds responsible for the majority of the perception of "heat." Sure enough, the chiles came back with wildly divergent amounts, the capsaicin ranging from 304 all the way up to 2,979 Scoville heat units (a common measure of chile heat) and the dihydrocapsaicin ranging from 105 to 1,135 units. Some chiles were nearly 10 times hotter than others—even though they all looked alike! So forget about size when trying to judge whether a chile pepper will be hot or mild.

One burning question remained: Is there any visual indicator of pungency? No, says Denise Coon of the Chile Pepper Institute, who explained that capsaicin production is tied to the environment. Chiles grown in sunny, arid weather undergo a lot of stress, and stressed chiles produce more capsaicin than chiles grown in temperate climates. (Hot, dry New Mexico is known for producing very hot chiles.) Chile plants have evolved to link stress and high capsaicin production as a protection mechanism. The hotter a pepper is, the less likely it is to be ingested by most animals. So the only surefire way to judge the heat level of a chile is to taste it.

QUICK AND EASY QUESADILLAS

WHAT WE WANTED: A toasty tortilla filled with melted cheese, easily made at a moment's notice.

A truly authentic quesadilla is just a humble kitchen snack: a fresh, handmade tortilla folded around mild melting cheese, quickly fried or crisped on a griddle, then devoured just as quickly. As the quesadilla migrated north of the border, however, it evolved into a greasy happy hour staple for beer and burger joints, becoming nothing more than bad Mexican pizza: stale and soggy supermarket tortillas filled with "buffalo chicken" or "Cajun shrimp" and sliced into big, floppy triangles.

Our quest focused on a quesadilla that would be authentic in spirit, if not quite in substance—that is, a quick and casual but still satisfying snack, ready at a moment's notice from supermarket staples. (We declined to hunt for exotic yet bona fide items, such as asadero cheese and squash blossoms, when Monterey Jack and jarred jalapeños were sitting in the fridge.) We tested a half-dozen techniques for cooking the quesadillas, including a deep fry, a shallow fry, a lightly oiled skillet, and a completely dry skillet. The fried versions were tasty but they were also messy and greasy. The lightly oiled nonstick skillet produced the best, though not perfect, results. While the exterior of the tortillas was nicely crisp and browned, the interior had a raw, doughy texture, and the cheese was not entirely melted. We lowered the flame and tried again, hoping to give the tortillas more time to heat through, but this batch exhibited a tough, leathery exterior.

What we needed was a way to preheat the tortillas so that we could assemble the quesadillas while they were still warm. We could then crisp them up quickly over fairly high heat without worrying that the filling would not be sufficiently heated. Some cookbooks suggest passing the tortillas over the flame of a gas burner to lightly char and soften them. This idea worked, but it excluded electric cooktops and demanded close attention to keep the tortillas from going up in flames. We got better results by simply toasting the tortillas in a hot dry skillet. As a tortilla heated up, it released its own steam, causing the tortilla to puff up and its layers to separate. Once filled and returned to the oiled skillet, this batch of tortillas made for quesadillas with a pleasing contrast in texture—their outer layer thin and crispy, their inner layer warm and soft, with just a little bit of chew.

We knew we didn't need much oil, but even a few drops tended to bead up and puddle in the nonstick skillet, resulting in uneven browning. A better approach, we found, was to brush the tortillas with oil before returning them to the skillet. We sprinkled the tortillas lightly with kosher salt after brushing them with oil, and tasters agreed that this made them seem crispier.

Our quesadillas were tasty, but they still suffered from a few design flaws. Our working recipe called for sandwiching cheese between two 10-inch flour tortillas. These were tricky to flip without spilling the fillings and oozed melted cheese all over the cutting board when cut into wedges. We switched to smaller 8-inch tortillas and began folding them in half around the filling, fitting them into the skillet two at a time. Cut in half instead of into multiple wedges, these "half moon" quesadillas were much sturdier and easier to eat, and, thanks to the folded edges, they kept their filling inside, where it belonged.

WHAT WE LEARNED: For tortillas with the best texture—a crisp outer layer and a soft, slightly chewy inner layer—toast them in a skillet prior to filling. Folding the tortilla in half around the cheese, rather than stacking one tortilla on top of the other, prevents the cheese from oozing out the sides. Brushing the quesadillas with oil and sprinkling them lightly with kosher salt further ensures a crisp crust.

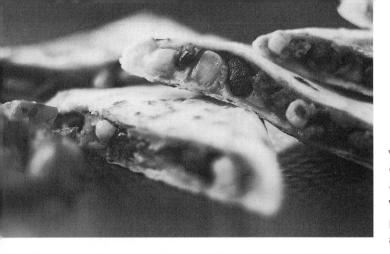

QUESADILLAS

Makes 2 folded 8-inch quesadillas

Cooling the quesadillas before cutting and serving is important; straight from the skillet, the melted cheese will ooze out. Finished quesadillas can be held on a baking sheet in a 200-degree oven for up to 20 minutes.

  2   (8-inch) flour tortillas
  2   ounces Monterey Jack or cheddar cheese,
      shredded (⅔ cup)
  1   tablespoon minced pickled jalapeños (optional)
      Vegetable oil for brushing the tortillas
      Kosher salt

1. Heat a 10-inch nonstick skillet over medium heat until hot, about 2 minutes. Place 1 tortilla in the skillet and toast until soft and puffed slightly at the edges, about 2 minutes. Flip the tortilla and toast until puffed and slightly browned, 1 to 2 minutes longer. Slip the tortilla onto a cutting board. Repeat to toast the second tortilla while assembling the first quesadilla. Sprinkle ⅓ cup of the cheese and half of the jalapeños, if using, over half of the tortilla, leaving a ½-inch border around the edge. Fold the tortilla in half and press to flatten. Brush the top generously with oil, sprinkle lightly with salt, and set aside. Repeat to form the second quesadilla.

2. Place both quesadillas in the skillet, oiled sides down; cook over medium heat until crisp and well browned, 1 to 2 minutes. Brush the tops with oil and sprinkle lightly with salt. Flip the quesadillas and cook until the second sides are crisp, 1 to 2 minutes. Transfer the quesadillas to a cutting board; cool about 3 minutes, halve each quesadilla, and serve.

VARIATIONS

CHEDDAR, BACON, AND SCALLION QUESADILLAS

Well-chilled bacon will be much easier to cut into small pieces than bacon that's been sitting out on the counter for a few minutes.

Cut 2 strips of bacon crosswise into ½-inch pieces; fry in a 10-inch nonstick skillet over medium heat until crisp, about 5 minutes. Using a slotted spoon, transfer the bacon to a paper towel–lined plate; pour the fat into a small bowl and reserve, if desired. Wipe out the skillet with paper towels. Follow the recipe for Quesadillas, using cheddar cheese and sprinkling the bacon and 1 tablespoon thinly sliced scallions over the cheese in each quesadilla. If desired, substitute the reserved bacon fat for the oil and omit the salt.

QUESADILLAS WITH QUESO FRESCO AND ROASTED PEPPERS

Queso fresco is a salty, crumbly Mexican cheese similar in flavor to farmer's cheese. It pairs well with sweet peppers.

Follow the recipe for Quesadillas, using queso fresco and adding 2 tablespoons chopped roasted red peppers, patted dry, along with ½ teaspoon minced fresh cilantro leaves to the filling.

CUBANO QUESADILLAS

In this Cuban-sandwich-inspired variation on a grilled ham and cheese, tortillas stand in for the traditional crusty French bread.

Follow the recipe for Quesadillas. After toasting the tortillas, spread 2 teaspoons mustard over half of one tortilla and then top with 2 slices deli ham, ⅓ cup shredded Gruyère cheese, and 1 tablespoon each minced red onion and chopped dill or sweet pickles, leaving a ½-inch border around the edge. Fold the tortilla in half and press to flatten. Brush the surface generously with oil, sprinkle lightly with salt, and set aside. Repeat to form the second quesadilla. Continue as directed in the recipe for Quesadillas.

CORN AND BLACK BEAN QUESADILLAS WITH PEPPER JACK CHEESE

Pantry staples like frozen corn and canned black beans make this hearty variation possible at a moment's notice. If desired, add a pinch of chile powder to the oil you use for brushing the tortillas. The flavored oil lends a spicy bite and attractive hue to the finished quesadillas.

- ⅓ cup frozen corn, thawed
- 2 teaspoons vegetable oil
- ⅓ cup minced red onion
- 1 medium garlic clove, minced or pressed through a garlic press (about 1 teaspoon)
- ½ teaspoon chili powder
- ⅓ cup canned black beans, drained and rinsed
- 2 teaspoons juice from 1 lime
- 1 recipe Quesadillas (page 20)

1. Heat a 10-inch nonstick skillet over medium-high heat until hot. Add the corn and cook, stirring occasionally, until the kernels begin to brown and pop, 3 to 5 minutes; transfer the corn to a bowl. Heat the vegetable oil in the now-empty skillet over medium heat until shimmering; add the onion and cook until softened, about 3 minutes. Add the garlic and chili powder and cook until fragrant, about 1 minute; stir in the black beans and cook until heated through, about 1 minute. Return the corn to the skillet; gently press the mixture with a spatula to lightly crush the beans. Transfer the mixture to the now-empty bowl, stir in the lime juice, and season with salt.

2. Wipe out the skillet with paper towels and return the pan to medium heat until hot. Follow the recipe for Quesadillas, using Pepper Jack cheese and dividing the corn and bean filling between the quesadillas.

TASTING LAB: Flour Tortillas

TO FIND OUT WHICH STORE-BOUGHT TORTILLAS TASTE best, we rounded up every flour tortilla we could find and headed into the test kitchen to taste them.

Tasters immediately zeroed in on texture, which varied dramatically from "doughy and stale" to "thin and flaky." The thinnest tortillas, Tyson Mexican Original, were the hands-down winner: Although not quite as tender, they boasted a more pronounced chew that tasters appreciated. Most brands had a mild, pleasantly wheaty flavor, but two of the doughier brands, Ole and La Banderita (both made by the same company), were panned for off, sour notes. Our advice is simple: Get the thinnest tortillas you can find at your local market.

EQUIPMENT CORNER: Quesadilla Makers

AS WE DEVELOPED OUR SKILLET METHOD FOR QUESA-dillas, the specter of the electric quesadilla maker weighed heavy upon us. While nobody wanted to believe that a glorified sandwich press could outperform a skillet, we had to acknowledge that the contraption does neatly sequester the cheesy fillings into six triangular sections and that it eliminates the need to flip the quesadilla. We decided it was worth a try and immediately ran into a problem.

The problem was that the recipes that came with this device advised limiting the amount of cheese to a paltry ¼ cup for two 10-inch flour tortillas. But when we ignored these stingy directions and added more cheese, the cheese flooded into the moat surrounding the heating plates. Though the nonstick heating plates clean up easily, the same cannot be said for the flooded drip reservoir. So for our quesadilla needs—which include generous amounts of queso—we'll stick with a skillet.

QUESADILLA MAKER
Can a quesadilla maker outperform a skillet?

BEEF TACOS

WHAT WE WANTED: A fresh-tasting crunchy corn taco shell filled with a spicy, well-balanced filling.

So maybe they're not authentic Mexican. They're Tex-Mex . . . maybe even gringo. But ground beef tacos have earned themselves a special place in the palates of at least a couple of generations of North Americans. We recall our mothers ripping open the seasoning packet, the colorful array of toppings in mismatched bowls that cluttered the tabletop, and, of course, the first bite that cracked the shell and sent a trickle of orange grease running down our wrists. Indeed, there is something appealing about the silly taco. It's a mix of spicy ground beef, shredded cheese, sweet chopped tomatoes (or, as some would have it, jarred salsa), and cool iceberg lettuce. Those in favor of more toppings can always add chopped onions, diced avocado, and sour cream. All this contained in a crisp and corny taco shell. Seems hard to go wrong.

But when we sampled a few tacos made from supermarket kits in the test kitchen, our happy memories faded. The fillings tasted flat and stale, reeking of dried oregano and onion powder. The store-bought shells tasted greasy and junky—too much like unwholesome snack food to be served at the dinner table. There's no denying that these seasoning packets, along with prefab taco shells, make taco-making ridiculously easy, but we thought that with only a little more effort we could produce a fiery, flavorful filling and crisp, toasty taco shells—tacos that even adults could enjoy.

We began by trying fillings made according to the few cookbook recipes we uncovered. There were two approaches. The first had us brown ground beef in a skillet; add spices, sometimes chopped onion and garlic, and water; and then simmer. The second directed us to sauté the onion and garlic before adding the beef to the pan. This is the technique we preferred. Sautéing the onion softened its texture and made its flavor full and sweet, while a quick minute of cooking helped bring out the garlic's flavor. For a pound of ground beef, a small chopped onion was enough; as for garlic, we liked the wallop of a tablespoon, minced.

For burgers we prefer the relatively fatty 80 percent lean ground chuck, and we expected we would like the same for the taco filling. After testing them all, though, we were surprised to discover that we preferred the leaner types: Anything fattier than 90 percent lean ground beef cooked into a slick, greasy mess.

The labels on taco seasoning packets indicate a hodge-podge of ingredients, including dehydrated onion and/ or garlic, MSG, mysterious "spices," and even soy sauce. However, they all include chili powder, so we started with one tablespoon and then quickly increased the total to two for more kick. A teaspoon each of ground cumin and ground coriander added savory, complex flavors. Dried oregano in a more modest amount, ½ teaspoon, provided just the right herbal note. For a little heat, we added cayenne.

The flavors were bold, but we wanted to make them fuller and rounder. From past experience we knew that exposing the spices to some heat—as is often done in various types of ethnic cooking—makes their flavors blossom, so we tried this technique with our taco filling. In one batch we simply sprinkled the spices over the beef as it simmered, and in the second we added the spices to the sautéed onion along with the garlic and gave them a minute to cook. The difference was marked. In the first batch the flavors seemed merely to sit in the liquid that surrounded the meat, and the beef itself tasted rather dull. The second batch, however, was richly and deeply flavored and the spices permeated the beef.

Since the meat was lean and we needed a sauce to carry the flavors of the spices, the filling required some liquid. Many recipes call only for water, but water produced a thin, hollow-tasting mixture. We also tried canned chicken broth, canned plain tomato sauce, and a combination of the two. A combination was best; the chicken broth offered backbone while the tomato sauce added viscosity and liveliness.

The final flavor adjustments to the filling came in the

form of sweet and sour. Tasters responded positively to a teaspoon of brown sugar; the slightest amount of sweetness expanded and enriched the flavor of the spices. Two teaspoons of cider vinegar picked up where the tomato sauce left off by adding just enough acidity to activate all the taste buds. Our taco filling was now "perfect," in the words of one taster. We moved on to the shell.

Store-bought taco shells are insipid, although so convenient that many home cooks may opt for them. We wondered, however, if it was worth the trouble to purchase store-bought corn tortillas that could then be fried at home, thereby producing a superior, homemade, taco shell. The flavor of the home-fried shells we tried was a revelation, so we went on to perfect a technique.

We began testing with the choice of oil for frying. Vegetable and canola oils worked fine, but corn oil edged out in front—its sweet flavor matched that of the tortillas. An 8-inch skillet held a tortilla comfortably and required a minimum of oil. We found that the shells fried up cleanly (not greasy) and evenly in ¾ cup oil heated to a temperature between 350 and 375 degrees. Cooler oil left the shells greasy and hotter oil browned them erratically and pushed the oil too close to the smoking point. Since the oil quantity was relatively small and the tortillas are fried one at a time, we settled on medium, instead of high, heat to maintain the correct oil temperature.

Because corn tortillas are like thin pancakes—they will not hold a shape—the question was how to fry them into the traditional wedge shape used for tacos. The method we settled on was simple enough. We fried one half of the tortilla until it stiffened, holding on to the other half with tongs. Next, the other half was submerged in the oil while we kept the shell mouth open (about 2 inches wide), again using the tongs. Finally, we slipped the first half back into the oil to finish. Each shell took about 2 minutes, not an unreasonable investment of time given the huge improvement in taste and texture that homemade taco shells offer.

Of course, what's offered as taco toppings is largely a matter of choice. Shredded cheese, however, is required—

Monterey Jack and cheddar were the obvious picks. We bypassed jarred salsa in favor of some simple chopped tomato and onions because we preferred their fresher, brighter flavors and textures. Shredded iceberg lettuce was favored over romaine for its crisper crunch. Sour cream and diced avocado were the other often-requested toppings. Finally, chopped fresh cilantro—never an option on our mothers' tables—was also welcomed. It helped to fast-forward the tacos of our pasts into the present. Truly these were tacos that tasted better than we remembered.

WHAT WE LEARNED: To avoid a greasy filling, use 90 percent lean (or leaner) ground beef. A little brown sugar and cider vinegar give the filling sweet and sour notes that round out its spicy flavor. Home-fried taco shells are a must for best flavor and texture.

TECHNIQUE: Making Your Own Taco Shells

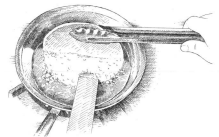

1. Using tongs to hold the tortilla, slip half of it into the hot oil. With a metal spatula in the other hand, submerge the half in the oil. Fry until just set, but not brown, about 30 seconds.

2. Flip the tortilla and, using tongs, hold the tortilla open about 2 inches while keeping the bottom submerged in the oil. Fry until golden brown, about 1 ½ minutes. Flip again and fry the other side until golden brown, about 30 seconds.

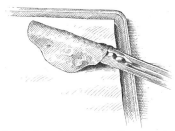

3. Transfer the shell, upside down, to the paper towel–lined baking sheet to drain. Repeat with the remaining tortillas, adjusting the heat as necessary to keep the oil between 350 and 375 degrees.

BEEF TACOS

Serves 4

Tomato sauce is sold in cans in the same aisle as canned whole tomatoes. Do not use jarred pasta sauce in its place. Taco toppings are highly individual: You need not offer all of the ones that we suggest below, but cheese, lettuce, and tomatoes are, in our opinion, essential.

beef filling

- 2   teaspoons corn or vegetable oil
- 1   small onion, chopped small
- 3   medium garlic cloves, minced or pressed through a garlic press (about 1 tablespoon)
- 2   tablespoons chili powder
- 1   teaspoon ground cumin
- 1   teaspoon ground coriander
- ½   teaspoon dried oregano
- ¼   teaspoon cayenne pepper
-     Salt
- 1   pound 90 percent lean (or leaner) ground beef
- ½   cup canned tomato sauce (not pasta sauce)
- ½   cup low-sodium chicken broth
- 1   teaspoon brown sugar
- 2   teaspoons vinegar, preferably cider vinegar
-     Ground black pepper

shells and toppings

- 8   Home-Fried Taco Shells (recipe follows) or store-bought shells (warmed according to package instructions)
- 4   ounces cheddar or Monterey Jack cheese, shredded (about 1 cup)
- 2   cups shredded iceberg lettuce
- 2   small tomatoes, chopped small
- ½   cup sour cream
- 1   avocado, peeled, pitted, and diced medium
- 1   small onion, chopped small
- 2   tablespoons chopped fresh cilantro leaves
-     Hot pepper sauce, such as Tabasco

1. FOR THE FILLING: Heat the oil in a medium skillet over medium heat until hot and shimmering. Add the onion and cook, stirring occasionally, until softened, about 4 minutes. Add the garlic, spices, and ½ teaspoon salt; cook, stirring constantly, until fragrant, about 1 minute. Add the ground beef and cook, breaking the meat up with a wooden spoon and scraping the pan bottom to prevent scorching, until the beef is no longer pink, about 5 minutes. Add the tomato sauce, broth, brown sugar, and vinegar; bring to a simmer. Reduce the heat to medium-low and simmer uncovered, stirring frequently and breaking the meat up so that no chunks remain, until the liquid has reduced and thickened (the mixture should not be completely dry), about 10 minutes. Adjust the seasonings with salt and pepper to taste.

2. Using a wide, shallow spoon, divide the mixture evenly among the taco shells; place 2 tacos on each plate. Serve immediately, passing the toppings separately.

HOME-FRIED TACO SHELLS

Makes 8 shells

Fry the taco shells before you make the filling, then rewarm them in a 200-degree oven for about 10 minutes before serving.

¾   cup corn, vegetable, or canola oil
8   corn tortillas (each 6 inches in diameter)

1. Heat the oil in a heavy-bottomed 8-inch skillet over medium heat to 350 degrees, about 5 minutes (the oil should bubble when a small piece of tortilla is dropped in; the piece should rise to the surface in 2 seconds and be light golden brown in about 1 minute). Meanwhile, line a rimmed baking sheet with a double thickness of paper towels.

2. Follow the illustrations on page 24 to fry the shells.

Follow the illustrations on page 24 to fry the shells.

TASTING LAB: Store-Bought Taco Shells

PREFAB TACO SHELLS SIMPLIFY THE PROCESS OF TACO making, but we wondered if all shells were created equal. We conducted a tasting to find out, trying six brands of store-bought taco shells (warmed according to package instructions) as well as home-fried shells. The runaway winner was the home-fried shells. Uneven and imperfect, they looked rustic and real, not manufactured. Most important, tasters preferred their clean, toasty corn flavor and crisp yet sturdy texture. One taster noted that the home-fried shells brought flavor and texture to the assembled taco, whereas most other taco shells seemed no more than convenient containers. Rating the store-bought shells seemed more a matter of choosing the lesser of evils. Old El Paso Taco Shells finished a distant second. They were described as "dry," and some tasters picked up "plastic" and "chemical" flavors, but a few appreciated their crispness and faint corny sweetness. El Rio Taco Shells and Ortega Taco Shells tied for third. The former were crisp but "too delicate" and "absolutely tasteless"; the latter were hard, dry, and tough, but some liked the "well-seasoned" corn flavor. Fourth place Taco Bell Taco Shells were bland, with a decidedly stale texture. Bearitos Taco Shells, made with organically grown blue corn and costing almost a dollar more than some other brands, took fifth. Their color was off-putting and their texture too brittle and delicate to support the taco filling. Old El Paso White Corn Taco Shells came in sixth place, disliked for a rancid flavor and stale texture.

BEST STORE-BOUGHT TACO SHELLS

Overall, home-fried taco shells can't be beat, but if you prefer the convenience of store-bought, Old El Paso Taco Shells came out ahead among the brands we tested.

For tortilla soup, we bake our tortilla strips instead of frying them, for great flavor without a greasy aftertaste.

SOUTH-OF-THE-

CHAPTER 3

border soups

The words "exciting" and "soup" don't often go hand in hand, but when it comes to two Latin American favorites, black bean soup and tortilla soup, we beg to differ. Black bean soup has a luxuriously rich texture—a silky broth thickened with pureed beans—and a hearty flavor with hints of smoky meat and a subtle citrusy kick, often accented with a cooling dollop of sour cream. Tortilla soup is a turbocharged Mexican chicken soup, enlivened by herbs, spices, heat from chiles, and the fresh crunch of crisp tortilla strips. These soups are just what the doctor ordered for tired palates.

These soups, however, are not without their challenges. Traditional recipes for black bean soup require a significant commitment of prep time, starting with soaking the beans a day ahead of preparing the soup. Tortilla soup includes a host of hard-to-find ingredients necessitating a special trip to a Latin market—if you can find one near your home. As terrific as these soups can be, our excitement waned at the prospect of all that work and shopping. We longed to make them fit modern time constraints and not involve any field-trips or research.

In this chapter, we tackle these challenges and more, to show you not only how terrific these Latin American soups can be, but how accessible, too.

IN THIS CHAPTER

THE RECIPES

Black Bean Soup
Black Bean Soup with Chipotle
  Chiles

Tortilla Soup

EQUIPMENT CORNER

Chef's Knives

SCIENCE DESK

Why Beans Cause Gas

TASTING LAB

Cumin

BLACK BEAN SOUP

WHAT WE WANTED: A rich, authentically flavored black bean soup that doesn't take all day to prepare.

Black beans (or turtle beans) have always been a staple in Mexican, Cuban, and Caribbean kitchens, but they really came into vogue in the United States with the introduction of black bean soup in the 1960s. The Coach House restaurant in New York City popularized the soup, the making of which was an all-day affair. It started with soaked beans that simmered for hours with, among other ingredients, parsnips, carrots, beef bones, and smoked ham hocks. The pureed soup was finished with a splash of Madeira, chopped hard-cooked eggs, and thinly sliced lemon. Refined? Yes. Realistic for the modern cook? No. The good news is that today's recipes, heavily influenced by Latin American cuisine, are easier to prepare. The bad news is that as restaurant recipes have been simplified, flavor has suffered.

Testing five soups shed light on specific problems. Asked to record their impressions, tasters chose the words "watery" and "thin" to describe the texture of most soups and either "bland" and "musty" or "over-spiced" and "bitter" to describe the taste. The soups were given low marks for appearance, too—all had unattractive purple and gray tones; none were truly black.

When beans are the star ingredient, it's preferable to use the dried variety, not canned—the former release valuable flavor into the broth as they cook, while the latter generally make vapid soup. We simmered five brands of dried beans, including an organic variety and beans from the bulk bin of a natural foods store, and there were only minor variations in flavor. In short, brand doesn't seem to matter. We've also learned that there's no reason to soak dried beans overnight—doing so only marginally reduces the cooking time and requires too much forethought. Similarly, the "quick-soak" method, in which the beans are brought to a boil and then soaked off the heat for an hour, is disappointing in that it causes many of the beans to explode during cooking.

As for seasoning, a teaspoon of salt added at the outset of cooking provided tastier beans than salt added at the end of cooking. We've found that salting early does not toughen the skins of beans, as some cooks claim. In addition to salt, we threw a couple of aromatic bay leaves into the pot.

We knew we didn't want to make from-scratch beef stock, so we focused on more time-efficient flavor builders, starting with a smoky ham hock. While tasters liked the meaty flavor offered by the ham hock, it also made them want more—not just more meat flavor (hocks are mostly bone) but real meat. We turned to untraditional (for black bean soup) cured pork products: salt pork, slab bacon, and ham steak. Ham steak contributed a good amount of smoky pork flavor and decidedly more meat than any of the other options, making it our first choice.

Aside from the ham flavor, the soup tasted rather hollow. We found improvement using a sofrito, a Spanish or Italian preparation in which aromatic vegetables and herbs (we used green pepper, onion, garlic, and oregano) are sautéed until softened and lightly browned. But our sofrito needed refinement. We replaced the oregano with cumin, which had a warmer, more likable taste. We slowly incorporated the ground spice, working our way up to 1½ tablespoons. (Freshly ground and toasted whole cumin seed was not worth the bother. See our recommendations on ground cumin on page 31.) Sound like a lot? It is, but we were after big flavor, and when we sautéed the cumin along with the aromatics, its pungency was tempered. We also replaced the bitter green pepper with minced carrot and celery for a sweeter, fresher flavor.

We decided not to be shy with minced garlic and red pepper flakes: We added five to six cloves and ½ teaspoon, respectively. The soup was now a hit, layered with sweet, spicy, smoky, and fresh vegetable flavors. While the Coach House recipe called for homemade beef stock, our aggressive seasonings meant that a mixture of water and store-bought broth was all that was needed.

We wanted partially pureed soup, refusing both ultra-smooth mixtures and chunky, brothy ones. Even after pureeing, though, a thickener seemed necessary. Simply using less liquid in the soup and mashing some of the beans improved the texture somewhat, but the soup still lacked body. A potato cooked in the soup pureed into an unpleasant, starchy brew. Flour, cooked with the oil in the sofrito to form a roux, and cornstarch, stirred into the soup at the end of cooking, both worked. We decided to call for cornstarch, which lets the cook control the thickness (or thinness) of the finished soup by adding more or less of the slurry (cornstarch and water paste) to the pot.

We were finally satisfied, save for the soup's unappealing gray color. As often happens, the solution came to us in a roundabout way. While our food scientist was looking into remedies for the gas-causing effects of beans in digestion (see "Why Beans Cause Gas" on page 32), we noticed that a side effect of cooking beans with baking soda is that the beans retain their dark color. The coating of the black beans contains anthocyanins (color pigments) that change color with changes in pH: A more alkaline broth makes them darker, and a more acidic broth makes them lighter. We experimented by adding various amounts of baking soda to the beans both during and after cooking. The winning quantity was a mere ⅛ teaspoon, which produced a great-tasting soup (there was no soapy aftertaste, as was the case with larger quantities) with a darker, more appetizing color than unadulterated beans. Problem solved.

Classic additions to black bean soup include Madeira, rum, sherry, or Scotch from the liquor cabinet and lemon, lime, or orange juice from the citrus bin. Given the other flavors in the soup, lime juice seemed the best fit. Because it is acidic, too much lime juice can push the color of the soup toward pink. Two tablespoons added flavor without marring the color.

Without an array of colorful garnishes, even the best black bean soup might be dull. Sour cream and diced

avocado offset the soup's heat, while red onion and minced cilantro contribute freshness and color. Finally, wedges of lime accentuate the bright flavor of the juice that's already in the soup.

WHAT WE LEARNED: Use dried beans, not canned. Add some baking soda to the bean cooking water to prevent the soup's color from turning gray. For layered flavor, be generous with the ground cumin, minced garlic, and red pepper flakes. A combination of pureed beans and cornstarch thickens the soup nicely, without it becoming overly chunky.

BLACK BEAN SOUP

Makes about 9 cups, serving 6

Dried beans tend to cook unevenly, so be sure to taste several beans to determine their doneness in step 1. For efficiency, you can prepare the soup ingredients while the beans simmer and the garnishes while the soup simmers. Though you do not need to offer all of the garnishes listed below, do choose at least a couple; garnishes are essential for this soup as they add not only flavor but texture and color as well. Leftover soup can be refrigerated in an airtight container for 3 or 4 days; reheat it in a saucepan over medium heat until hot, stirring in additional chicken broth if it has thickened beyond your liking.

beans

1	pound (2 cups) dried black beans, rinsed and picked over
4	ounces ham steak, trimmed of rind
2	bay leaves
5	cups water
⅛	teaspoon baking soda
1	teaspoon salt

soup

3	tablespoons olive oil
2	large onions, chopped fine (about 3 cups)
1	large carrot, chopped fine (about ½ cup)
3	celery ribs, chopped fine (about 1 cup)
½	teaspoon salt
5–6	medium garlic cloves, minced or pressed through a garlic press (about 1½ tablespoons)
½	teaspoon red pepper flakes
1½	tablespoons ground cumin
6	cups low-sodium chicken broth
2	tablespoons cornstarch
2	tablespoons water
2	tablespoons juice from 1 to 2 limes

garnishes

	Lime wedges
	Minced fresh cilantro leaves
	Red onion, diced fine
	Avocado, peeled, pitted, and diced medium
	Sour cream

1. FOR THE BEANS: Place the beans, ham, bay leaves, water, and baking soda in a large saucepan with a tight-fitting lid. Bring to a boil over medium-high heat; using a large spoon, skim the scum as it rises to the surface. Stir in the salt, reduce the heat to low, cover, and simmer briskly until the beans are tender, 1¼ to 1½ hours (if necessary, add another 1 cup water and continue to simmer until the beans are tender); do not drain the beans. Discard the bay leaves. Remove the ham steak (ham steak darkens to the color of the beans), cut it into ¼-inch cubes, and set aside.

2. FOR THE SOUP: Heat the oil in an 8-quart Dutch oven over medium-high heat until shimmering but not smoking; add the onions, carrot, celery, and salt and cook, stirring occasionally, until the vegetables are soft and lightly browned, 12 to 15 minutes. Reduce the heat to medium-low and add the garlic, pepper flakes, and cumin; cook, stirring constantly, until fragrant, about 3 minutes. Stir in the beans, bean cooking liquid, and chicken broth. Increase the heat to medium-high and bring to a boil, then reduce the heat to low and simmer, uncovered, stirring occasionally, to blend flavors, about 30 minutes.

3. TO FINISH THE SOUP: Ladle 1½ cups of the beans and 2 cups liquid into a food processor or blender, process until smooth, and return to the pot. Stir together the cornstarch and water in a small bowl until combined, then gradually stir about half of the cornstarch mixture into the soup; bring to a boil over medium-high heat, stirring occasionally, to fully thicken. If the soup is still thinner than desired once boiling, stir the remaining cornstarch mixture to recombine and gradually stir the mixture into the soup;

return to a boil to fully thicken. Off the heat, stir in the lime juice and reserved ham; ladle the soup into bowls and serve immediately, passing the garnishes separately.

VARIATION

BLACK BEAN SOUP WITH CHIPOTLE CHILES

The addition of chipotle chiles in adobo—smoked jalapeños packed in a seasoned tomato-vinegar sauce—makes this a spicier, smokier variation on Black Bean Soup.

Follow the recipe for Black Bean Soup, omitting the red pepper flakes and adding 1 tablespoon minced chipotle chiles in adobo plus 2 teaspoons adobo sauce along with the chicken broth in step 2.

TASTING LAB: Cumin

WE TASTED FIVE BRANDS OF CUMIN, AND ALL WERE DEEMED fine. If you like to order spices by mail, Penzeys India Ground Cumin Seed (left) is a best buy at $1.50 per ounce, plus shipping. If you prefer to buy spices at the supermarket, McCormick Gourmet Collection Ground Cumin (right) is a best buy at $2.99 per ounce.

TECHNIQUE: Storing Spices Efficiently

It is best to store spices away from heat and light (not on the counter in a spice rack), but if your chosen spot is a drawer, then you have to either label the lid or lift up the jar to determine its contents. You can, however, easily fashion a rack inside the drawer so that the bottles are held at an angle and their labels are visible at a glance. Here's how:

A. For a wide drawer of 24 inches or more, fit two or three expansion curtain rods into the drawer and lean the spice bottles against them.

B1. For narrower drawers, cut three pieces from a ¼-inch-diameter wooden dowel to the width of the drawer. Cut two pieces of corrugated cardboard to the depth and length of the drawer, then cut three small X's in each, at 2½-inch intervals, to hold the dowels in place.

B2. Place one piece of cardboard against each sidewall of the drawer. Position the dowels across the drawer and insert them into the small X's.

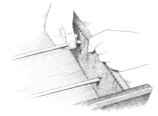

B3. Lean the spice bottles against the dowels in the drawer, with the labels facing up.

SCIENCE DESK: Why Beans Cause Gas

FOR SOME, THE GREATEST RESISTANCE TO PREPARING BLACK beans comes not from the lack of a good recipe but from an aversion to the discomfort associated with digestion. The creation of unwanted intestinal gas begins when small chains of carbohydrates called oligosaccharides enter the large intestine. People cannot digest these molecules efficiently, but bacteria residing at the end of the gut do and produce gas as a byproduct. Some sources say presoaking or precooking beans alleviates the gaseous aftermath by removing these carbohydrates. We decided to put this to the test.

We measured the amount of the most prevalent oligosaccharide in black beans, stachyose, that remained in cooked beans that had been treated using different methods. An overnight soak in water reduced the amount of stachyose remaining in the beans by 29.8 percent. The quick-soak method, consisting of a one-minute boil followed by a soak for an hour, was more effective, removing 42.5 percent of the stachyose, although many of the beans did explode during cooking. We tested several ingredients that are purported to "neutralize" the offending compounds as the beans cook; epazote, kombu (giant kelp), bay leaf, and baking soda. None of these seemed to do much in the pot, though it is possible that they act only during digestion.

Our conclusion: Though the quick-soak method is not our first choice because of its negative effect on the texture of the beans, if beans cause you significant discomfort, this approach is the most effective at reducing the amount of offending compounds.

EQUIPMENT CORNER: Chef's Knives

OUR TEST KITCHEN IS STOCKED WITH PREMIUM KNIVES THAT cost $100 or more. These knives are pretty good—and for that price, they ought to be. But could we find a decent knife for significantly less money? To find out, we rounded up eight 8-inch chef's knives (the best size for most cooks) and headed into the test kitchen to give each knife a workout.

When we cut butternut squash in half, some of our nine test knives (including one of the two Henckels tested, the International) felt dangerously flimsy. Others managed this task but cut crookedly as the blade bent (such as the Oxo). A few knives (especially the Forschner and Wüsthof) completed this task without a hitch.

We then chopped onions and minced parsley with all nine knives. These tasks were much easier to perform if the cutting edge was curved rather than perfectly straight. Try this test to understand why: Start with the knife tilted up on its tip, with the heart of the blade sitting on the food to be cut. From there, slide the knife forward while lowering the handle until the knife sits flat on the cutting board. If the edge is rounded, the knife almost "rocks" back to the starting position when you lift it; a flat blade (like those on both Henckels knives tested) falls to the board with a rhythm-breaking thump and doesn't "rock" back up.

Some say a heavy blade does some of the work for you. We think a heavy blade is awkward. A heavy handle is no better and can quickly tire your elbow and wrist. The weight should be equally balanced between the handle and blade.

All of the knives started out sharp enough to slice a ripe tomato. At the end of testing, the same could not be said for several knives, especially the Chicago and Farberware entries.

Smooth, polished handles became dangerously slick when we tried cutting up a chicken, but textured handles helped us keep a good grip, even when our hands were greasy. Blades on some knives were so narrow that our testers' knuckles kept crashing into the cutting board. At the store, hold the knife in your hand. If the handle is too smooth or if there doesn't seem to be enough clearance room for your knuckles, move on to another knife.

Do you need to fork over $100 for a good knife? Not even close. The Forschner Victorinox, which costs just $25, was the clear winner in these trials, and it rivals the best of the pricey knives in our test kitchen.

Rating Chef's Knives

WE TESTED EIGHT CHEF'S KNIVES AND PUT THEM THROUGH A VARIETY OF TASKS, FROM CUTTING HARD WINTER SQUASH and butchering whole chickens to mincing parsley and slicing ripe tomatoes. They were rated for cutting ability, blade shape, weight, sharpness, and handle comfort. The knives are listed in order of preference. See www.americastestkitchen.com for up-to-date prices and mail-order sources for top-rated products.

HIGHLY RECOMMENDED

Forschner Victorinox Fibrox Chef's Knife $25.33

One tester summed it up: "Premium-quality knife at a bargain price." Knives costing four times as much would be hard pressed to match its perform-ance. The blade is curved and sharp; the handle comfortable. Overall, "sturdy" and "well balanced."

NOT RECOMMENDED

Oxo Good Grips Chef's Knife $12.99

A delicate knife not suited for even the most delicate tasks. The blade bowed and twisted even when used to chop parsley and it bent permanently when put to strenuous jobs such as splitting squash.

RECOMMENDED

Wüsthof Gourmet Cook's Knife $49.99

Best suited for cooks with smaller hands. Testers with large hands complained that their knuckles hit the board before the blade did. The spine of the knife was thought to be "unnecessarily sharp," but this knife per-formed well in all tests.

NOT RECOMMENDED

J. A. Henckels International Fine Edge Pro Chef's Knife $11.40

We found nothing to like about the cheapest knife of the bunch. This "overgrown paring knife" left absolutely no room for knuckles. The perfectly flat blade and shiny, slick handle make this contender a shoo-in for the junk drawer.

RECOMMENDED WITH RESERVATIONS

J. A. Henckels Twin Signature Chef's Knife $29.95

Described as hefty and bulky, this knife also has a contoured handle that can get slippery and "didn't feel comfortable" in all testers' hands. The blade borders on being "too flat."

NOT RECOMMENDED

Farberware Pro Forged Chef's Knife $19.99

Feels unfinished, and the rough seams between the blade and handle are uncomfortable. Forget slicing—we could only "bruise" onions.

NOT RECOMMENDED

Calphalon Contemporary Cutlery Chef's Knife $31.99

A dead ringer for expensive German knives, but the thick blade on this knife is heavy enough to tax even the strongest cook. "Feels more like an ax" than a kitchen knife.

NOT RECOMMENDED

Chicago Walnut Tradition Chef's Knife $13.05

"Shaggy" wooden handle needs some sanding. Dull knives bruise vegetables; this one doesn't even scratch the surface. One tester realized, "this is why folks cut themselves."

TORTILLA SOUP

WHAT WE WANTED: A spicy full-flavored version of this Mexican classic that doesn't rely on hard-to-find ingredients.

Tortilla soup is a classic south-of-the-border chicken soup, a spicy chicken-tomato broth full of shredded chicken and overflowing with garnishes (fried tortilla strips, crumbled cheese, diced avocado, and lime wedges). All in all, an intensely flavored soup with rich flavors and contrasting textures. Authentic recipes call for at least one, if not several, uniquely Mexican ingredients, such as cotija, epazote, and crema Mexicana, none of which is available in local markets—unless you live in Mexico. In addition, traditional recipes demand a major investment of time, requiring you to make homemade chicken stock and fry tortilla strips, which seems beyond the pale for home cooks wanting to whip up a batch for a weeknight meal.

We made a few of these authentic recipes (after a long hunt for ingredients). They tasted great, but the preparation was arduous at best. Yet when we cooked a few "Americanized" recipes, we ended up with watery brews of store-bought chicken broth and canned tomatoes topped with stodgy, off-the-shelf tortilla chips. Quick, but definitely not what we would call great-tasting.

We started anew and broke the soup down into its three classic components: a flavor base made with fresh tomatoes, garlic, onion, and chiles; chicken stock; and an array of garnishes, including fried tortilla strips. We zeroed in on the flavor base first, recalling that the best of the soups we had made called for a basic Mexican cooking technique in which the vegetables are charred on a comal, or griddle, then pureed and fried to create a concentrated paste that flavors the soup.

Without a comal in the test kitchen, we used a cast-iron skillet for charring, and the results were superb, even with mediocre supermarket tomatoes. The downside was that it took 25 attentive minutes to complete the task. We wondered if we could skip charring altogether by adding smoke-flavored

dried chiles to a puree of raw tomatoes, onion, and garlic. (We used guajillo chiles, which are often used to spice up tortilla soup.) The answer was yes, but toasting and grinding these hard-to-find chiles didn't bring us any closer to a quick and easy recipe. Chipotle chiles (smoked jalapeños) seemed like a more practical choice. Canned in a vinegary tomato mixture called adobo sauce, chipotles pack heat, roasted smoky flavor, and, more important, convenience. We also found that aggressively frying the raw tomatoes, onion, and chipotle puree over high heat forced all of the water out of the mixture and further concentrated its flavor.

With the vegetable-charring step eliminated, we moved on to the chicken stock. Yes, the test kitchen does have an excellent recipe for homemade stock, but we were hoping to move this recipe into the express lane. The obvious alternative was to doctor supermarket low-sodium chicken broth, especially since this soup is awash with so many other vibrant flavors. We tried cooking chicken in broth bolstered with onion and garlic, reasoning that the chicken would

---

GETTING IT RIGHT: Corn Tortillas

We tasted six brands of corn tortillas and found that thicker tortillas didn't brown as well in the oven and became more chewy than crisp. Thin tortillas, either white or yellow, quickly became feather-light and crisp when oven-fried. Flavor differences between brands were slight, but locally made tortillas did pack a bit more corn flavor than national brands. Our advice? Purchase the thinnest tortillas you can find and choose a locally made brand, if possible.

Thick:
Too Chewy

Thin:
Just Right

both release and take on flavor while it poached. (We chose bone-in chicken as it has more flavor than boneless.) Split chicken breasts poached in just 20 minutes and could then be shredded and stirred back into the soup before serving. (Rich-flavored chicken thighs are an equally good choice, but, if poorly trimmed, they can turn the soup greasy.) Cooked this way, the chicken retained its juiciness and tender texture and the broth was nicely flavored.

Every authentic recipe for tortilla soup calls for fresh epazote, a common Mexican herb that imparts a heady, distinctive flavor and fragrance to the broth. Unfortunately, while epazote is widely available in the Southwest, it is virtually nonexistent in the Northeast. Still, we managed to track some down for testing purposes. Its wild, pungent flavor is difficult to describe, but after careful tasting we decided that it most closely resembles fresh cilantro, mint, and oregano. Using a broth steeped with epazote as a control, we sampled broths made with each of these herbs. The winner was a pairing of strong, warm oregano with pungent cilantro. It was not identical to the flavor of epazote, but it scored highly for its intensity and complexity. We now had deeply flavored broth that when stirred together with the tomato mixture made for a soup that was starting to taste like the real thing.

Flour tortillas, whether fried or oven-baked, tasted fine on their own but quickly disintegrated in hot soup. That left us with corn tortillas. The classic preparation is frying, but cooking up two or three batches of corn tortilla strips took more time and attention than we wanted to muster. Tasters flatly rejected the notion of raw corn tortillas—a recommendation we found in more than one recipe—as they rapidly turned gummy and unpalatable when added to the hot soup. Corn tortillas require some sort of crisping. After much testing, we came across a technique in a low-fat cookbook that was both fast and easy: Lightly oiled tortilla strips are simply toasted in the oven. The result? Chips that are just as crisp, less greasy, and much less trouble to prepare than their fried cousins.

As for the garnishes, we worked through the list one ingredient at a time. Lime added sharp, fresh notes to an already complex bowl, as did cilantro leaves and minced jalapeño. Avocado was another no-brainer. Thick, tart crema Mexicana (a tangy, cultured cream) is normally swirled into individual soup bowls, too. If it's unavailable, sour cream is a natural stand-in. Crumbled cotija or queso fresco cheese is great but hard to find. Cotija (the test kitchen favorite) is sharp and rich, while queso fresco is mild and milky. If you can't find cotija, use Monterey Jack, which melts nicely.

WHAT WE LEARNED: In place of tomatoes charred on a comal, or special Mexican griddle, use canned chipotle chiles packed in adobo sauce mixed with pureed fresh tomatoes to give the broth a spicy, smoky kick. A combination of fresh oregano and cilantro most closely mimics the flavor of an herb crucial to authentic tortilla soup, hard-to-find epazote. Use corn tortillas, not flour tortillas, for crispy strips with the best flavor and texture. And baking the tortilla strips, rather than frying them, crisps the strips quickly without a greasy aftertaste.

TORTILLA SOUP

Makes about 9 cups, serving 6

Despite its somewhat lengthy ingredient list, this recipe is very easy to prepare. If you desire a soup with mild spiciness, trim the ribs and seeds from the jalapeño (or omit the jalapeño altogether) and use the minimum amount of chipotle in adobo sauce (1 teaspoon, pureed with the tomatoes in step 3). Our preferred brand of low-sodium chicken broth is Swanson's Certified Organic Free Range (see details of our tasting on page 78). If advance preparation suits you, the soup can be completed short of adding the shredded chicken to the pot at the end of step 3. Return the soup to a simmer over medium-high heat before proceeding. The tortilla strips and the garnishes are best prepared the day of serving.

tortilla strips

8 (6-inch) corn tortillas, cut into ½-inch-wide strips
1 tablespoon vegetable oil
   Salt

soup

2 split bone-in, skin-on chicken breasts (about 1½ pounds) or 4 bone-in, skin-on chicken thighs (about 1¼ pounds), skin removed and well trimmed of excess fat
8 cups low-sodium chicken broth
1 very large white onion (about 1 pound), trimmed of root end, quartered, and peeled
4 medium garlic cloves, peeled
2 sprigs fresh epazote or 8 to 10 sprigs fresh cilantro plus 1 sprig fresh oregano
   Salt
2 medium tomatoes, cored and quartered
½ medium jalapeño chile (see note)
1 chipotle chile in adobo, plus up to 1 tablespoon adobo sauce
1 tablespoon vegetable oil

garnishes

   Lime wedges
   Avocado, peeled, pitted, and diced fine
   Cotija cheese, crumbled, or Monterey Jack cheese, diced fine
   Fresh cilantro leaves
   Jalapeño chile, minced
   Crema Mexicana or sour cream

1. FOR THE TORTILLA STRIPS: Adjust an oven rack to the middle position; heat the oven to 425 degrees. Spread the tortilla strips on a rimmed baking sheet; drizzle with the oil and toss until evenly coated. Bake until the strips are deep golden brown and crisped, about 14 minutes, rotating the pan and shaking the strips (to redistribute) halfway through baking. Season the strips lightly with salt; transfer to a plate lined with several layers of paper towels.

2. FOR THE SOUP: While the tortilla strips bake, bring the chicken, broth, 2 onion quarters, 2 garlic cloves, the epazote, and ½ teaspoon salt to a boil over medium-high heat in a large saucepan; reduce the heat to low, cover, and simmer until the chicken is just cooked through, about 20 minutes. Using tongs, transfer the chicken to a large plate. Pour the broth through a fine-mesh strainer; discard the solids in the strainer. When cool enough to handle, shred the chicken into bite-size pieces; discard the bones.

3. Puree the tomatoes, 2 remaining onion quarters, 2 remaining garlic cloves, jalapeño, chipotle chile, and 1 teaspoon adobo sauce in a food processor until smooth. Heat the oil in a Dutch oven over high heat until shimmering; add the tomato-onion puree and ⅛ teaspoon salt and cook, stirring frequently, until the mixture has darkened in color, about 10 minutes. Stir the strained broth into the tomato mixture, bring to a boil, then reduce the heat to low and simmer to blend the flavors, about 15 minutes. Taste the soup; if desired, add up to 2 teaspoons additional adobo sauce. Add the shredded chicken and simmer until heated through, about 5 minutes. To serve, place portions of tortilla strips in the bottom of individual bowls and ladle the soup into the bowls; pass the garnishes separately.

GETTING IT RIGHT: Translating Tortilla Soup

Authentic tortilla soup is chock-full of hard-to-find Mexican ingredients. We tested dozens of widely available substitutes. Here are our favorites.

| Epazote | Fresh Cilantro and Oregano |

| Comal-Roasted Chile | Chipotles in Adobo Sauce |

Cilantro and oregano replicate the pungent flavor of fresh epazote better than dried epazote does.

Smoked jalapeños in a tomato-vinegar sauce take the place of skillet-charred chiles and tomatoes.

| Cotija | Monterey Jack |

| Crema Mexicana | Sour Cream |

Monterey Jack doesn't crumble like cotija, but it melts better than other choices, such as feta.

Sour cream is milder than cultured Mexican cream, but it's close enough.

Chris removes the thin skin from butternut squash with a sharp peeler and then dices the trimmed squash with a sharp chef's knife.

COOKING with squash

IN THIS CHAPTER

THE RECIPES

Butternut Squash Soup
Curried Squash Soup
Squash Soup with Cinnamon-
    Sugar Croutons

Butternut Squash Risotto
Butternut Squash Risotto
    with Spinach and Toasted
    Pine Nuts

EQUIPMENT CORNER

Nutmeg Graters

What could be more synonymous with fall than butternut squash, with its vivid orange color and sweet, earthy flavor? We enjoy butternut squash simply: on its own, roasted in chunks, or pureed with a little butter until smooth. But we don't stop there. In this chapter, we explore two main-course recipes: a creamy, comforting soup perfect for serving on a busy weeknight and a rich, hearty risotto suitable for entertaining.

The bad butternut squash soups we've tasted (and prepared) can run the gamut from thin and insipid to thick, fibrous, and overly sweet. We needed to find a way to strike just the right balance between flavor and texture to show off the merits of this vegetable in a soup setting. Nor is incorporating butternut squash into risotto without its challenges (such as how to prepare and cook the squash so that it complements, rather than overwhelms, the risotto).

But don't let this large vegetable intimidate you. With a cleaver and several novel cooking methods, you can easily incorporate butternut squash into your seasonal repertoire.

COOKING WITH SQUASH **39**

BUTTERNUT SQUASH SOUP

WHAT WE WANTED: A silky smooth soup rich with not-too-sweet nutty squash flavor.

Many squash soups do not live up to their potential. Rather than being lustrous, slightly creamy, and intensely "squashy" in flavor, they are vegetal or porridge-like, and sometimes taste more like a squash pie than a squash soup.

Knowing that our basic method would be to cook the squash and then puree it with a liquid, our first test focused on how to cook the squash for the soup. Some recipes suggest boiling the squash in a cooking liquid, others roasting it in the oven, and still others sautéing it on the stovetop.

We tried boiling the squash, but having to peel the tough skin away before dicing it seemed unnecessarily tedious. We eliminated the sauté technique for the same reason. While roasting was infinitely more simple than our attempts at boiling or sautéing (all we had to do was slice the squash in half, scoop out the seeds, and roast it on a rimmed baking sheet), it produced a caramel-flavored soup with a gritty texture. Roasting also took at least one hour—too long for what should be a quick, no-nonsense soup.

In an effort to conserve time without sacrificing the quick preparation we liked from the roasting test, we decided to try steaming the squash. In a large Dutch oven, we sautéed shallots in butter (we tried garlic and onion but found them too overpowering and acrid with the sweet squash), then added water to the sautéed shallots and brought the mix to a simmer. We seeded and quartered the squash and placed it into a collapsible steaming insert, then added the squash and insert to the Dutch oven. We covered the pan and let the squash steam for 30 minutes, until it was tender enough to show no resistance to a long-pronged fork. This method proved to be successful. We liked it because all of the cooking took place in just one pot and, as a bonus, we ended up with a squash-infused cooking liquid that we could use in the soup.

But there was a downside. Essentially, steaming had the opposite effect of roasting: whereas roasting concentrated the sugars and eliminated the liquid in the squash (which is

---

TECHNIQUE: Cutting Up Butternut Squash

With its thick skin and odd shape, butternut squash is notoriously difficult to cut, even with the best chef's knife. We prefer to use a cleaver and mallet.

1. Set the squash on a damp kitchen towel to hold it in place. Position the cleaver on the skin of the squash.

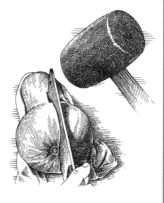

2. Strike the back of the cleaver with a mallet to drive the cleaver deep into the squash. Continue to hit the cleaver with the mallet until the cleaver cuts completely through the squash.

what made the roasted squash soup gritty), steaming added liquid to the squash and diluted its flavor.

As we were preparing squash one morning, it occurred to us that we were throwing away the answer to more squash flavor—the seeds and fibers. Instead of trashing the scooped-out remnants, we added them to the sautéed shallots and butter. In a matter of minutes, the room became fragrant with an earthy, sweet squash aroma, and the butter in our Dutch oven turned a brilliant shade of saffron. We added the water to the pan and proceeded with the steaming preparation. After the squash was cooked through, we strained the liquid of seeds, fibers, and spent shallot, then blended the soup.

To intensify the sweetness of the squash (but not make the soup sweet), we added a teaspoon of dark brown sugar to the blender jar. Not only was this batch of squash soup brighter in flavor, but it was more intense in color as well. To round out the flavor and introduce some richness to the soup, we added ½ cup of heavy cream. Now the soup was thick, rich, and redolent with pure squash flavor.

As is true with many creamed soups, texture is almost as important as flavor. We found blending the squash in batches with just enough liquid to make a thick puree worked best—the thicker base provided more friction and made it easier for the blender to smooth out any lumps or remaining squash fibers. Once all the squash was pureed to a silken texture, we added the remaining liquid and cream and briefly pulsed the soup to combine. We heated the soup briefly over a low flame and stirred in a little freshly grated nutmeg. In under one hour and with only one pot, we made a squash soup that offered nothing less than autumn in a bowl.

WHAT WE LEARNED: For the best flavor, use every bit of squash, including the seeds and stringy fibers. Sautéing the seeds and fibers as well as steaming the whole squash ensures big squash flavor. Steaming also produces a tender, creamy squash. Pureeing the soup in batches easily smoothes out any lumps or squash fibers, resulting in a velvety texture.

BUTTERNUT SQUASH SOUP

Serves 4 to 6

Other squash varieties that work well in this soup are delicata and carnival. Delicata is shaped like a zucchini and can be yellow or white with long green stripes. Carnival is shaped like an acorn squash but has a yellow skin with green and orange stripes. Lightly toasted pumpkin seeds, a drizzle of aged balsamic vinegar, or a sprinkle of paprika make appealing accompaniments to this soup.

4   tablespoons (½ stick) unsalted butter
1   large shallot, chopped fine
3   pounds butternut squash (about 1 large squash), cut in half lengthwise (see the illustrations on page 40), each half cut in half widthwise; seeds and fibers scraped out and reserved
6   cups water
    Salt
½   cup heavy cream
1   teaspoon dark brown sugar
    Pinch grated nutmeg

1. Melt the butter in a large, heavy-bottomed stockpot or Dutch oven over medium-low heat until foaming. Add the shallot and cook, stirring frequently, until translucent, about 3 minutes. Add the seeds and fibers from the squash and cook, stirring occasionally, until the butter turns a saffron color, about 4 minutes.

2. Add the water and 1 teaspoon salt to the pot and bring to a boil over high heat. Reduce the heat to medium-low, place the squash cut-side down in a steamer basket, and lower the basket into the pot. Cover and steam until the squash is completely tender, about 30 minutes. Take the pot off the heat and use tongs to transfer the squash to a rimmed baking sheet. When cool enough to handle, use a large spoon to scrape the flesh from the skin. Reserve the squash flesh in a bowl and discard the skin.

CURRIED SQUASH SOUP

If you like your curry spicy, choose madras curry powder for this soup.

Mix 4 tablespoons plain yogurt, 2 tablespoons minced fresh cilantro leaves, 1 teaspoon lime juice, and ⅛ teaspoon salt together in a small bowl. Refrigerate until needed. Follow the recipe for Butternut Squash Soup, adding 2 teaspoons curry powder to the blender when pureeing the squash and liquid. Finish the soup as directed and ladle it into individual bowls. Spoon some of the cilantro-yogurt mixture into each bowl and serve immediately.

SQUASH SOUP WITH CINNAMON-SUGAR CROUTONS

A sprinkle of spicy but sweet croutons is a nice foil for the rich soup.

Adjust an oven rack to the middle position and heat the oven to 350 degrees. Remove the crusts from 4 slices of white sandwich bread and cut the bread into ½-inch cubes (you should have about 2 cups). Toss the bread cubes with 2 tablespoons melted butter in a medium bowl. In a small bowl, combine 4 teaspoons sugar and 1 teaspoon ground cinnamon; sprinkle over the bread cubes and toss to combine. Spread the bread cubes in a single layer on a parchment-lined baking sheet and bake until crisp, 8 to 10 minutes. (The croutons can be stored in an airtight container for several days.) Follow the recipe for Butternut Squash Soup, sprinkling some of the croutons over the bowls of soup just before serving.

3. Strain the steaming liquid through a mesh strainer into a second bowl; discard the solids in the strainer. (You should have 2½ to 3 cups liquid.) Rinse and dry the pot.

4. Puree the squash in batches in a blender, pulsing on low speed and adding enough reserved steaming liquid to obtain a smooth consistency. Transfer the puree to the clean pot and stir in the remaining steaming liquid, the cream, and brown sugar. Warm the soup over medium-low heat until hot, about 3 minutes. Stir in the nutmeg and adjust the seasonings, adding salt to taste. Serve immediately. (The soup can be refrigerated in an airtight container for several days. Warm over low heat until hot; do not boil.)

EQUIPMENT CORNER: Nutmeg Graters

BEFORE TESTING NUTMEG GRATERS, WE RAN A COUPLE of tests to see if grating fresh nutmeg is worth the effort. In baked goods that call for lots of spices, such as spice cookies, we found that the signature flavor of fresh-ground nutmeg was lost; ground nutmeg from a jar works just fine in such recipes. However, in something like a béchamel sauce or eggnog, where there are no other spices to compete with it, fresh-ground nutmeg contributes a distinctively heady flavor that we really like. It also proved worthwhile in our butternut squash soup, where a pinch of nutmeg is added at the very end to finish the soup.

We purchased the following: three nutmeg mills, which work just like pepper mills and so keep your fingers completely safe; a new-style grater from Zyliss designed especially to keep your fingers out of harm's way; an old-style nutmeg grater; and a Microplane grater for spices.

Only one of the mills, the Cole & Mason acrylic mill, produced a neat and even grind in good time. It is pricey, though, at $21.50. The new Zyliss Nutmeg Grater, which costs $14.99, does protect your fingers, but it produced painfully little grated nutmeg. To use it, you put a whole nutmeg in a plastic hopper, secure the spring-loaded cap on top, and then slide the cap back and forth to grate the nutmeg. The old-style nutmeg grater comes in the form of a metal cylinder; the curves are intended to keep your fingertips away from the teeth as you grate. We tested one from Norpro that cost just $2, but it brought our fingers perilously close to the grating teeth.

Microplane takes the idea of a cylinder even further. In addition to a comfortable handle, this $9.50 grater has a slender, tightly curled, 5-inch-long grating surface that provides a good margin of safety for your fingertips. It produced mounds of nutmeg in no time flat and can also be used for grating nuts and chocolate. Perhaps not as elegant as the Cole & Mason for garnishing eggnog, it is nonetheless our top choice based on price, ease of use, and output.

BEST NUTMEG GRATERS

Grater
Microplane 40016 Spice Grater **$9.50**
Comfortable, safe, and efficient—and a fraction of the price of a mill.

Mill
Cole & Mason Nutmeg Mill **$21.50**
Expensive, but perfect for garnishing eggnog.

BUTTERNUT SQUASH RISOTTO

WHAT WE WANTED: A creamy, well-balanced version of the classic Italian rice dish.

Risotto can be challenging enough on its own, but throw butternut squash into the mix and, well, the stakes get even higher. Still, we know squash and rice have a natural affinity for each other, and this dish is a classic found in many Italian cookbooks. The most pressing issue we started with was how to cook the squash. Many recipes suggest roasting it ahead of time and then folding it into the finished rice. This was fine as far as it went, but the risotto and the squash never married properly. Somehow, we had to find a way to integrate the cooking of the two ingredients while preserving their individual personalities. We had high expectations for a recipe calling for pureed cooked squash added to the sautéed aromatics and cooked along with the rice, but those hopes were dashed when, instead, gluey squash paste emerged from the saucepan. The most obvious approach was to sauté the squash along with the aromatics and then leave it in the pan to cook down with the rice. This was no winner either, the squash being reduced to mushy, unidentifiable orange blobs.

What we sought was a creamy, orange-tinged rice fully infused with deep (but not overly sweet) squash flavor, flecked with bits of broken down squash as well as more substantial (but still soft) cubes. Quick, forced integration wouldn't work; the results would be too jarring. We would need a multi-step approach to coax the two elements together.

To maintain the textural integrity of the squash pieces, we found that dicing then cooking the flesh yielded better results than roasting the squash halves and removing the flesh afterward (this method caused the squash to fall apart). As for cooking method, roasting the diced squash in a 450-degree oven worked fairly well, but most tasters found the concentrated sweetness that resulted from the dry, intense heat too distracting. The other obvious method, sautéing the

squash pieces in a skillet, did not produce the color and flavor development we had hoped for. The solution? We gave one side of the squash pieces enough time to caramelize slightly before gently and occasionally stirring them during cooking. This produced the color and flavor we were after without the overt sweetness that was typical of the oven-roasting approach. We also found that olive oil was better than butter for sautéing since the latter caused the squash to darken more than we wanted.

Based on previous tests, we knew that the squash could not be added all at once to the rice. Added early on, the squash dissolved and lost its personality; added later in the cooking, it never became sufficiently integrated. Our first approach was to mash half of the cooked squash pieces and then sauté them with the toasted rice, folding in the rest of the intact pieces in at the end. Although the rice now had a ton of squash flavor, it also took on an unappealing gummy texture as the starches from the squashy paste immediately bound to the rice like glue. The final solution was actually quite simple—we added half of the cooked squash pieces in with the toasted rice (without mashing them) and then gently folded the remaining half in at the end. Now we had a perfect marriage—separate but equal.

In an effort to further elevate the squash flavor, we borrowed a surprising test kitchen technique we discovered when developing our Butternut Squash Soup (page 41). We sautéed the seeds and fibers (the scrapings) and then added them to the saucepan with the broth. A simple step, perhaps, but it yielded a complex and easy-to-detect boost in flavor without more sweetness.

All the butternut squash needed now was a rich, creamy rice base upon which it could be layered. In keeping with risotto-making tradition, we began by sautéing the basic aromatics of onion and garlic in some melted butter before adding short-grained Arborio rice, the test kitchen's grain of choice for achieving creamy, al-dente risotto. While this is normally done in a saucepan or saucier, we knew we could probably get away with using the same nonstick skillet we'd used for cooking the squash. In addition to having one less pot to wash, this not uncommon technique reduces sticking.

After the rice was toasted in the garlic-onion mixture, we added a cup of white wine (most basic risotto recipes call for half that) for extra acidity and brightness. Due to the strong flavors in the risotto, the wine flavor was faint at best. The addition of lemon juice, apple cider vinegar, and white wine vinegar all lent unwelcome, off flavors to the dish, but increasing the wine to triple the standard amount—1½ cups—gave the rice the acidity and complexity needed to balance the sweetness of the squash. Once the rice grains fully absorbed the wine, we stirred in half of the cooked squash.

Traditional risotto recipes are time-consuming since small amounts of broth or water are added to the pan, which must be stirred constantly for over half an hour. The test kitchen had already discovered a more streamlined, quicker method, which calls for preheating the chicken broth in a separate saucepan and then adding a whopping 3 cups to the rice once the wine has been absorbed. This speeds up the cooking and means less stirring at the outset. The remaining liquid is then added in smaller ½-cup increments and the rice stirred more frequently to prevent the bottom of the skillet from drying out.

While half-chicken, half-beef broth adds richness to some rice dishes, tasters disliked how the additional salt and meatiness from the beef broth competed with the flavor of the squash. Plus, the darker, muddier tinge was unappetizing. Plain chicken broth cut with a bit of water won out for its cleaner, fresher flavor. While vegetable broth is an acceptable alternative should the dish need to be kept vegetarian, it also lends a noticeably sweeter flavor to the risotto.

As for other ingredients, tasters preferred the traditional sage to thyme—1 tablespoon provided barely enough flavor but 2 tablespoons was perfect. Parmesan (a generous 1½ ounces) was the overwhelming favorite cheese, followed by the slightly sweeter Asiago. Pecorino

Romano was ruled out for its "funky, stinky, off taste." After stirring in ¼ teaspoon of freshly grated nutmeg for a hint of warm spice, we folded in the remaining squash. We had finally achieved the balance we were looking for in this classic Italian dish.

WHAT WE LEARNED: Buy whole squash, not pre-cut squash, so you can make a flavorful broth with the squash's seeds and fibers. Sauté the squash before starting the risotto to intensify flavor. Add the broth to the risotto in a large sum at the beginning, then when finishing, stir often for a creamy texture. Increase the standard amount of wine to balance the sweetness of the squash. For risotto with pleasing, contrasting textures, reserve a portion of the sautéed squash pieces to fold in just before serving.

TECHNIQUE: Dicing Squash

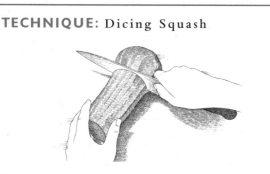

1. After removing the skin with a peeler, cut the squash in half.

2. Cut the bulb in half through the base and remove the seeds with a spoon.

3. Cut each piece into ½-inch half-moons, then into ½-inch dice.

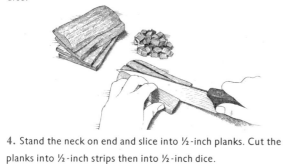

4. Stand the neck on end and slice into ½-inch planks. Cut the planks into ½-inch strips then into ½-inch dice.

BUTTERNUT SQUASH RISOTTO

Serves 4 as a main course or 6 as a first course

Infusing the chicken broth with the squash's seeds and fibers helps to reinforce the earthy squash flavor without adding additional squash. To make this dish vegetarian, vegetable broth can be used instead of chicken broth, but the resulting risotto will have more pronounced sweetness. See the illustrations at left for tips on preparing the squash.

2	tablespoons olive oil
1	medium butternut squash (about 2 pounds), peeled, seeded (reserve fibers and seeds), and cut into ½-inch cubes (about 3½ cups)
¾	teaspoon salt
¾	teaspoon ground black pepper
4	cups low-sodium chicken broth
1	cup water
4	tablespoons (½ stick) unsalted butter
2	small onions, chopped very fine (about 1½ cups)
2	medium garlic cloves, minced or pressed through a garlic press (about 2 teaspoons)
2	cups Arborio rice
1½	cups dry white wine
1½	ounces Parmesan cheese, grated fine (about ¾ cup)
2	tablespoons minced fresh sage leaves
¼	teaspoon grated nutmeg

1. Heat the oil in a 12-inch nonstick skillet over medium-high heat until shimmering but not smoking. Add the squash in an even layer and cook without stirring until golden brown, 4 to 5 minutes; stir in ¼ teaspoon of the salt and ¼ teaspoon of the pepper. Continue to cook, stirring occasionally, until the squash is tender and browned, about 5 minutes longer. Transfer the squash to a bowl and set aside.

2. Return the skillet to medium heat; add the reserved squash fibers and seeds and any leftover diced squash. Cook, stirring frequently to break up the fibers, until lightly browned, about 4 minutes. Transfer to a large saucepan and add the chicken broth and water; cover the saucepan and bring the mixture to a simmer over high heat, then reduce the heat to medium-low to maintain a bare simmer.

3. Melt 3 tablespoons of the butter in the now-empty skillet over medium heat; when the foaming subsides, add the onions, garlic, remaining ½ teaspoon salt, and remaining ½ teaspoon pepper. Cook, stirring occasionally, until the onions are softened, 4 to 5 minutes. Add the rice to the skillet and cook, stirring frequently, until the grains are translucent around the edges, about 3 minutes. (To prevent the rice from spilling out of the pan, stir inward, from the edges of the pan toward the center, not in a circular motion.) Add the wine and cook, stirring frequently, until the liquid is fully absorbed, 4 to 5 minutes. Meanwhile, strain the hot broth through a fine-mesh strainer into a medium bowl, pressing on the solids to extract as much liquid as possible. Return the strained broth to the saucepan and discard the solids in the strainer; cover the saucepan and set over low heat to keep the broth hot.

4. When the wine is fully absorbed, add 3 cups of the hot broth and half of the reserved squash to the rice. Simmer, stirring every 3 to 4 minutes, until the liquid is absorbed and the bottom of the pan is almost dry, about 12 minutes.

5. Stir in about ½ cup of the hot broth and cook, stirring constantly, until absorbed, about 3 minutes; repeat with additional broth until the rice is al dente, 2 or 3 more times. Off the heat, stir in the remaining 1 tablespoon butter, the Parmesan, sage, and nutmeg; gently fold in the remaining cooked squash. If desired, add up to ¼ cup additional broth to loosen the texture of the risotto. Serve immediately.

VARIATION

BUTTERNUT SQUASH RISOTTO WITH SPINACH AND TOASTED PINE NUTS

Keep a close eye on the pine nuts when toasting them; they can go from toasted to burned very quickly.

1. Toast ¼ cup pine nuts in a small, dry skillet over medium heat until golden and fragrant, about 5 minutes; set aside.

2. Follow the recipe for Butternut Squash Risotto; in step 2, after transferring the sautéed squash seeds and fibers to the saucepan, add 1 teaspoon olive oil to the empty skillet and swirl to coat. Add 4 ounces baby spinach and cook, covered, over medium heat, until the leaves begin to wilt, about 2 minutes. Uncover and cook, stirring constantly, until fully wilted, about 30 seconds. Transfer the spinach to a mesh strainer; set aside. Proceed with the recipe as directed. Drain the excess liquid from the spinach and stir the spinach into the risotto along with the remaining squash in step 5. Top individual servings of risotto with the toasted pine nuts.

We tested a variety of inexpensive steaks to find out which delivered good beefy flavor and tender texture.

STRIP LOIN

FLAP MEAT

BOTTOM ROUND

TOP SIRLOIN

DINNER on a dime

CHAPTER 5

IN THIS CHAPTER

THE RECIPES
Pan-Seared Inexpensive Steak
Tomato-Caper Pan Sauce
Mustard-Cream Pan Sauce

Buttermilk Mashed Potatoes
Buttermilk Mashed Potatoes with
    Leeks and Chives
Buttermilk Ranch Mashed
    Potatoes

EQUIPMENT CORNER
Sauciers

TASTING LAB
Inexpensive Steaks

There's something to be said about the convenience of serving steak for dinner. It's relatively easy to prepare and needs little embellishment beyond seasoning with salt and pepper. And side dishes for steak needn't be complicated—they can be as simple as potatoes and a green vegetable or salad. But does steak for dinner mean splurging on a $12 porterhouse? For those of us feeding a family, that price tag adds up, and such an indulgence just doesn't always make sense. We decided to investigate inexpensive steaks and find out which were worth eating and how best to prepare them.

We also wanted to take a look at a classic accompaniment to steak—mashed potatoes. Not a complicated dish, but we wanted something a little different from the same-old, without turning to fancy cheeses or roasted garlic. We found our answer in a rather humble ingredient—buttermilk—which lends the potatoes tang and richness. They're nothing fancy, but they taste just right alongside our steak.

GREAT CHEAP STEAKS

WHAT WE WANTED: An inexpensive steak with the flavor and texture to rival its pricey counterparts.

It's far too easy to spend lots of money on steak. Many people use the barometer of price to make their choice at the meat counter—the more expensive the better. But is this necessarily true? Are there any tricks to cooking less expensive cuts that could make them comparable in flavor and texture to the pricier cuts out there?

We began at the supermarket meat counter. Staring at the confusing array of steaks, we had several questions. What did the names mean? Where did these cuts come from? Which ones really tasted best?

Before narrowing down the choices, we needed to understand a bit more about what makes certain cuts of beef inexpensive. In simple terms, steak is muscle and cost is driven primarily by tenderness. As the animal grows and exercises, the fibers within each muscle grow, making the muscles bigger and tougher. Within each steer, the more tender meat comes from the least exercised part of the animal—the middle. This is why the cuts of beef from the rib and the loin are so tender compared with any cut from the chuck (shoulder/front arms) or the round (back legs). Another factor that affects the perception of tenderness is fat content. Marbled fat adds to the tenderness of meat. During cooking, this kind of fat (as opposed to exterior fat) melts into the muscle and helps separate fiber from fiber.

Armed with this knowledge, we went back to the supermarket (four stores in all) with an upper price limit of $6.99 per pound. We bought every cut within our price range and quickly found our first challenge was identifying them by name. While there is a national identification system (called the Uniform Retail Meat Identity Standards, or URMIS) that assigns a number and specific name to every retail cut of red meat, regional nomenclature is still common. For example, top butt, a steak sold in New Jersey, is a boneless shell sirloin steak in New England and a top

sirloin steak in northern California. Even within a small geographic area, the same steak can be called by various names. Once we figured out the naming conventions, we were left with a list of 12 cheap steaks.

Back in the test kitchen, we quickly discovered that most of these steaks were too tough and/or lacked beefy flavor, but a few showed tremendous potential. Tasters were particularly enthusiastic about boneless shell sirloin steak and flap meat steak. Both of these cuts come from the sirloin, which is right behind the middle of the cow. In fact, when we compared these steaks with porterhouse ($12.99 per pound), they held their own, especially the boneless shell sirloin. Not bad for a steak that retails here in Boston for $4.29 per pound.

We wondered if some sort of preparation could improve the flavor and texture of cheap steak. We tried salting the meat, dry aging, wet aging, soaking in vinegar, sprinkling with meat tenderizer, soaking in pineapple juice, and even cutting the meat in half horizontally to shorten the strands of protein that can make it tough to chew. None of these methods noticeably improved the texture. We also tried marinating the meat from one to 24 hours. While some of these methods worked to enhance the beef flavor, they made no significant impact on tenderness. In fact, when these steaks went head to head with one that had not been tenderized, tasters almost always preferred the plain steak.

Now the trick was to fine-tune our cooking method. We were looking for good overall browning on both sides of the steak and a generous fond—the browned bits that cling to the bottom of the skillet after searing and are crucial to a flavorful pan sauce. Sounds easy, but the challenges here are the same as for any pan-seared steak, expensive or not. What's important is to obtain a nice sear on both sides without overcooking the steak or allowing the fond to burn. This was achieved by starting with a very hot pan and hot oil and cooking one side of the steak until it was perfectly browned (without any moving or peeking). Once the first

side was done, we reduced the heat to avoid burning the fond (or the steak's crust). Many experienced cooks will agree that knowing when to take the steak out of the pan is the trickiest part. From prior kitchen tests, we've found that inserting an instant-read thermometer through the side of the steak (avoiding the bone) is the most accurate way to gauge doneness. (See "How to Tell When a Steak Is Done" at right for guidelines.) Once the steak is done, it should be transferred to a plate, covered with foil, and allowed to rest for 12 to 15 minutes before slicing. This helps the steak retain its juices. Lastly, the steak should be sliced thin, against the grain and on the bias to ensure the most tender meat. There you have it: a steak that's as tasty as it is affordable.

WHAT WE LEARNED: Choose boneless shell sirloin steaks (also called top butt) or whole flap meat steaks. Start with a very hot, conventional (not nonstick) skillet. Allow the meat to rest before slicing. Slice the steak thin, against the grain and on the bias, to ensure the most tender meat.

TECHNIQUE: How to Tell When a Steak Is Done

A great steak starts at the supermarket and ends with proper timing in the kitchen. Chefs who cook hundreds of steaks a week seem to know when a steak is done almost by intuition. Here are some of the more intriguing methods of determining doneness and our assessment of their practicality for home cooks.

Method: Press the meat and compare to parts of the body. Rare meat will feel like the flesh between your thumb and forefinger. Make a fist and touch the same part of your hand—medium meat will feel like this. Well-done meat will feel like the tip of your nose.
Our Assessment: You look funny touching your hand and nose when cooking a steak. Besides, this method is of no help to most home cooks.

Method: Nick and peek. Slice into the steak with a paring knife and check the color.
Our Assessment: The steak has already been butchered once—why do it a second time in the pan and risk a loss of juices? Fine in an emergency, but not our first choice.

Method: Take the temperature. Hold the steak aloft with a pair of tongs and slide an instant-read thermometer through the side, making sure to avoid any bones.
Our Assessment: The most reliable method. Works the first time you try it—and every time thereafter.

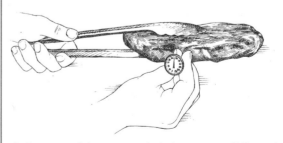

An instant-read thermometer is the best way to tell if a steak is done.

Rating Inexpensive Steaks

FIFTEEN MEMBERS OF THE AMERICA'S TEST KITCHEN STAFF TASTED 12 INEXPENSIVE STEAKS, ALL PRICED AT $6.99 PER POUND OR LESS. Because the same steak can be sold under many different names, for each entry, we've listed both the "technical name" (according to the Uniform Retail Meat Identity Standards) and the alternate names often used by supermarkets. With the exception of two specialty cuts, all of these steaks are regularly available in supermarkets.

RECOMMENDED
Boneless Shell Sirloin Steak

Alternate Names: Top butt, butt steak, top sirloin butt, top sirloin steak, center cut roast

Shopping Tips: One of the two main muscles from the hip. Can be quite large. Look for a 1-pound piece of even 1¼-inch thickness.

Tasters' Comments: "Tremendous beef flavor" coupled with "very tender" texture make this steak a winner. "Just like butter."

RECOMMENDED
Flap Meat Steak

Alternate Names: Top sirloin tips, beef sirloin tips, sirloin tip steak, sirloin flap meat for tips

Shopping Tips: Varies widely in size. Ask for a 1-pound steak of even thickness. Avoid small strips of meat or large steaks that taper drastically at one end.

Tasters' Comments: "Great beefy flavor" is the main selling point. Praised as "tender and fun to chew" and "never mushy."

RECOMMENDED (for grilling only)
Flank Steak

Alternate Names: Jiffy steak, London broil

Shopping Tips: This wide, thin steak doesn't fit easily in a pan but works great on the grill.

Tasters' Comments: "Pleasant," "mild" flavor with "just enough chew."

RECOMMENDED (for grilling only)
Skirt Steak

Alternate Names: Philadelphia steak, fajitas meat

Shopping Tips: This thin steak can measure more than a foot long, making it better suited for grilling than pan-searing.

Tasters' Comments: Tasters gush "wonderful" and "beefy heaven." The meat is "rich and fatty."

RECOMMENDED (available at butcher shops only)
Hanger Steak

Alternate Names: Hanging tenderloin, butcher's steak

Shopping Tips: Usually a restaurant cut, but your butcher may be able to procure this thick steak that "hangs" between the last rib and the loin.

Tasters' Comments: "Bold, brash beef flavor," with a texture that's "moderately tender" and "a little chewy."

RECOMMENDED (available at butcher shops only)
Flat-Iron Steak

Alternate Name: Blade steak

Shopping Tips: This restaurant cut comes from the same muscle as the blade steak, but the muscle is cut in such a way that the vein is removed at the same time.

Tasters' Comments: "Great beef flavor" and "awesome combination of tender and chewy." Like blade steaks, can be livery on occasion.

NOT RECOMMENDED
Top Blade Steak, Boneless

Alternate Names: Blade steak, book steak, butler steak, lifter steak, petit steak, flat-iron steak, boneless top chuck steak

Tasters' Comments: "Tender and juicy" but very undependable. Often tastes "like liver." But "when it's good, it's really good." A gamble.

NOT RECOMMENDED
Shoulder Steak, Boneless

Alternate Names: Chuck for swissing, boneless clod steak, London broil, boneless shoulder cutlet

Tasters' Comments: "Strong taste veers toward liver," but the texture has "decent bite."

NOT RECOMMENDED
Top Round Steak

Alternate Name: Inside round cut

Tasters' Comments: "Nice basic beef flavor," but the texture is "like bubblegum."

NOT RECOMMENDED
Bottom Round Steak

Tasters' Comments: "Lean and mild" is the overall assessment. Also found to be "gummy, with flat flavor."

NOT RECOMMENDED
Eye Round Steak

Tasters' Comments: "Not much meat flavor," while the texture is "tough," "chewy," and "like sawdust."

NOT RECOMMENDED
Tip Steak

Alternate Names: Sirloin tip steak, round tip steak, knuckle steak, top sirloin steak

Tasters' Comments: "Spongy," "shallow" beef flavor. "Tough as shoe leather."

PAN-SEARED INEXPENSIVE STEAK

Serves 4

A pan sauce can be made while the steaks rest after cooking (sauce recipes follow); if you intend to make a sauce, make sure to prepare all of the sauce ingredients before cooking the steaks. To serve two instead of four, use a 10-inch skillet to cook a 1-pound steak and halve the sauce ingredients. Bear in mind that even those tasters who usually prefer rare beef preferred these steaks cooked medium-rare or medium because the texture is firmer and not quite so chewy. Shopping can be confusing, as steaks are often haphazardly labeled at the supermarket. See the chart on page 52 for alternate names. The times in the recipe are for 1¼-inch-thick steaks.

2   tablespoons vegetable oil
2   whole boneless shell sirloin steaks (top butt) or whole flap meat steaks, each about 1 pound and 1¼ inches thick
    Salt and ground black pepper

1. Heat the oil in a heavy-bottomed 12-inch skillet over medium-high heat until smoking. Meanwhile, season both sides of the steaks with salt and pepper. Place the steaks in the skillet; cook, without moving the steaks, until well browned, about 2 minutes. Using tongs, flip the steaks; reduce the heat to medium. Cook until well browned on the second side and the internal temperature registers 125 degrees on an instant-read thermometer for medium-rare (about 5 minutes) or 130 degrees for medium (about 6 minutes).

2. Transfer the steaks to a large plate and tent loosely with foil; let rest until the internal temperature registers 130 degrees for medium-rare or 135 degrees for medium, 12 to 15 minutes. Meanwhile, prepare the pan sauce, if making.

3. Using a sharp chef's knife or carving knife, slice the steak about ¼ inch thick against the grain on the bias, arrange on a platter or on individual plates, and spoon some sauce (if using) over each steak; serve immediately.

until beginning to brown, 2 to 3 minutes. Sprinkle the flour over the shallot; cook, stirring constantly, until combined, about 1 minute. Add the wine and increase the heat to medium-high; simmer rapidly, scraping up the browned bits on the pan bottom with a wooden spoon. Simmer until the liquid is reduced to a glaze, about 30 seconds; add the broth and simmer until reduced to ⅔ cup, about 4 minutes. Reduce the heat to medium; add the capers, tomato, and any meat juices that have accumulated on the plate and cook until the flavors are blended, about 1 minute. Stir in the parsley and season to taste with salt and pepper; spoon the sauce over the sliced steak and serve immediately.

MUSTARD-CREAM PAN SAUCE

Makes ¾ cup

- 1   medium shallot, minced (about 3 tablespoons)
- 2   tablespoons dry white wine
- ½   cup low-sodium chicken broth
- 6   tablespoons heavy cream
- 3   tablespoons grainy Dijon mustard
      Salt and ground black pepper

Follow the recipe for Pan-Seared Inexpensive Steak; after transferring the steaks to a large plate, pour off all but 1 tablespoon of the fat from the now-empty skillet. Return the skillet to low heat and add the shallot; cook, stirring frequently, until beginning to brown, 2 to 3 minutes. Add the wine and increase the heat to medium-high; simmer rapidly, scraping up the browned bits on the pan bottom with a wooden spoon. Simmer until the liquid is reduced to a glaze, about 30 seconds; add the broth and simmer until reduced to ¼ cup, about 3 minutes. Add the cream and any meat juices that have accumulated on the plate; cook until heated through, about 1 minute. Stir in the mustard; season to taste with salt and pepper. Spoon over the sliced steak and serve immediately.

TOMATO-CAPER PAN SAUCE

Makes ¾ cup

If ripe fresh tomatoes are not available, substitute 2 to 3 canned whole tomatoes, seeded and cut into ¼-inch pieces.

- 1   medium shallot, minced (about 3 tablespoons)
- 1   teaspoon unbleached all-purpose flour
- 2   tablespoons dry white wine
- 1   cup low-sodium chicken broth
- 2   tablespoons capers, drained
- 1   medium ripe tomato, seeded and cut into
      ¼-inch dice (about ¼ cup)
- ¼   cup minced fresh parsley leaves
      Salt and ground black pepper

Follow the recipe for Pan-Seared Inexpensive Steak. After transferring the steaks to a large plate, pour off all but 1 tablespoon of the fat from the now-empty skillet. Return the skillet to low heat and add the shallot; cook, stirring frequently,

BUTTERMILK MASHED POTATOES

WHAT WE WANTED: Smooth, lush mashed potatoes, highlighted with the tang of buttermilk and easy enough to prepare on a busy weeknight.

Recipe writers like to tout buttermilk as a miracle ingredient, claiming that the naturally lean product (made by adding bacteria to skim or low-fat milk) creates the illusion of butter and cream where there actually is none. Buttermilk is commonly used in mashed potatoes because of these supposed low-fat/high-flavor qualities. But would any butterless mashed potato recipes really deliver?

In a word, no. The recipes we tried produced potatoes that were curdled, crumbly, chalky, and dry. In fact, other than a low calorie count, the grainy, thirsty potatoes only had one thing going for them: the distinctive tang of buttermilk. This trademark tart flavor was in fact so alluring (the low-fat notion was nice but not at the expense of flavor) that we decided to continue our investigation.

We sketched out a plan: First and foremost, we were going to add some butter! Because of the flavorful, creamy buttermilk, we wouldn't need to add a truckload, but we had decided that fat-free potatoes just weren't worth choking down. Second, we wanted an everyday recipe, streamlined enough for frequent dinner-table appearances. We also had to develop a curdle-proof technique. While most recipes instruct the cook to heat the buttermilk, what resulted was an unappealing mix of watery, coagulated liquid and grainy curds.

Tackling the curdling problem first, our thought was to skip the heating step, but that wasn't the answer: Buttermilk curdles at 160 degrees, a temperature reached almost instantly when the cold liquid hits steaming-hot potatoes. We pulled out an instant-read thermometer and started adding buttermilk to the potatoes when they dropped below the 160-degree mark. This worked, but talk about fussy! We kept searching for a viable solution and came across sources suggesting pinches of baking soda (to neutralize acidity) or cornstarch (for stability). Neither trick worked. We knew that high-fat dairy products like half-and-half aren't prone

to curdling. Since we were planning to add butter anyway, what if we fattened up the buttermilk with some melted butter? Bingo. When mixed with room-temperature buttermilk, the melted butter acted as an insulating agent, coating the proteins in the buttermilk and protecting them from heat shock.

In the past, the test kitchen has found that simmering whole russet potatoes in their skins (and peeling them while they're hot) yields true potato flavor and a rich, silky texture; peeled and cut russets cook up with a thin taste and texture. Could we simplify the cooking method by switching our choice of potatoes? Peeled and cut red potatoes were dense and pasty when mashed, but peeled and cut Yukon Golds made creamy, smooth mashed potatoes.

Why do Yukon Gold potatoes respond better to this technique than russets? Russet potatoes have more starch and therefore absorb a lot more water than lower-starch Yukon Golds. So while mashed russets become soggy if peeled and cut before cooking, the less absorbent Yukon Golds turn out just right. We also found it important to cook the potatoes sufficiently.

Settling on amounts of butter and buttermilk was a balancing act. Too much butter obscured the buttermilk flavor; too little tasted too lean. After many trials, we settled on 6 tablespoons butter and ⅔ cup buttermilk. These amounts allowed plenty of tartness to shine through—and while this wasn't diet food, we didn't have to think twice about going back for seconds. So when it comes to buttermilk mashed potatoes, all you need is the right potato and the right technique. (And a little butter.)

WHAT WE LEARNED: Lower-starch Yukon Gold won out over russet potatoes. Yukon Golds can be cut and peeled before being boiled and still won't become waterlogged, unlike russets, which must be boiled in their jackets, then peeled while hot, which can be cumbersome. Bring the buttermilk to room temperature and combine with the cooled melted better before adding them to the potatoes—this will prevent the buttermilk from curdling.

BUTTERMILK MASHED POTATOES
Serves 4

To achieve the proper texture, it is important to cook the potatoes thoroughly; they are done if they break apart when a knife is inserted and gently wiggled. Buttermilk substitutes like clabbered milk do not produce sufficiently tangy potatoes. To reduce the likelihood of curdling, the buttermilk must be brought to room temperature and mixed with cooled melted butter.

- 2 pounds Yukon Gold potatoes, peeled and cut into 1-inch chunks
   Salt
- 6 tablespoons (¾ stick) unsalted butter, melted and cooled
- ⅔ cup buttermilk at room temperature
   Ground black pepper

1. Place the potatoes in a large saucepan and cover with 1 inch cold water; add 1 tablespoon salt. Bring to a boil over high heat, then reduce the heat to medium and simmer until the potatoes break apart very easily when a paring knife is inserted, about 18 minutes. Drain the potatoes briefly, then immediately return them to the saucepan set on the still hot burner.

2. Using a potato masher, mash the potatoes until a few small lumps remain. Gently mix the melted butter and buttermilk in a small bowl until combined. Add the butter-buttermilk mixture to the potatoes; using a rubber spatula, fold gently until just incorporated. Adjust the seasonings with salt and pepper to taste; serve immediately.

BUTTERMILK MASHED POTATOES WITH LEEKS AND CHIVES

Follow the recipe for Buttermilk Mashed Potatoes, adding 1 bay leaf to the potato cooking water in step 1. Discard the bay leaf after draining the potatoes. While the potatoes cook, melt 1 tablespoon unsalted butter in a small nonstick skillet over medium heat. Add 1 medium leek, white and light green parts only, rinsed well, quartered, and cut into ¼-inch slices; cook, stirring occasionally, until lightly browned and wilted, about 8 minutes. Continue with the recipe from step 2, adding the sautéed leeks and 3 tablespoons minced fresh chives to the potatoes along with the butter-buttermilk mixture.

BUTTERMILK RANCH MASHED POTATOES

Remove the sour cream from the refrigerator at the same time as the buttermilk so that both will be at room temperature when they're added to the potatoes.

Follow the recipe for Buttermilk Mashed Potatoes, adding 1 small garlic clove, minced or pressed through a garlic press (about ½ teaspoon), 3 scallions, sliced very thin (about ⅓ cup), 2 tablespoons minced fresh parsley leaves, and ⅓ cup sour cream to the potatoes along with the butter-buttermilk mixture in step 2.

EQUIPMENT CORNER: Sauciers

THE TEST KITCHEN IS DIVIDED FAIRLY EVENLY INTO two distinct groups: Those who count sauciers among their most essential pans and those who never use them, who basically think of a saucier as nothing more than a souped-up saucepan. The two noticeable differences between a saucier and a sauce pan are a slightly wider mouth and rounded, flared sides—the latter designed expressly to accommodate wire whisks and to eliminate any distinct edge at the bottom of the pan where a sauce might seek temporary refuge and overcook.

To better ascertain the potential benefits of the saucier, we conducted a survey of the test kitchen's most zealous saucier mavens. "I love cooking in my saucier," proclaimed one exuberant test cook. "It's used so frequently that it rarely gets put away." Tasks for which the saucier camp reported reaching for this pan rather than a saucepan included preparations demanding constant stirring—custards, risottos, sauces—as well as those requiring poaching (especially fruit) and braising. One staffer praised the saucier for combining the best qualities of a saucepan and a skillet: "It's got depth and capacity but also width and easy interior access."

Anecdotal enthusiasm was all well and good. But how would sauciers fare in objective kitchen tests? To find out, we brought seven leading brands into the kitchen to perform typical stovetop tasks.

TECHNIQUE: Cleaning Leeks

Leeks are often quite dirty and gritty, so they require thorough cleaning. There are two ways to do this. Both methods require that you first cut the dark green portion into quarters lengthwise, leaving the root end intact.

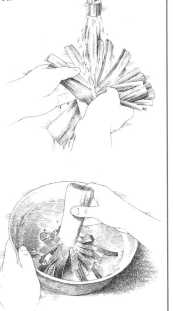

A. Hold the leek under running water and shuffle the cut layers like a deck of cards.

B. Slosh the cut end of the leek up and down in a bowl of water.

We'll cut to the chase. Except for one model, every pan performed each task brilliantly, including the test kitchen's favorite saucepan, which we included for comparison. (See the chart on page 59.) Risotto after risotto, béchamel after tedious béchamel, our daily stovetop sessions spent hunting for illuminating signs of variation invariably ended with a tidy row of virtually identical preparations. "This third risotto may be a bit more watery," one of us would venture aloud. (It wasn't.) "Gravy number six—does it have a slightly darker hue?" (It didn't.) An extra minute of cooking time here, a more conspicuously caramelized piece of onion there, but the results were all safely within our parameters for good performance. Given that our trusty saucepan was among these good performers, these tests raised the question: Why purchase a saucier if you already have a good saucepan?

The quick (and honest) answer is that you don't have to, especially if you already have a large, high-quality saucepan such as the test kitchen favorite, All-Clad. Sauciers have their advantages to be sure: easy access to the corners (thanks to the rounded bottom) and a wide-mouth design that encourages evaporation and eases stirring, allowing for wider, lazier circles with the whisk. Though these are not deal breakers when it comes to using a traditional saucepan, if you don't have the ideal saucepan you might consider purchasing a saucier instead. The question is, which one?

After several weeks of stirring and studying, we had developed some pretty clear preferences. First, we liked a lip around the edge to facilitate pouring. Although two of the lipless pans—the All-Clads—appeared to be deliberately curved to promote tidy pours, the others made a mess.

Second, the wider the pan, the easier and more luxuriant seemed the task at hand. The large diameters of the All-Clad and Viking sauciers allowed for loose, relaxed, forearm-powered rounds rather than tight circles directed mostly by the wrist—a notable difference between our saucepan and the best sauciers. One guest risotto stirrer, who'd missed the gravy and béchamel sessions, praised the open feel of the Sitram, which tied with the All-Clad for widest diameter. By contrast, the KitchenAid saucier was only slightly wider than the saucepan, making the task of stirring a tighter operation.

Less subjective than "luxuriant whisk feel" was the direct relationship between the width of the bottom of the pan and the amount of heat that wafted up its sides during cooking. The narrower pans (such as the KitchenAid), which covered a smaller area of the gas burner, allowed more heat to escape. And this residual heat proved uncomfortable after about 10 minutes of cooking—a legitimate concern when using a saucier, which is designed primarily for tasks that demand a cook's constant proximity to the pan.

We also preferred long, substantial handles: After 15 minutes on moderate heat, most pans were plagued by about 4½ inches of unusable handle. The Viking and All-Clads each had plenty of cool handle to spare; the rest were all but untouchable. (The KitchenAid, with the shortest handle of the lot and the narrowest diameter, was the least touchable of all, as the handle heated up very quickly.)

Weight was also a significant factor. Cooking proceeded more evenly in the heavier pans, and their heft also gave us a greater sense of security at the stovetop. Three of the four heaviest sauciers—the Viking, then the All-Clad, and the two Calphalons—all made it to the top of our chart.

Only one pan, the Sitram, stood out as "Not Recommended." When we browned butter and flour for béchamel sauce and mirepoix (finely chopped vegetables) for gravy, a dark ring quickly formed around the Sitram's interior. The ring went from deep brown to smoking black minutes before the mirepoix was done, and the uneven heat produced gloppy béchamel with unsightly brown flecks. Thus, the Sitram didn't make the cut. So, after weeks of testing, where did we come out? There are four pans (the All-Clad, Viking, and the two Calphalon pans) that are all recommended.

Rating Sauciers

WE TESTED AND EVALUATED SEVEN MEDIUM-SIZE SAUCIERS (2½ TO 3½ QUARTS), SUFFICIENT FOR A RISOTTO DINNER for four or multiple servings of sauce or gravy. Because manufacturers differ on nomenclature, our criterion for selecting pans was the mixing-bowl shape rather than the product name. Tests were performed over gas burners on the ranges in our test kitchen. The pans are listed in order of preference. See www.americastestkitchen.com for up-to-date prices and mail-order sources for top-rated products.

RECOMMENDED
All-Clad Stainless
3-Quart Saucier Pan with Lid
$145

This pan's wide mouth, wide interior cooking area, and great interior contours scored points with our testers. The long, substantial handle also stayed cool, bringing this pan to the head of the pack.

RECOMMENDED
Viking Professional Cookware
3½-Quart Reduction Sauce Pan
$160

The extra-long handle remained cool, but some testers thought it was set at an awkward angle. This pan was a pound heavier than any others, making one-handed pouring a bit challenging. Still, this pan works well.

RECOMMENDED
Calphalon Contemporary Stainless Steel
3½-Quart Sauce Pan
$135

Testers found this pan to be extra roomy; it did a fine job of containing splashes from vigorous whisking and its extra-long handle stayed exceptionally cool.

RECOMMENDED
Calphalon Infused Anodized
3-Quart Chef's Pan with Lid
$160

Deep and roomy and nicely shaped for whisking, but this pan's dark interior surface makes it difficult to judge the state of the fond.

RECOMMENDED WITH RESERVATIONS
KitchenAid Hard Anodized
2½-Quart Covered Saucier
$145

The smallish size sent residual heat from gas burners set to high up the sides of the pan toward testers' hands. The handle also got blazing hot over high heat and could not be touched without a potholder.

RECOMMENDED WITH RESERVATIONS
Anolon Commercial Clad
2½-Quart Covered Saucier
$50

Some testers found this pan too light. The handle was also criticized for being too bulky.

NOT RECOMMENDED
Sitram Cybernox2
3.3-Quart Saucier Pan with Cover
$74

The pan's light weight caused some food to burn. The handle became far too hot to touch without a potholder.

Chris and Bridget serve up a tasty weeknight rendition of jambalaya made in a nonstick skillet.

ONE-SKILLET dinners

CHAPTER 6

When most people think of dishes like lasagna and jambalaya, they think of labor-intensive weekend meals. In this chapter, however, we aimed to develop versions that could be prepared on a busy weeknight.

Lasagna, for example, is traditionally a layered baked pasta dish that relies on a slow-cooked sauce. The tomato sauce is made in one pot and the noodles cooked in another. The sauce and noodles are then transferred, layer by layer, to a third dish where cheese is added (between the layers) and the whole is baked. Condensing the cooking of all these components into one skillet posed many difficulties.

Jambalaya is often made in a Dutch oven. Translating it to a skillet shouldn't be difficult—or so we thought. But finding a way to retain the dish's complex Creole flavor, while ensuring that the rice, chicken, sausage, and shrimp finished cooking simultaneously, was a true test of patience.

After much trial and error (and many a bland and overcooked dish), we learned not only how to pair the ingredients in these recipes but also the order in which they should be added to the skillet. Our efforts produced estimable versions of these classics that are accessible any night of the week.

IN THIS CHAPTER

THE RECIPES

Skillet Lasagna
Skillet Lasagna with Sausage
 and Peppers

Skillet Jambalaya

EQUIPMENT CORNER

Celebrity Skillets

TASTING LAB

Canned Diced Tomatoes

SKILLET LASAGNA

WHAT WE WANTED: An easy-to-prepare stovetop version of the baked Italian classic.

Lasagna is a crowd-pleasing dish that never goes out of style. With layers of chewy pasta, hearty sauce, and rich, creamy cheese, it is so good that second helpings are nearly always mandatory. But lasagna is not a dish you throw together at the last minute. Even with the advent of no-boil noodles, it still takes a good chunk of time to make the components and assemble and bake the casserole.

While lasagna is traditionally made with fully or partially cooked components that meld together during baking, we wondered if it would possible to take the same flavors and components of lasagna and cook them on the stovetop in a skillet instead of in the oven. Our plan was simple. We would first brown the meat and remove it from the pan, then build a thin but flavorful sauce. Then we'd add the pasta (regular lasagna noodles broken into 2-inch lengths), which we figured could be slowly simmered while the pan was covered, giving us some "walk away" time. We would finish the dish by adding ricotta cheese, Parmesan, and any other flavors we deemed necessary.

Most lasagna sauces simmer for hours, which allows the ingredients to meld and their flavors to develop. But in this skillet version, we wanted to forgo a long-simmered sauce, so we limited the time that it took to simmer the sauce to the time that it took to cook the pasta. Aiming to keep our ingredient list to a minimum, we started with onions and garlic, which gave the sauce its depth. Since this recipe was meant to be a one-dish meal, we felt it necessary to add some protein. We tried ground beef, which was good, but we thought that meatloaf mix (a combination of ground beef, pork, and veal sold in one package at most supermarkets) was even better. For a flavor variation, tasters liked a combination of Italian sausage and sweet red peppers.

With the aromatics and meat decided, we next turned to the type of tomatoes we would use in the sauce. We started our tests with tomato puree, but found that the sauce was a tad too heavy and the pasta tended to sit on top of the sauce, making it cook unevenly. We tried adding a little water to give the pasta a better medium in which to cook, but the resulting lasagna was too bland. Abandoning tomato puree, we switched to a large can of diced tomatoes thinned out with a little extra water. This gave the sauce a nicely chunky and substantial texture—and there was just enough liquid to cook the pasta. A small can of tomato sauce fortified the tomato flavor and helped hold the lasagna together.

To replicate the cheesiness of a traditional lasagna, we stirred in the ricotta, but this didn't give us the results we were looking for. Once mixed in, the sweet creaminess of the ricotta became lost and only succeeded in making the sauce appear grainy and shockingly pink. Instead we placed dollops of ricotta on top of the lasagna and then re-covered the pan, allowing the added cheese to heat through. This way, the ricotta remained distinct from the other ingredients. The ricotta also created an attractive pattern over the top of the dish, while a sprinkling of freshly chopped basil gave it the flavor of authentic, oven-baked lasagna.

WHAT WE LEARNED: Use meatloaf mix (a combination of ground beef, pork, and veal) for a meat sauce with full flavor in less time. Use juicy diced canned tomatoes, rather than tomato puree, so that your sauce contains enough liquid for the noodles to absorb and cook through. Break traditional lasagna noodles into 2-inch lengths so that they fit into the skillet and are easier to eat.

SKILLET LASAGNA

Serves 4 to 6

Meatloaf mix is combination of ground beef, pork, and veal, sold pre-packaged in many supermarkets. If it's unavailable, use ground beef. A 12-inch nonstick skillet with a tight-fitting lid works best for this recipe.

1   (28-ounce) can diced tomatoes
    Water
1   tablespoon olive oil
1   medium onion, minced
    Salt
3   medium garlic cloves, minced or pressed
    through a garlic press (about 1 tablespoon)
⅛   teaspoon red pepper flakes
1   pound meatloaf mix
10 curly-edged lasagna noodles, broken into
    2-inch lengths
1   (8-ounce) can tomato sauce
½   cup plus 2 tablespoons grated Parmesan cheese
    Ground black pepper
1   cup ricotta cheese
3   tablespoons chopped fresh basil leaves

1. Pour the tomatoes with their juices into a 1-quart liquid measuring cup. Add water until the mixture measures 1 quart.

2. Heat the oil in large nonstick skillet over medium heat until shimmering. Add the onion and ½ teaspoon salt and cook until the onion begins to brown, about 5 minutes. Stir in the garlic and pepper flakes and cook until fragrant, about 30 seconds. Add the ground meat and cook, breaking apart the meat, until no longer pink, about 4 minutes.

3. Scatter the pasta over the meat but do not stir. Pour the diced tomatoes with their juices and tomato sauce over the pasta. Cover and bring to a simmer. Reduce the heat to medium-low and simmer, stirring occasionally, until the pasta is tender, about 20 minutes.

4. Remove the skillet from the heat and stir in the ½ cup Parmesan. Season with salt and pepper. Dot with heaping tablespoons of the ricotta, cover, and let stand off the heat for 5 minutes. Sprinkle with the basil and the remaining 2 tablespoons Parmesan. Serve.

VARIATION

SKILLET LASAGNA WITH SAUSAGE AND PEPPERS

Follow the recipe for Skillet Lasagna, substituting 1 pound Italian sausage, removed from its casing, for the meatloaf mix. Add 1 chopped red bell pepper to the skillet with the onion in step 2.

GETTING IT RIGHT: Building Skillet Lasagna

To cook all of the ingredients in one pan, a little attention to the ordering of the layers is necessary. It may not look like much as you begin the cooking process, but, after 20 minutes and an occasional stir, a layered lasagna appears almost as if by magic.

1. Start by sautéing the onion, garlic, and meat in the skillet. Scatter the broken lasagna noodles over the meat.

2. Pour the diced tomatoes and tomato sauce over the noodles. Cover and cook for about 20 minutes.

3. Add the Parmesan, dot with the ricotta, cover the skillet, and let the cheese soften off the heat.

TASTING LAB: Canned Diced Tomatoes

THE CONVENTIONAL WISDOM HOLDS THAT CANNED tomatoes surpass fresh for much of the year because they are packaged at the height of ripeness. After holding side-by-side tests of fresh, off-season tomatoes and canned tomatoes while we were developing recipes for cream of tomato soup, pasta all'Amatriciana (pasta with tomatoes, bacon, and onion), and skillet lasagna, among others, we agree. But with so many brands of canned tomatoes available, there is an obvious question: Which brand tastes best? Having sampled eight brands of canned diced tomatoes, both plain and cooked into a simple sauce, we have the answer.

According to both Bob Graf, president of the California League of Food Processors, and representatives of Small Planet Foods, distributors of Muir Glen tomato products, canned diced tomatoes emerged on the market in the early 1990s. Sales of diced tomatoes have since come to dominate the category of canned processed tomato products, outselling tomato paste, whole and crushed tomatoes, and tomato sauce and puree, all of which have been around for generations.

Depending on the season and the growing location, more than 50 varieties of tomato are used to make these products, according to Graf and Dr. Diane Barrett, fruit and vegetable products specialist in the department of food science and technology at the University of California, Davis. Graf said that while tomato varieties are generally not genetically engineered, they are refined for traits that will satisfy growers (yield and harvesting characteristics), processors (ease of skinning and solid-to-liquid ratio), and consumers (color and flavor) alike.

Packers generally reserve the ripest, best-colored specimens for use as whole, crushed, and diced tomatoes, as these are the products in which consumers demand vibrant color and fresher flavor. Lower-grade tomatoes are generally used in cooked products, such as paste, puree, and sauce.

Before further processing, the tomatoes are peeled by means of either steam—always the choice of Muir Glen, the only organic brand in our lineup—or a hot lye bath, which many processors currently favor. Because temperatures in lye peeling are not as high as those in steaming, many processors believe that lye leaves the layer of flesh just beneath the skin in better condition, giving the peeled tomato a superior appearance. Tasters, however, could not detect specific flavor differences in the canned tomatoes based on this aspect of processing. Two of our three highly recommended products, Muir Glen and S&W, use steam, while the third, Redpack, uses lye.

After peeling, the tomatoes are sorted again for color and the presence of any obvious deficiencies, and then they're diced and sorted. The cans are then filled with the tomatoes and topped off with salt and filler ingredients (usually tomato juice, but sometimes puree—read on). Finally, the lids are attached to the cans and the cans are cooked briefly for sterilization, then cooled and dried so that they can be labeled.

The flavor of a ripe, fresh tomato balances elements of sweetness and tangy acidity. The texture should be somewhere between firm and pliant, and certainly not mushy. Ideally, canned diced tomatoes should reflect the same combination of characteristics. Indeed, tasters indicated that excessive sweetness or saltiness (from the salt added during processing), along with undesirable texture qualities, could make or break a can of diced tomatoes. If the tasters thought that any one of these characteristics was out of whack, they downgraded that sample. In fact, two of the eight brands in the tasting were deemed to have major flaws in both flavor and texture that landed them in the lowest echelon of the ratings.

The downfall of Hunt's, the lowest-rated brand of the eight, was saltiness. According to the label on the can, one serving of Hunt's diced tomatoes contains 380 milligrams of sodium; the other brands tested average just over 240 milligrams per serving. That's a good 50 percent more salt, a characteristic that tasters easily detected and didn't appreciate.

Cento, the other brand that received low ratings, was the only product in the bunch that is packed in tomato puree rather than tomato juice. This led to complaints about the flavor, which some tasters perceived as "way cooked," "like candy," and "ketchupy." By comparison, the thin, watery juice in which the other canned diced tomatoes are packed tasted lighter and more natural. Puree is heavier and pulpier than juice, and it must be heated longer to achieve its specified concentration. In short, more cooking equals less freshness. The heavy puree is probably also responsible for tasters' impressions that Cento tomatoes were overly sweet, another significant point against them.

Cento was also the only brand in the lineup that didn't include calcium chloride among its ingredients. According to Barrett, the calcium in this compound helps the tomato pieces maintain a firm texture by stabilizing the pectin network in the tomato tissue. Because calcium is divalent—that is, it has an electrical charge of +2—it acts as a bridge between two long chains of pectin, in effect bonding them together. Based on our results, the absence of added calcium made a difference, as tasters described the Cento tomatoes as "mealy," "very broken down," and "squishy."

Oddly, no one flavor profile dominated. The three highly recommended brands, Muir Glen, S&W, and Redpack, displayed a range of flavor characteristics. Muir Glen led the ratings with a favorable balance of sweetness and saltiness and a notably "fresh" flavor in the sauce. Redpack also ranked high for its fresh flavor in the sauce. The same group of tasters, however, gave the thumbs up to S&W tomatoes, a brand noted for its bracing acidity and powerful, almost exaggerated tomato flavor. What links these three brands, then? Well, it's more about what characteristics they don't have than what they do have. None of them exhibited major flavor flaws, the likes of which landed some other brands lower in the ratings. The three winners were neither too sweet, like Cento, nor too salty, like Hunt's. Likewise, they tasted neither bitter nor metallic.

As for texture, tasters preferred a moderately firm diced tomato. Both Muir Glen and S&W placed in the middle of the pack in terms of firmness, while Redpack was rated firmest of all. Clearly, our tasters frowned on mushy canned tomatoes.

Rating Canned Diced Tomatoes

TWENTY MEMBERS OF THE AMERICA'S TEST KITCHEN STAFF TASTED EIGHT BRANDS OF CANNED DICED TOMATOES plain (to get opinions on overall flavor, texture, and size) and cooked (in a simple sauce with garlic, olive oil, sugar, and salt). The tomatoes are listed in order of preference based on their scores in these two tastings. All brands are available in supermarkets.

RECOMMENDED
Muir Glen Organic Diced Tomatoes
$1.50 for 14.5 ounces/$1.99 for 28 ounces

A few tasters found these organic tomatoes "mellow" when tasted plain, but for the same reason this brand rated number one in the sauce tasting.

RECOMMENDED
S&W "Ready-Cut" Premium, Peeled Tomatoes
$1.50 for 14.5 ounces/$2.50 for 28 ounces

This West Coast brand was liked for its "tangy," "vibrant" flavor. It was rated as "very acidic" in both the plain and the sauce tasting, and it made one of the saltiest sauces.

RECOMMENDED
Redpack "Ready-Cut" Diced Tomatoes (known as Redgold on the West Coast)
$0.79 for 14.5 ounces/$1.19 for 28 ounces

These tomatoes did not score highly in the plain tasting and were considered "bland" by some. But they were also judged the firmest, which may have contributed to their jump to second place in the sauce tasting.

RECOMMENDED WITH RESERVATIONS
Del Monte Diced Tomatoes
$0.99 for 14.5 ounces/$1.79 for 28 ounces

The flavor of these tomatoes was deemed slightly "musty" and "sweet" to some and "bright and balanced" to others when eaten raw but likened to "stewed tomatoes" when cooked in sauce.

RECOMMENDED WITH RESERVATIONS
Contadina Diced Tomatoes
$0.99 for 14.5 ounces/$1.39 for 28 ounces

While some tasters thought these tomatoes tasted "bright and fresh," the overall consensus was that they were too "soft and fleshy." The sauce had a "nice balance of sweet/salty" but was "very broken down" and looked as if "it had cooked for a very long time."

RECOMMENDED WITH RESERVATIONS
Furmano's Diced Tomatoes
$1.39 for 28 ounces

This highly acidic and salty brand secured a decent rating in the sauce tasting because the "tomatoes retained their texture" and "bright flavor" when cooked. When tasted raw, however, they were generally viewed as "bitter" and "like a tin can."

NOT RECOMMENDED
Cento "Chef's Cut" Tomatoes
$1.49 for 28 ounces

The only brand without calcium chloride in the ingredient list was very mushy. Tasters commented on the addition of basil only in the raw tasting; some welcomed it, others thought it tasted of "stale herbs." The sauce was described as too sweet, "like ketchup."

NOT RECOMMENDED
Hunt's Diced Tomatoes
$1.19 for 14.5 ounces/$1.59 for 28 ounces

The word "hypersalty" sums up these diced tomatoes. Eaten raw they tasted like V-8, with an unpleasant metallic aftertaste. And things only got worse in the sauce, which tasted "like soy sauce" to several different people.

SKILLET JAMBALAYA

WHAT WE WANTED: A quicker, easier-to-prepare version of this Creole classic.

Originating in the bayous of Louisiana, jambalaya has become synonymous with Creole cooking. A hearty mix of shredded chicken, spicy andouille sausage, and plump shrimp all cooked together with rice and vegetables, it seemed like a natural one-dish meal. Considering that jambalaya could be easily prepared in a skillet, and having already developed a reliable recipe and technique for skillet chicken and rice, we hoped to simply incorporate the ingredients that make jambalaya so distinct and develop a pretty good rendition of this Creole classic.

While some jambalaya recipes use a whole chicken, we felt using packaged chicken pieces would be a sure time-saver. We found bone-in, skin-on chicken thighs to be the best choice. Their robust flavor didn't get lost in the other flavors in the dish, and their tender meat was easy to shred and remained moist.

Next we tackled the andouille sausage, a key ingredient in any jambalaya. In order to extract the most flavor from the sausage, we found that a quick browning in the pan, after we had browned and removed the chicken, was essential. Once we browned the sausage and removed it from the pan, we then used some of the rendered fat to cook the vegetables, which further enhanced the flavor of the dish.

To re-create the flavors of jambalaya, we added a chopped red pepper to the pan along with chopped onion and a significant amount of garlic. We also added a can of diced tomatoes; their acidity helped brighten the dish, contrasting nicely with the spicy andouille. We assumed we'd need both wine and chicken broth to cook the rice, but we discovered that the liquid and acidity of the tomatoes made the wine superfluous. We also found that using clam juice in addition to the chicken broth helped to heighten the flavor of the shrimp and give the dish its classic briny overtones. We added the browned chicken thighs back to the pan along with the rice, cooking them together for about 25 minutes before adding the shrimp.

We learned it was best to remove the chicken from the skillet at this point and add the shrimp and browned sausage to the pan last. We cooked the shrimp (and warmed the sausage) very briefly over direct heat, and then removed the pan from the heat. The residual heat of the rice and vegetables cooked the shrimp through gently without the risk of overcooking. While the shrimp was cooking, we removed the meat from the chicken thighs, shredding it easily using two forks (see the illustration on page 68). After five minutes, the shrimp were cooked and the chicken was ready to be stirred back in. A couple of tablespoons of chopped parsley provided the finishing touch to our Creole casserole.

WHAT WE LEARNED: Bone-in, skin-on chicken thighs are your best bet for moist meat and minimal work. For long-simmered flavor, use the rendered fat from the chicken and andouille sausage to sauté the vegetables. To prevent dried-out shrimp, cook the shrimp briefly over direct heat, then remove the skillet from the heat and allow the residual heat from the rice and vegetables to cook the shrimp through.

SKILLET JAMBALAYA

Serves 4 to 6

If you cannot find andouille sausage, either chorizo or linguiça can be substituted. For a spicier jambalaya, you can add ¼ teaspoon of cayenne along with the vegetables, and/or serve it with Tabasco.

4	bone-in, skin-on chicken thighs (about 1½ pounds), trimmed of excess skin and fat
	Salt and ground black pepper
5	teaspoons vegetable oil
½	pound andouille sausage, halved lengthwise and sliced into ¼-inch pieces
1	medium onion, chopped medium
1	medium red bell pepper, stemmed, seeded, and chopped medium
5	medium garlic cloves, minced or pressed through a garlic press (about 1½ tablespoons)
1½	cups long-grain white rice
1	(14.5-ounce) can diced tomatoes, drained
1	(8-ounce) bottle clam juice
2½	cups low-sodium chicken broth
1	pound large shrimp (31 to 40 count), peeled, deveined, and rinsed
2	tablespoons chopped fresh parsley leaves

1. Dry the chicken thoroughly with paper towels, then season generously with salt and pepper. Heat 2 teaspoons of the oil in a 12-inch skillet over medium-high heat until just smoking. Carefully lay the chicken thighs in the skillet, skin-side down, and cook until golden, 4 to 6 minutes. Flip the chicken over and continue to cook until the second side is golden, about 3 minutes. Remove the pan from the heat and transfer the chicken to a plate. Using paper towels, remove and discard the browned chicken skin.

2. Pour off all but 2 teaspoons of the fat left in the skillet and return to medium-high heat until shimmering. Add the andouille and cook until lightly browned, about 3 minutes; transfer the sausage to a small bowl and set aside.

3. Add the remaining 3 teaspoons oil to the skillet and return to medium heat until shimmering. Add the onion, bell pepper, garlic, and ½ teaspoon salt; cook, scraping the browned bits off the bottom of the skillet, until the onion is softened, about 5 minutes. Add the rice and cook until the edges turn translucent, about 3 minutes. Stir in the tomatoes, clam juice, and chicken broth; bring to a simmer. Gently nestle the chicken into the rice. Cover, reduce the heat to low, and cook until the chicken is tender and cooked through, 30 to 35 minutes.

4. Transfer the chicken to a plate and cover with foil to keep warm. Stir the shrimp and sausage into the rice and continue to cook, covered, over low heat for 2 more minutes. Remove the skillet from the heat and let stand, covered, until the shrimp are fully cooked and the rice is tender, about 5 minutes. Meanwhile, following the illustration below, shred the chicken using two forks. Stir the parsley and shredded chicken into the rice and season with salt and pepper to taste. Serve immediately.

TECHNIQUE: Shredding Chicken

Hold one fork in each hand, with the tines facing down. Insert the tines into the chicken meat and gently pull the forks away from each other, breaking the meat apart and into long, thin strands.

EQUIPMENT CORNER: Celebrity Skillets

CHEFS ARE PUTTING THEIR NAMES ON MUCH MORE than restaurants. We purchased six large skillets, each emblazoned with the name of a television cooking personality. All of these pans are relatively affordable, but would their performance be worthy of the famous names on the handle?

T-Fal's Jamie Oliver line and Wolfgang Puck's own Bistro line from the Home Shopping Network are good choices whose results approached those of the test kitchen favorite, All-Clad, in every test. But even these winning pans possess design flaws that keep them out of All-Clad's league. Meanwhile, both Emerilware pans delivered only adequate results, and Martha Stewart's Everyday Skillet delivered unacceptable results.

Rating Celebrity Skillets

WE PREPARED OUR PAN-SEARED PORK TENDERLOINS (TO JUDGE BROWNING AND FOND DEVELOPMENT), cooked onions (to check sauté speed), and made crêpes (to gauge uniformity of heat transfer) in each skillet. As a basis of comparison, we ran the same tests in our favorite traditional and nonstick skillets, both made by All-Clad. The results are listed in order of preference. See www.americastestkitchen.com for up-to-date prices and mail-order sources for top-rated products.

RECOMMENDED
Jamie Oliver T-Fal Professional Series 12½-Inch Stainless Steel Sauté Pan $59.99
Exceptional heat retention and browning can be attributed to this nonstick pan's excessive weight. At 4 pounds and 6 ounces, it's more than a pound heavier than our favorite All-Clad skillet and provides an unwelcome kitchen workout.

RECOMMENDED
Wolfgang Puck Bistro 12-Inch Open Omelet Pan
$29.50
Excellent browning and superior fond at a bargain price, but when heating up and cooling down, this pan mysteriously snaps and pops. On gas burners, the handle heats up enough to require potholders.

RECOMMENDED
Wolfgang Puck Bistro 12-Inch Nonstick Omelet Pan
$35
Sautéed evenly at a moderate pace. Nice price, but this pan has the same problems as its traditional (not nonstick) counterpart.

RECOMMENDED WITH RESERVATIONS
Emerilware 12-Inch Frypan
$70
This nonstick, hard-anodized aluminum pan was a middle-of-the-pack performer that delivered lackluster browning.

RECOMMENDED WITH RESERVATIONS
Emerilware Stainless 12-Inch Frypan
$59.95
This pan required a good deal of babysitting as the sauté speed ran very fast. Slow heat recovery left a light fond.

NOT RECOMMENDED
Martha Stewart Everyday Stainless Steel 12-Inch Nonstick Skillet
$31.50
This pan ran too hot on high heat and too slow on low heat, keeping the cook on a short leash. It also retained heat poorly and burned the onions.

Julia uses two forks to easily shred the chicken into bite-sized pieces for chicken and dumplings.

AMERICAN classics

The beauty of many old-fashioned dishes is that they defy being simplified. These dishes often beg to be prepared on the weekend, when life slows down a bit, which is all the better for enjoying them. Take chicken and dumplings. A Sunday dinner dish popular in the South, this American classic can be as idiosyncratic to prepare as pie dough, but its rewards, as is the case with tender flaky pie crust, are well worth the effort. We did not seek to streamline this dish, but rather to foolproof it—after the time and effort involved, there would be no room for error resulting in leaden dumplings or lackluster chicken and broth.

Baked beans are another case. Sure, you can buy baked beans in a can, but in both flavor and texture they are not comparable to the slow-cooked version you can make yourself. The choices of recipes are staggering, and many left us with overly sweet versions that yielded mushy or, worse, undercooked beans. Again, if we were rolling up our sleeves to prepare this dish, we wanted guarantees of its success.

In developing these dishes, we found that neither requires fancy ingredients or expensive equipment, just a little time and effort. It may be an old-fashioned notion, but we can't agree more that simpler is often best.

IN THIS CHAPTER

THE RECIPES
Chicken and Dumplings
Chicken and Dumplings with
    Leeks and Tarragon

Boston Baked Beans

EQUIPMENT CORNER
Zipper-Lock Bags

TASTING LAB
Supermarket Chicken Broths

confirmed in our tasting because we could not be certain about how a particular bird was processed.

Our first solid clue to any possible connection between processing method and flavor emerged when we discovered that Empire, the only kosher chicken in our tasting, was also the best tasting. Both Empire and Murray birds are hand-slaughtered rather than killed by machine, which ensures both a clean kill and a quick and efficient "bleed-out." (Murray birds are not kosher but are processed under similar conditions in accordance with Muslim law.) Industry experts indicated that machine-processed chickens are more likely to be subject to improper slaughtering, which can cause blood to clot, resulting in tough meat or a livery flavor.

Because tasters far preferred the Empire chicken to Murray's, however, it followed that more was at work here than slaughtering technique. For one thing, kosher chickens like Empire's are dunked in cold water to remove feathers after slaughter. Cold water firms both the skin and the fat layer beneath it. In contrast, most other producers scald birds in hot water to remove the feathers. The experts we talked to said that scalding can "solubilize" the chicken's fat, leading to excessive moisture loss and a wrinkled appearance in the chicken skin after cooking. Uneven scalding can also cause "barking," or a blotchy appearance in the skin.

Appearance aside, perhaps the most noticeable difference between the Empire bird and the others we sampled was that the Empire bird tasted juicy and well seasoned.

To remove as many impurities as possible, the chickens are buried in salt for one hour and then rinsed off with cold spring water. The combination of salt and water acts like a brine, encouraging the fibers in the meat to open and trap the salt and water, leading to a juicier, more flavorful bird. This single factor, more than any other, seems to have put the Empire bird ahead of the pack.

If you are looking for advice on purchasing a high-quality chicken, we recommend kosher. All the other adjectives—free-range, natural, lean, organic, and the like—don't necessarily translate into a better-tasting chicken. Empire, the brand that won our current contest, was followed by Bell & Evans, winner of our 1994 tasting. You can't go wrong with either. Tyson, a mass-produced bird that costs $1.29 per pound, came in third, ahead of birds costing twice as much.

Because the winning bird in our tasting is packed in salt and then rinsed, we wondered what would happen if we brined the runner-up, Bell & Evans, as well as the last-place Perdue chicken, tasting them alongside the first-place Empire bird. To find out, we put three more chickens into the oven. The Empire and Bell & Evans birds still finished on top, but the Perdue chicken wasn't far behind. The brined Perdue chicken was milder and less toothsome than the other two birds, but it was certainly acceptable. Our conclusion: If your local market doesn't carry kosher chickens, you can use a quick saltwater soak to improve the quality of just about any chicken.

Rating Chickens

THIRTY MEMBERS OF THE AMERICA'S TEST KITCHEN STAFF TASTED NINE BRANDS OF CHICKEN, ALL roasted without additional seasonings. The chickens are listed in order of preference based on their scores in this tasting. All brands are available in supermarkets.

HIGHLY RECOMMENDED
Empire Kosher Roasting Chicken
$1.99 per pound

Many tasters found this bird to be the most flavorful of the tasting, calling it "perfectly seasoned" and "well balanced." The meat tasted "natural" and "sweet," while the texture was "firm," "moist," and "tender." During processing the Empire bird is covered with salt to draw out impurities in the meat, so it never needs to be brined in a saltwater solution to pump up flavor or juiciness.

RECOMMENDED
Bell & Evans Fresh Young Chicken
$2.69 per pound

Tasters found the Bell & Evans chicken to be "pretty," as well as flavorful, with its meat tasting "clean," "fresh," and "natural." The texture of the white meat was called "firm" and "moist," whereas the dark meat was described as "moist" and "tender." This bird is fed an all-vegetable diet that contains no animal byproducts or antibiotics.

RECOMMENDED
Tyson Fresh Young Chicken
$1.29 per pound

One taster said this "tastes like chicken," while another found it lacking in flavor. Its white meat was described as "firm," albeit slightly "mealy," while its dark meat was well liked for its tenderness. The Tyson bird was downgraded by some tasters for the "uneven" color of its skin.

RECOMMENDED
D'Artagnan Free Range Organic Chicken
$3.75 per pound

Described as "golden," "glossy," and "archetypically beautiful," this free-range bird wowed tasters with its good looks. Although the white meat was called "dry" and "stringy," tasters felt it had a "natural flavor." The dark meat was called "moist" and "tender," although some panelists thought it had "livery" undertones. This chicken is raised on an organic, all-vegetable, antibiotic-free feed.

RECOMMENDED
Eberly's Free Range Young Natural Chicken
$3.99 per pound

Tasters described this free-range bird as "golden and gorgeous," but many thought the white meat was "stringy." "Bland" and "boring" to some, others loved its "natural" and "buttery" flavor. Eberly's raises all of its chickens on an organic, all-vegetable feed free of any antibiotics.

NOT RECOMMENDED
Murray's Whole Chicken
$2.29 per pound

Tasters thought this chicken was somewhat "bland" and generally "unremarkable." The skin was described as "golden" and "speckled," while the meat was "slightly metallic," "tough," "dry," and "chewy." This chicken is raised on an all-vegetable, antibiotic-free feed.

NOT RECOMMENDED
Foster Farms Young Chicken
$1.29 per pound

The dark meat tasted "gamey" and "livery," the white meat "off" and "metallic." Both dark and white meat were "overly moist." The bird itself appeared to have "puffed and deflated," leaving it with "wrinkled" skin.

NOT RECOMMENDED
Rocky Junior Frying Chicken
$2.29 per pound

Tasters described this sample as being "bland" and "tasteless," with "gamey" dark meat; its texture was called "chewy," "wet," and "stringy." Tasters also objected to its "anemic" appearance. This bird is raised on an all-vegetable, antibiotic-free feed.

NOT RECOMMENDED
Perdue Whole Chicken
$1.79 per pound

Tasters objected to the look, texture, and flavor of this chicken. They described the skin as "shriveled." The texture was "pithy," "chalky," and "stringy." The flavor was "a bit off," with a "sour quality that kicks in at the end."

PAN-ROASTED ASPARAGUS

WHAT WE WANTED: Browned, crisp asparagus, similar in flavor to grilled, but done on the stovetop.

Although we consider grilling to be the ultimate method for cooking asparagus, there are plenty of rainy weekday nights when asparagus is on the menu. Rather than waste time heating a finicky broiler, we were hoping that a simple stovetop method might deliver crisp, nicely browned spears.

We turned up several promising recipes, but the results were disappointing. In most cases, the spears were indeed browned but also limp, greasy, and shriveled. Equally daunting were the logistics of cooking enough asparagus to feed four people. All the recipes we consulted suggested laying the spears out in a single layer, then individually rotating them to ensure even browning. This seemed like a lot of meticulous fuss for one measly bunch of asparagus, which, with these restrictions, was all we could fit into a 12-inch pan.

After testing different-sized spears, heat levels, pan types, and cooking fats, a few things became clear. As in grilling, the thinner spears would have to be eliminated. They overcooked so quickly that there was no way to get a proper sear. Selecting thicker spears helped to solve this problem, but we were still a long way from getting them to brown properly. Over moderate heat, the spears took so long to develop a crisp, browned exterior that they overcooked. But cranking up the burner was not a good alternative—the spears skipped brown altogether and went straight to spotty and blackened.

We knew that in restaurants, line cooks sometimes blanch off pounds of asparagus before service, then toss them into the pan or onto the grill to order for a quick sear. They do this primarily to save time, but we wondered if parcooking would also enhance browning. We didn't want to have to blanch asparagus in one pan and then sauté in another, so we wondered about finding a way to combine the steps.

We cooked two batches, covering the skillets for the first five minutes and adding a few tablespoons of water to one of them. The latter batch was definitely steamed, but the extra moisture inhibited its browning after we removed the lid. The asparagus in the other skillet, which had contained nothing besides olive oil, steamed very little. When we replaced the oil with butter, however, the results were quite different: A small cloud of steam escaped the pan when the lid was lifted, and the asparagus had softened and turned bright green. Evidently, the small amount of moisture in the butter was enough to start steaming the asparagus. Tasters eventually agreed that a mixture of olive oil and butter provided the best combination of flavor and browning.

Once the lid was removed, however, it was a race against the clock to try to get all the spears turned and evenly browned before they overcooked and turned limp. In the course of this round of tests, however, we made a fortunate discovery. Citing the pleasing contrast of textures, tasters actually preferred the spears that were browned on only one side and remained bright green on the other.

This finding also helped to solve the problem of how to fit more asparagus into the skillet. The rationale behind not crowding the pan—it causes the food to steam and brown unevenly—no longer applied. In fact, it was precisely the result we were after. Carefully positioning the asparagus in the pan also helped. A better fit and better browning were possible with half of the spears pointed in one direction and the other half pointed in the opposite direction. Now just an occasional toss was enough to ensure that all the spears became partially browned.

WHAT WE LEARNED: Choose thick spears because thinner spears overcook too quickly. Positioning half the spears in one direction and the other half in the opposite direction ensures a better fit in the pan. Brown just one side of the asparagus to provide a contrast in texture and guarantee that the asparagus remains firm and tender, but never limp.

2. Uncover and increase the heat to high; season the asparagus with salt and pepper. Cook until the spears are tender and well browned along one side, 5 to 7 minutes, using the tongs to occasionally move the spears from the center of the pan to the edge of the pan to ensure all are browned. Transfer the asparagus to a serving dish, adjust the seasonings with salt and pepper, and, if desired, squeeze the lemon half over the spears. Serve immediately.

VARIATIONS

PAN-ROASTED ASPARAGUS WITH TOASTED GARLIC AND PARMESAN

Heat 2 tablespoons olive oil and 3 medium garlic cloves, sliced thin, in a 12-inch skillet over medium heat; cook, stirring occasionally, until the garlic is crisp and golden but not dark brown, about 5 minutes. Using a slotted spoon, transfer the garlic to a paper towel–lined plate. Follow the recipe for Pan-Roasted Asparagus, adding the butter to the oil in the skillet. After transferring the asparagus to a serving dish, sprinkle with 2 tablespoons grated Parmesan, the toasted garlic, and the lemon juice; adjust the seasonings and serve immediately.

PAN-ROASTED ASPARAGUS WITH WARM ORANGE-ALMOND VINAIGRETTE

Heat 2 tablespoons olive oil in a 12-inch skillet over medium heat until shimmering; add ¼ cup slivered almonds and cook, stirring frequently, until golden, about 5 minutes. Add ½ cup fresh orange juice and 1 teaspoon chopped fresh thyme leaves; increase the heat to medium-high and simmer until thickened, about 4 minutes. Off the heat, stir in 2 tablespoons minced shallot, 2 tablespoons sherry vinegar, and salt and pepper to taste; transfer the vinaigrette to a small bowl. Wipe out the skillet; follow the recipe for Pan-Roasted Asparagus. After transferring the asparagus to a serving dish, pour the vinaigrette over and toss to combine; adjust the seasonings and serve immediately.

PAN-ROASTED ASPARAGUS

Serves 3 to 4

This recipe works best with asparagus that is at least ½ inch thick near the base. If using thinner spears, reduce the covered cooking time to 3 minutes and the uncovered cooking time to 5 minutes. Do not use pencil-thin asparagus; it cannot withstand the heat and overcooks too easily.

1	tablespoon olive oil
1	tablespoon unsalted butter
2	pounds thick asparagus spears (see note), ends trimmed
	Kosher salt and ground black pepper
½	lemon (optional)

1. Heat the oil and butter in a 12-inch skillet over medium-high heat. When the butter has melted, add half of the asparagus to the skillet with the tips pointed in one direction; add the remaining spears with the tips pointed in the opposite direction. Using tongs, distribute the spears in an even layer (the spears will not quite fit into a single layer); cover and cook until the asparagus is bright green and still crisp, about 5 minutes.

EQUIPMENT CORNER: Remote Thermometers

THE ONLY WAY TO ENSURE PERFECTLY COOKED MEAT is through constant temperature monitoring, but repeatedly opening the oven door or lifting the lid off a grill wreaks havoc on cooking times. Could a remote thermometer—which transmits the temperature from the thermometer to a cordless console—solve this problem? To find out, we rounded up four models.

What separated the best from the worst were the transmission range and the temperature-setting options. Some models transmitted up to 200 feet, while the shortest range was a mere 30 feet. Our favorite models clearly indicated when we had moved out of transmission range (sounding a series of warning beeps); the others simply ceased flashing a display light—a bit too subtle.

More important is that some models are restricted to factory-determined temperature settings. If you want to pull off a turkey at 165 degrees (which we recommend) using the Weber Barbecue Digital Thermometer, the best you can do is set it to "Beef—Medium" (160 degrees) or "Beef—Well Done" (170 degrees). It can't be set to 165. We urge you not to use the "Turkey" setting (programmed at a parchingly dry 180 degrees).

In the end, we liked the Taylor thermometer best. The provided temperature guidelines can be overridden to set any temperature, the range is ample (up to 150 feet), and the clippable pager is small enough not to hinder an impromptu game of catch.

Rating Remote Thermometers

WE TESTED FOUR REMOTE THERMOMETERS IN THE $35 to $75 range. The first test involved setting the thermometers to remote mode and using them to check the internal temperature of grilled whole beef tenderloins, a cut that suffers badly if cooked just a couple of degrees past the target temperature, which for us is no higher than 125 degrees for medium-rare. Next, we tested how well we could receive the transmitter signal based on three different scenarios: a straight, uninterrupted shot from the transmitter; around a sharp corner from the transmitter; and into a building, around corners and through four doors (which we closed). In addition, we checked accuracy in both an ice-water slurry (32 degrees) and boiling water (212 degrees). The remote thermometers are listed below in order of preference. See www.americastestkitchen.com for up-to-date prices and mail-order sources for top-rated products.

HIGHLY RECOMMENDED
Taylor Wireless Oven Thermometer with Remote Pager
$34.99

A decent range, and there's a clear indication when you move out of it. Plus, you can set it to any temperature.

RECOMMENDED
Maverick Remote Smoker Thermometer
$39.99

The range (advertised at 100 feet, 30 feet in testing) limits its usefulness, but a second probe measures ambient grill temperature, making it better for outdoor cooking.

RECOMMENDED WITH RESERVATIONS
Weber Barbecue Beeper Digital Thermometer
$34.95

Great range, but it's not obvious when you've left it. Preset temperature alerts are limiting.

RECOMMENDED WITH RESERVATIONS
Brookstone Grill Alert Talking Remote Thermometer
$75

Same problems as the Weber. For the extra $30, a computerized voice says, "Your entrée is ready." Creepy.

If you don't have a roasting pan deep enough to accommodate a large turkey, use two large disposable roasting pans placed on a baking sheet.

LET'S TALK turkey

CHAPTER 10

IN THIS CHAPTER

THE RECIPES

Roast Turkey for a Crowd

Giblet Pan Gravy for a Crowd

Classic Bread Stuffing with Sage
  and Thyme
Bread Stuffing with Sausage,
  Pecans, and Apricots
Bread Stuffing with Bacon and
  Apples

Candied Sweet Potato Casserole
Candied Sweet Potato Casserole
  with Toasted Marshmallow
  Topping

EQUIPMENT CORNER

Turkey Gadgets

TASTING LAB

Packaged Stuffings

Thanksgiving can strike fear into the heart of even the most proficient cook. First, there's the turkey to contend with—in no other meal is the main course paraded in front of guests with as much fanfare. And what if you're cooking for a crowd? Most recipes recommend roasting a 12- to 14-pound turkey, but this only feeds about 10 to 12. What's the cook to do when cooking for more: roast two turkeys? Most ovens simply won't accommodate two birds. This leaves the cook with roasting one large turkey, but that poses its own challenges. We set out to find a way to roast a turkey big enough to feed a crowd.

In addition to the turkey, there's the matter of side dishes—and pleasing everyone at the table with their favorites. Sweet potato casserole is often claimed as a must-have at Thanksgiving. Kids love this sweet, sticky dish—it's a no-brainer—but many adults find it overly sweet and cloying, more along the lines of dessert than side dish. We set out to develop a sweet potato casserole with a bit of a savory accent to please everyone. And best of all, with these Thanksgiving recipes, we minimized the work involved so that the cook can enjoy the holiday as much as everyone else seated at the table.

ROAST TURKEY FOR A CROWD

WHAT WE WANTED: A moist and juicy bird large enough to feed a crowd.

Most recipes recommend roasting 12- to 14-pound turkeys, a size that is easy to handle and that delivers, according to many tasters, superior flavor. But what if you have more than 10 people coming to dinner? Roasting two turkeys is not an option for most home cooks. We set out to find a way to roast a massive 18- to 22-pound bird, enough to feed the most crowded Thanksgiving table.

Our first step was to select the right brand at the market. Two years ago, the test kitchen conducted a turkey taste test and came up with an interesting—and totally unexpected—result. The frozen Butterball turkey finished ahead of the fresh Butterball entry as well as more than one fresh premium brand. The reason? Frozen Butterball turkeys are injected with a salt solution; in other words, they are brined. Although the flavor of the meat was a bit on the bland side, many tasters commented that this bird "tastes just like Thanksgiving." We performed another taste test just to be sure and found that the meat was, indeed, moist and tender. So now we had a turkey that had been brined for us, eliminating a step that would be all but impossible with a huge bird.

Other techniques had to be eliminated from the start, given the size of the bird. We chose not to air-dry (another favored test kitchen technique that would be unworkable with a huge bird) or stuff the turkey (which would add to the already long cooking time). Finally, we wanted to keep this bird as traditional as possible, so we opted not to rub it with spices or massage it with flavored butter.

Our next task was to determine the proper cooking temperature. We roasted it, per the instructions included with the Butterball, at 350 degrees until the thigh registered 170 to 180 degrees, approximately 4½ hours. Although the breast meat was tender, the dark meat was surprisingly fatty and the skin a tad blond and springy. Next we cooked a turkey at 400 degrees. We began it breast-side down and, after an hour, flipped it breast-side up, hoping for a deeply browned showstopper. (This technique yields great results for smaller turkeys. As the fat renders out of the dark meat, it flows down into and bastes the breast.) Although it looked great, the breast meat turned out chalky and parched, as if it had spent the day at the beach.

Because high temperature had yielded a prettier bird and low temperature a more tender one, we decided to try a combination of both. After roasting a dozen or so birds, we finally hit on the right combination of temperatures for a large turkey: 425 degrees for the first hour (breast-side down) and 325 degrees thereafter (breast-side up). The breast meat was firm and juicy, the dark meat rich and tender, and the skin a breathtaking rosy mahogany brown.

After we had cooked and turned 200 pounds of turkey, a test cook pointed out that her mother would never be able to rotate a turkey of this weight. We tried yet another turkey, with the same combination of high and low heat, but we kept the turkey breast-side up the entire time. It was slightly inferior to the turned bird but still good enough to eat, so those not up to the task can skip this step. (We also tried this same method breast-side down, and the skin turned out mottled and undercooked.)

Although we had opted not to stuff the bird, we wondered if a simple aromatic mix in the cavity might add flavor to the meat. We started with the classic onion, carrot, and celery combination and, while this turkey was better, something was still missing. Lemon added freshness to the meat closest to the bone and gave the pan juices a cleaner taste. Sprigs of fresh thyme added the scent of Thanksgiving. More vegetables went into the roasting pan to flavor the drippings. We added a little water to ensure that the vegetables didn't dry out.

After roasting several birds, trussed and untrussed, we concluded that trussing added a fussiness we didn't want as well as an unwelcome 15 to 20 minutes in cooking time. (To cook the inner thigh fully, which is hidden by trussing, you inevitably overcook the white meat.) We also investigated the best way to treat the skin, leaving it as is versus brushing it with unsalted butter, olive oil, or vegetable oil. The difference was not significant, but the turkey with the butter tasted better and more, well, buttery. The next question was whether regular basting is worth the effort. It turned out that basting actually makes the skin soggy, so we simply brushed the turkey with melted butter once prior to cooking.

Tenting the turkey either during or after roasting was also abandoned: The foil traps the steam and softens the skin. Instead, letting the roasted bird sit at room temperature, uncovered, for 35 to 40 minutes allows the juices, which rise to the surface during cooking, to flow back into the meat. This was more successful than the usually

recommended 20 minutes, probably because of the size of the bird.

For those who don't want to buy a Butterball, we wondered if this method would work on another brand of turkey. We tested an organic turkey, which wasn't injected, and a kosher turkey, which is essentially brined by the koshering process. All the testers preferred the Butterball for its juicier meat. The kosher bird came in second, and the organic turkey took last place because the meat was dry. If you prefer to avoid a frozen, injected bird, try a kosher brand.

WHAT WE LEARNED: Choose a frozen Butterball turkey, which has already been brined for juicy flavor. A combination of high and low heat results in a tender, juicy bird with deeply browned skin. The meat and pan drippings are made more flavorful by the addition of onion, carrot, and celery. A quartered lemon adds a bright, clean flavor. After roasting, allow the turkey to rest to allow the juices to redistribute, but don't tent it with foil or the skin will get soggy.

ROAST TURKEY FOR A CROWD

Serves about 20

You can use any roasting pan to roast the turkey, even a disposable one, but make sure to use a V-rack to elevate it. Be sure to dry the skin thoroughly before brushing the bird with butter; otherwise, it will have spotty brown skin. Rotating the bird helps produce moist, evenly cooked meat, but for the sake of ease, you may opt not to rotate it. In that case, skip the step of lining the V-rack with foil and roast the bird breast-side up for the entire cooking time. Because we do not brine the bird, we had the best results with a frozen Butterball (injected with salt and water) and a kosher bird (soaked in salt water during processing).

2   medium onions, chopped coarse
2   medium carrots, chopped coarse
2   celery ribs, chopped coarse
1   lemon, quartered
2   sprigs fresh thyme
1   frozen Butterball or kosher turkey (18 to 22 pounds gross weight), rinsed thoroughly; giblets, neck, and tailpiece removed and reserved for gravy (recipe follows)
4   tablespoons (½ stick) unsalted butter, melted
1   teaspoon salt
1   teaspoon ground black pepper

1. Adjust an oven rack to the lowest position; remove the remaining racks. Heat the oven to 425 degrees. Line a large V-rack with heavy-duty foil and poke holes in the foil; set the V-rack in a 15 by 12-inch roasting pan.

2. Toss the onions, carrots, celery, lemon, and thyme in a medium bowl; set aside. Brush the turkey breast with 2 tablespoons of the melted butter, then sprinkle with half of the salt and half of the pepper. Set the turkey breast-side down on the V-rack. Brush with the remaining 2 tablespoons butter and sprinkle with the remaining salt and pepper. Fill the cavity with half the onion mixture; scatter the rest in the roasting pan and pour 1 cup water into the pan.

3. Roast the turkey 1 hour; remove the roasting pan with the turkey from the oven. Lower the oven temperature to 325 degrees. Using a clean dish towel or 2 potholders, turn the turkey breast-side up; return the roasting pan with the turkey to the oven and continue to roast until the legs move freely and an instant-read thermometer inserted into the thickest part of the thigh registers 170 to 180 degrees, about 2 hours longer.

4. Remove the turkey from the oven. Gently tip the turkey up so that any accumulated juices in the cavity run into the roasting pan. Transfer the turkey to a carving board, and transfer the vegetables from the cavity to the roasting pan. Let the turkey rest until ready to carve, 35 to 40 minutes.

GIBLET PAN GRAVY FOR A CROWD

Makes about 2 quarts

Complete step 1 up to a day ahead, if desired. Begin step 3 once the bird has been removed from the oven and is resting on a carving board.

1   tablespoon vegetable oil
       Reserved turkey giblets, neck, and tailpiece
1   medium onion, unpeeled and chopped
1   quart low-sodium chicken broth or turkey stock mixed with 3 cups water
2   sprigs fresh thyme
8   sprigs fresh parsley
5   tablespoons unsalted butter
¼   cup plus 2 tablespoons unbleached all-purpose flour
1½   cups dry white wine
       Salt and ground black pepper

1. Heat the oil in a stockpot; add the giblets, neck, and tailpiece, and sauté until golden and fragrant, about 5 minutes. Add the onion and continue to sauté until softened, 3 to 4 minutes longer. Reduce the heat to low, cover, and cook until the turkey and onion release their juices, about

20 minutes. Add the broth and herbs, bring to a boil, and adjust the heat to low. Simmer, uncovered, skimming any scum that may rise to the surface, until the broth is rich and flavorful, about 30 minutes longer. Strain the broth into a large container and reserve the neck, heart, and gizzard. When cool enough to handle, shred the neck meat, remove the gristle from the gizzard, and dice the reserved heart and gizzard. Refrigerate the giblets and broth until ready to use. (The broth can be stored in the refrigerator up to 1 day ahead.)

2. While the turkey is roasting, return the reserved turkey broth to a simmer. Heat the butter in a large, heavy-bottomed saucepan over medium-low heat. Vigorously whisk in the flour (the roux will froth and then thin out again). Cook slowly, stirring constantly, until nutty brown and fragrant, 10 to 15 minutes. Vigorously whisk all but 3 cups of the hot broth into the roux. Bring to a boil, then continue to simmer, stirring occasionally, until the gravy is lightly thickened and very flavorful, about 30 minutes longer. Set aside until the turkey is done.

3. When the turkey has been transferred to a carving board to rest, spoon out and discard as much fat as possible from the roasting pan, leaving the caramelized herbs and vegetables. Place the roasting pan over two burners set on medium-high heat (if the drippings are not a dark brown, cook, stirring constantly, until they caramelize). Return the gravy to a simmer. Add the wine to the roasting pan of caramelized vegetables, scraping up any browned bits with a wooden spoon, and boil until reduced by half, about 5 minutes. Add the remaining 3 cups turkey broth and continue to simmer for 15 minutes; strain the pan juices into the gravy, pressing as much juice as possible out of the vegetables. Stir the reserved giblets into the gravy and return to a boil. Adjust the seasonings, adding salt and pepper to taste, if necessary. Serve with the carved turkey.

CLASSIC BREAD STUFFING WITH SAGE AND THYME

Serves 16

Drying the bread before making the stuffing is crucial for texture and flavor. If you plan ahead, you can simply leave the bread cubes out on the counter for a few days to become stale. Otherwise, spread them out on baking sheets and dry in a 300-degree oven for 30 to 60 minutes. Let the bread cool before using in the stuffing.

You can substitute three 14-ounce bags of plain dried bread cubes for the homemade dried bread cubes, but you'll need to increase the amount of chicken broth to 7 cups. This recipe can easily be halved and baked in a 13 by 9-inch baking dish for a smaller crowd.

12	tablespoons (1½ sticks) unsalted butter plus extra for the dish
4	celery ribs, chopped fine
2	medium onions, minced
½	cup minced fresh parsley leaves
3	tablespoons minced fresh sage leaves or 2 teaspoons dried
3	tablespoons minced fresh thyme leaves or 2 teaspoons dried
1	tablespoon minced fresh marjoram leaves or 1 teaspoon dried
3	pounds high-quality white sandwich bread, cut into ½-inch cubes and dried (see note)
5	cups low-sodium chicken broth
4	large eggs, lightly beaten
2	teaspoons salt
2	teaspoons ground black pepper

1. Adjust an oven rack to the middle position and heat the oven to 400 degrees. Melt the butter in a 12-inch skillet over medium-high heat. Add the celery and onions and cook until softened, about 10 minutes. Stir in the parsley, sage, thyme, and marjoram and cook until fragrant, about 1 minute. Transfer to a very large bowl.

2. Add the dried, cooled bread, broth, eggs, salt, and pepper to the vegetables and toss to combine. Turn the mixture into a buttered 15 by 10-inch baking dish.

3. Cover with foil and bake for 25 minutes. Remove the foil and continue to bake until golden, about 30 minutes longer. Cool for 10 minutes before serving.

VARIATIONS

BREAD STUFFING WITH SAUSAGE, PECANS, AND APRICOTS

Follow the recipe for Classic Bread Stuffing with Sage and Thyme. Before cooking the vegetables in step 1, cook 1½ pounds bulk sausage in a large skillet over medium heat, breaking it up into smaller pieces with a wooden spoon, until lightly browned, 5 to 10 minutes. If desired, substitute the rendered sausage fat for an equal amount of butter in step 1. Add the cooked and crumbled sausage, 3 cups chopped pecans, toasted, and 2 cups dried apricots, sliced thin, to the bread mixture with the vegetables in step 2.

BREAD STUFFING WITH BACON AND APPLES

Follow the recipe for Classic Bread Stuffing with Sage and Thyme. Before cooking the vegetables in step 1, cook 1½ pounds bacon, chopped fine, in a 12-inch skillet over medium heat until crisp and brown, about 12 minutes. Transfer the bacon with a slotted spoon to a paper towel–lined plate. If desired, substitute the bacon fat for an equal amount of butter in step 1. Add 2 Granny Smith apples, peeled, cored, and cut into ½-inch cubes (about 2 cups), to the skillet with the celery and onions. Stir the crisp bacon into the bread cubes with the vegetables in step 2.

TASTING LAB: Packaged Stuffings

EACH YEAR, AMERICANS SPEND ALMOST $300 MILLION on stuffing products. Obviously, supermarket stuffing isn't as good as homemade, but it does offer unbelievable ease—just boil water and butter, add stuffing mix, and serve. But how much quality must you sacrifice for that convenience? We held a blind tasting to find out.

Of eight popular brands of herb-flavored stuffing, only two were deemed passable. Why is this stuff so bad? Just look at the ingredient list—it looks more like a chemist's inventory than a recognizable recipe. MSG, high fructose corn syrup, yeast, partially hydrogenated soybean and/or cottonseed oils, caramel color, BHT, propyl gallate—you get the idea. Chicken stock appeared in just three brands and flavorful herbs were few and far between. Only Arnold contained herbs other than parsley (rosemary, thyme, sage, and basil), but those were down at the bottom of the list. Though Kellogg's bag promised that it was seasoned with "five savory herbs," only "spices" were listed as an ingredient. The rest of the brands contained just parsley—not exactly a big flavor booster.

In addition to poor flavor, the stuffing textures suffered from the extremes, all panned as either "pasty" and "gummy" or "dry" and "chewy." While textural and flavor issues could be fixed with a little doctoring—add some cooked diced vegetables, use more or less liquid, substitute chicken stock for water, and finish with fresh herbs—it simply isn't worth it.

In the end, the "winners" of our tasting were chosen not because of great flavor or texture but because they were "not objectionable." As one taster wrote, "The best, but so what?" Even our best-rated brands would need some serious doctoring to earn a space on our table. And with great homemade stuffing only an hour away, why bother trying to fix something that is so obviously broken?

Rating Packaged Stuffings

TWENTY-FIVE MEMBERS OF THE AMERICA'S TEST KITCHEN STAFF TASTED EIGHT BRANDS OF STUFFING, ALL prepared according to the package instructions. The stuffings are listed in order of preference based on their scores in this tasting. All brands are available in supermarkets nationwide.

PASSABLE IN A PINCH
Stove Top Stuffing Mix Savory Herbs
$1.69 for 6 ounces

"Not objectionable," wrote one taster of this familiar staple, and others agreed, with some going so far as to say it "tastes fairly homemade." Many, however, were turned off by the "bad artificial aftertaste."

PASSABLE IN A PINCH
Bell's Traditional Stuffing
$2.79 for 16 ounces

More than one taster praised the "balanced herb flavor," though many found this stuffing "too wet" and "mushy." Most agreed that this stuffing was simply "okay."

NOT RECOMMENDED
Arnold Premium Stuffing Herb Seasoned
$2.79 for 14 ounces

Most tasters found this "basic" stuffing "too dry and chewy," though a few praised it as "not too mushy." "Holy poultry seasoning!" wrote one taster and others agreed, noting the overpowering "artificial herb flavor."

NOT RECOMMENDED
Kellogg's Stuffing Mix
$2.19 for 6 ounces

"Is this Elmer's?" questioned one taster of this "mushy," "paste-like" stuffing. Though some tasters liked the "nice meaty flavor," the best most tasters could say was that it was "not terrible."

NOT RECOMMENDED
Pepperidge Farm Cubed Herb Seasoned Stuffing
$2.79 for 14 ounces

"Tastes fake," wrote one taster of this "average," "one-dimensional" stuffing that was "chalky and very wet at the same time."

NOT RECOMMENDED
Pepperidge Farm One Step Stuffing Mix Garden Herb
$1.99 for 6 ounces

Tasters agreed that this "dry and chewy" stuffing "needs some help." Bread pieces were "too fine" and had "not much flavor other than bread."

NOT RECOMMENDED
Manischewitz Homestyle Stuffing Stove Top Mix
$3.69 for 6 ounces

This matzo-based stuffing was described as "overcooked oatmeal" and "funky, and not in a good way." Most agreed with the taster who described this as "nothing like stuffing."

NOT RECOMMENDED
Zatarain's New Orleans Style French Bread Stuffing Mix
$2 for 6.6 ounces

"Tastes like the Oodles of Noodles flavoring packet," wrote one taster of this bright yellow, "strangely sweet" stuffing that was deemed "fake in every way."

CANDIED SWEET POTATO CASSEROLE

WHAT WE WANTED: A sweet potato side dish that is savory enough for an adult's palate, but still sweet enough to please the kids at the table.

Candied sweet potatoes are a traditional dish served alongside a roast ham or Thanksgiving turkey. All too often, however, they turn out watery, overseasoned, and overly sweet, tasting more like a loose, crustless pumpkin pie than a savory side dish. We wanted lightly seasoned and perfectly cooked sweet potatoes soft enough to slice with a fork, yet resilient enough not to fall through the fork tines while being eaten. And we wanted a topping that adds another dimension to the dish, instead of one that just weighs it down with sweetness.

To start, we followed the method touted in many cookbooks, and boiled peeled pieces of sweet potato before tossing them with a brown-sugar-and-butter sauce. Despite the popularity of this method, we found these sweet potatoes to be watery and lacking in flavor. Boiling the sweet potatoes washed away vital flavors and added moisture that was difficult to get rid of. We tried partially cooking the sweet potatoes in the microwave before mixing them with the sauce but found that they overcooked easily, while the sauce still lacked substantial flavor. Next we tossed raw, peeled pieces of sweet potato with brown sugar and butter and baked them in a covered casserole dish. This method also produced a watery sauce as well as unevenly cooked sweet potatoes. As the brown sugar and butter began to melt, the potatoes leached some of their liquid, making a watery cooking solution in which the potatoes began to float. It was difficult to keep these floating sweet potatoes completely submerged, and any unsubmerged parts of the potatoes dried out.

We had better luck once we tried cooking the sweet potatoes on the stovetop. When we cooked the potatoes in a Dutch oven with butter and brown sugar, the flavors of the potatoes and the sauce melded. Moistened with a little water and covered, the sweet potatoes cooked perfectly in about 50 minutes, resulting in the ultimate candied sweet potatoes, with a rich and complex sauce. Although the sauce was still a bit watery when we removed the lid, it was easy to crank up the heat and reduce it quickly to a thicker consistency.

We then tested adding chicken broth, wine, and cider, but tasters preferred the clean taste of the sweet potatoes on their own, seasoned with only a little salt and pepper. While a few tasters preferred the flavor of dark brown sugar to light brown, most found it overpowering. White sugar, on the other hand, was unanimously deemed too bland. We also tried all sorts of spices and herbs, but tasters once again preferred the simple flavors of sweet potatoes seasoned only with salt and pepper.

Now that the potatoes were done, we could focus on the topping. Pecans are a natural with sweet potatoes. We decided to leave them whole instead of chopping them, and this made for a nice presentation. Mixed with a beaten egg white, brown sugar, and some cayenne and cumin, this was a topping that could hold its own against the robust sweet potatoes. After just 15 minutes in a hot oven, this casserole was cooked through and the flavors had melded.

WHAT WE LEARNED: For the best texture and flavor, steam the sweet potatoes on the stovetop with a little water, butter, and brown sugar. Keep other flavorings simple—just salt and pepper. In the topping, use whole pecans instead of chopped; this provides a better texture and appearance. A little cayenne and cumin lend a hit of spice to the topping that offsets the sweetness of the potatoes.

CANDIED SWEET POTATO CASSEROLE

Serves 10 to 12

For a more intense molasses flavor, use dark brown sugar in place of light brown sugar.

sweet potatoes

8	tablespoons (1 stick) unsalted butter, cut into 1-inch chunks
5	pounds sweet potatoes (about 8 medium), peeled and cut into 1-inch cubes
1	cup packed light brown sugar
1½	teaspoons salt
½	teaspoon ground black pepper
½	cup water

pecan topping

2	cups pecan halves
½	cup packed light brown sugar
1	egg white, lightly beaten
⅛	teaspoon salt
	Pinch cayenne pepper
	Pinch ground cumin

1. FOR THE SWEET POTATOES: Melt the butter in a large Dutch oven over medium-high heat. Add the sweet potatoes, brown sugar, salt, pepper, and water; bring to a simmer. Reduce the heat to medium-low, cover, and cook, stirring often, until the sweet potatoes are tender (a paring knife can be slipped into and out of the center of the potatoes with very little resistance), 45 to 60 minutes.

2. When the sweet potatoes are tender, remove the lid and bring the sauce to a rapid simmer over medium-high heat. Continue to simmer until the sauce has reduced to a glaze, 7 to 10 minutes.

3. FOR THE TOPPING: Meanwhile, mix all the ingredients for the topping together in a medium bowl; set aside.

4. Adjust an oven rack to the middle position and heat the oven to 450 degrees. Pour the potato mixture into a 13 by 9-inch baking dish (or a shallow casserole dish of similar size). Spread the topping over the potatoes. Bake until the pecans are toasted and crisp, 10 to 15 minutes. Serve immediately.

VARIATION

CANDIED SWEET POTATO CASSEROLE WITH TOASTED MARSHMALLOW TOPPING

Follow the recipe for Candied Sweet Potato Casserole, substituting 4 cups mini marshmallows for the pecan topping. Bake until the marshmallows are crisp and golden, about 5 minutes.

EQUIPMENT CORNER: Turkey Gadgets

NEED A HAND WITH THAT TURKEY? DURING THE HOLIDAYS, you'll find an array of tools and equipment to help hold it, move it, stuff it, roast it, baste it, take its temperature, and more. We tested more than 20 items designed to make roasting a turkey easier. We were surprised to find that many don't live up to their promises. Here's what you need, what you might want to consider, and what to avoid.

ESSENTIAL

A roomy, sturdy roasting pan, preferably the Calphalon Contemporary Roasting Pan ($99).

A heavy-duty, nonadjustable V-rack, preferably the Norpro Nonstick Roasting Rack, model #270 ($9.95).

An instant-read thermometer, preferably the Thermapen, model #211-006 ($75).

A fat separator to defat drippings for grease-free gravy, preferably the Trudeau Gravy Separator with Integrated Strainer, model #099-1105 ($9.99).

WORTH CONSIDERING

Turkey Forks: Roasting the turkey breast-side down for part of the cooking time helps to protect the delicate white meat, but it also necessitates the turning of a piping-hot, greasy, half-cooked bird. In the test kitchen, we use big wads of paper towels or oven mitts (covered with plastic bags to keep them clean). As an alternative, some testers appreciated pitchfork-like Turkey Lifters ($15 for a set of two). When inserted into either end of the bird, they provide firm handles and plenty of leverage. The only disadvantage is that the prongs leave holes in the meat through which juices can escape easily.

TOTALLY USELESS

Flavor Injector: The syringe-like flavor injector made us feel like large-animal veterinarians as we injected brine into the bird in hope of saving the time spent on traditional brining. That hope faded when we discovered we had to give the brine time to become evenly dispersed throughout the turkey.

Easy-Read Thermometer: Pop-up thermometers (yes, you can buy these without the bird) are reliable only if you like white meat cooked to 180 degrees, which leaves it too dry for our taste (we opt for 165 degrees). Color-key thermometers look like tongue depressors and change color as the bird cooks, but give no indication of exact temperature, making it difficult to know when the turkey is done.

Coil Fasteners: These spring-like metal fasteners are designed to sew the skin shut around the cavity, but they require four hands to get the job done.

Bulb Baster: We've found that basting a bird (with a bulb baster or by any other means) runs counter to efforts to crisp the skin.

Roasting Bag: Roasting a turkey inside a plastic bag is supposed to make the bird especially juicy. It also ensures soft, flabby skin.

Lifting Rack: This flat rack with huge handles seemed like a good idea, but because it failed to lift the turkey high enough off the pan, the turkey steamed in its own juices. What's more, the handles barely fit in the 30-inch test kitchen ovens.

Roast Turkey for a Crowd **page 110**

Asparagus, Ham, and Gruyère Frittata **page 5**

Skillet Lasagna **page 63**

Barbecued Pulled Chicken **page 276**

Fettuccine Alfredo **page 177**

Paella **page 214**

Pan-Seared Oven-Roasted Pork Tenderloins **page 143** and Smashed Potatoes **page 92**

Butternut Squash Risotto **page 46**

Chicken Teriyaki **page 209**

Orange-Flavored Chicken **page 204**

Beef Braised in Barolo **page 181**

Fish Meunière with Browned Butter and Lemon **page 166**

Tortilla Soup **page 36**

Pan-Seared Inexpensive Steak **page 53**

Pan-Seared Sesame-Crusted Tuna Steaks **page 149**

Pork Chops with Vinegar and Sweet Peppers **page 136**

132

PORK CHOPS

CHAPTER 11

& tenderloin

IN THIS CHAPTER

THE RECIPES

Pork Chops with Vinegar and
    Sweet Peppers
Pork Chops with Balsamic
    Vinegar and Sweet Peppers

Pan-Seared Oven-Roasted Pork
    Tenderloins
Dried Cherry-Port Sauce with
    Onions and Marmalade
Banana-Date Chutney
Garlicky Lime Sauce with Cilantro

SCIENCE DESK

Why Meat Should Rest Before
    Slicing

TASTING LAB

Gourmet White Wine Vinegars
Supermarket White Wine
    Vinegars

The "other white meat" might be leaner than the pork enjoyed by our parents, but it's more difficult to cook. Pork has one-third less fat than it did 20 years ago, but lost with the fat is much of the meaty flavor. For this reason, choosing the right cut and the right cooking method make a big difference when preparing pork.

In this chapter, we decided to take a look at two pork cuts—chops and tenderloin. First, we sought to develop a foolproof preparation for pork chops with vinegar and peppers—a modern version tangy and juicy enough to rival that prepared by any Italian grandmother. Next, we turned to pan-roasted pork tenderloin—a sleekly sophisticated dish popular in today's restaurants, but not without its challenges. After trying these recipes, we think you'll agree that cooking with today's leaner pork isn't so bad for the taste buds after all.

In general, the soy sauces that did well in our testing were pleasingly distinct and balanced in flavor. They were neither overpowering nor bland. Saltiness was acceptable so long as this was not the only personality trait. All of the soy sauces that were disliked in the plain tasting failed to gain approval in the stir-fry test. Not all of the soy sauces recommended performed consistently in both tastings. The clear favorite, however, an organic Japanese soy sauce by Eden Foods, was remarkably consistent.

It was interesting to find out that the winner, Eden Selected Shoyu Soy Sauce, which is made in Japan, is brewed outdoors in cedar vats for about three years so that the fermenting soy sauce is subjected to seasonal changes in temperature. Sally Gralla, a spokesperson for Eden Foods, explained that most soy sauces are brewed indoors in steel tanks for a shorter period of time, about one year.

According to Dr. Daniel Y. C. Fung, professor of food science at Kansas State University, the amount of time a soy sauce is given to ferment can be a contributing factor to its palatability. But that's not everything. Wheat and soybeans are very complex food systems, he says. When bacteria, yeast, and mold start growing, they produce a large variety of compounds that will create a great diversity of flavors. The grade of wheat or soybean, the type or quality of mold starter, the temperature at which the wheat is roasted, the amount of salt used in the brine, the amount of air let into the vats during aging . . . all can affect the fine balance of flavors in soy sauce. "It is a science as well as an art to make soy sauce," says Fung. "Much like winemaking."

All of the above can also contribute to the ability of the sauce to retain its flavor during cooking (or, as we found with many soy sauces, the inability to retain flavor). At the heart of soy sauce flavor are amino acid compounds, some of which are volatile. These are the compounds that give the sauce its aroma, says Dr. Ronald Schmidt, professor of food science at the University of Florida in Gainesville. Add heat to the mix, and these aromatic compounds quickly dissipate. Depending on the soy sauce, this can significantly reduce the taste experience—which tasters actually found to be

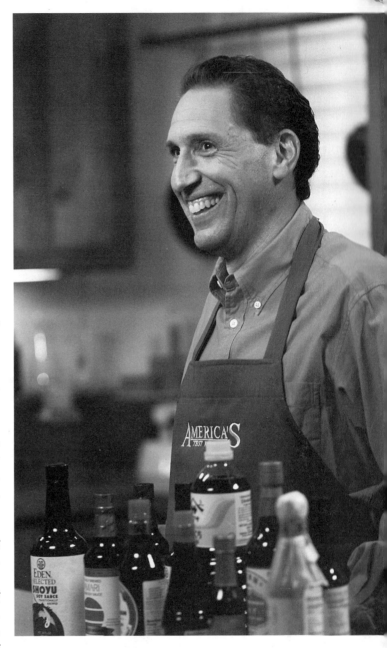

advantageous with the particularly awful-tasting products.

Finally, it was no surprise that the one synthetic soy sauce in the tasting ranked miserably low. Sadly, this is the sort of soy sauce most Americans were first able to access. Fortunately, we found, plenty of other choices are now available.

Rating Soy Sauces

FIFTEEN MEMBERS OF THE AMERICA'S TEST KITCHEN STAFF TASTED 10 BRANDS OF SOY SAUCE PLAIN WITH UNSEASONED SWEET rice and cubes of silken tofu for dipping. In the second tasting, cubes of chicken were tossed in a measured amount of each soy sauce as well as a small amount of sugar. The chicken was then stir-fried along with a modest amount of minced garlic and ginger. The soy sauces are listed in order of preference based on their scores in these taste tests. All brands are available in supermarkets, natural food stores, or Asian markets.

HIGHLY RECOMMENDED
Eden Selected Shoyu Soy Sauce
$2.59 for 10 ounces

Tasters decisively ranked this "distinct" soy sauce number 1 in both taste tests. The flavor was "toasty, caramel-y, and complex," not wimpy. The salt flavor was tangible but not overpowering.

RECOMMENDED
San-J Reduced Sodium Tamari Natural Soy Sauce
$3.99 for 10 ounces

Although this soy sauce contains 25 percent less sodium than most tamaris, tasters ranked it as the saltiest of the sauces when tasted plain. The salty edge subsided significantly in the stir-fry. Though it's labeled as a tamari, its makers do add a trace amount of wheat to this sauce.

RECOMMENDED
Naturally Brewed Higeta Honzen Soy Sauce
$7.50 for 12.6 ounces

The tag on the fancily packaged bottle touts this soy sauce as "the preferred seasoning of chefs in the finest and most exclusive restaurants in Japan." One taster described this pricey soy sauce as "enhancing the flavor without standing out or under-representing itself" in the stir-fry. As a dipping sauce, it was more "intense," with a somewhat bitter finish. For certain, no other soy sauce neared it in price.

RECOMMENDED
Eden Organic Tamari Soy Sauce Traditionally Brewed
$4.49 for 10 ounces

Brewed for two years, this tamari was full-bodied, complex, and "almost fruity," but it still "doesn't set off all my taste buds," wrote one taster. "A respectable level of salt."

RECOMMENDED
Kikkoman Naturally Brewed Soy Sauce
$1.59 for 10 ounces

This was the best among the supermarket standards and tied for first in the dipping sauce taste test, where it was described as "more rounded than others." It was definitively salty, but when tasted in a stir-fry, it lost its pizzazz.

RECOMMENDED
San-J Organic Whole Soybean Shoyu
$2.49 for 10 ounces

This Japanese-style soy sauce (brewed in Virginia) stood out as saltier than many of the others, even though its sodium level was no different. There was nothing objectionable about this soy sauce, but nothing great to say about it either.

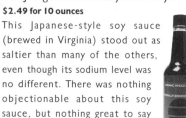

NOT RECOMMENDED
Pearl River Bridge Superior Soy Sauce
$2.55 for 18.6 ounces

When tasted plain, this Chinese soy sauce was described as unpalatably fishy, "like the parking lot of a wholesale fish pier." Tasters also complained of metallic notes and too much salt flavor.

NOT RECOMMENDED
Yamasa Naturally Brewed Soy Sauce
$2.99 for 34 ounces

Popular in Japanese restaurants, this rich, amber-colored soy sauce contradicted itself. When tasted plain as a dipping sauce, tasters objected to it, saying it was "too strong," "harsh," "spikey," and "a bit chemical." In the stir-fry it was mild and shallow.

NOT RECOMMENDED
Eden Organic Tamari Soy Sauce Naturally Brewed
$2.99 for 10 ounces

Unlike Eden's traditionally brewed tamari (see middle column), this tamari was aged for just six months in an accelerated brewing process. The drawbacks were glaring. One taster thought it tasted "like burnt bacon," others found it "harsh" and "overpowering." These offenses dissipated when the sauce was heated up in a stir-fry; there, however, it had "hardly any flavor."

NOT RECOMMENDED
La Choy Soy Sauce
$1.99 for 10 ounces

This was the only synthetically made soy sauce in the tasting, and it showed. Tasters did not mince words in their descriptions: "awful," "crude," "chemical," and "heinous"; like "very bad jarred beef" or "burnt wood." Maybe we should have tried using it for dipping french fries or fish sticks, as is recommended on the bottle's inside label.

PAN-ROASTED HALIBUT

WHAT WE WANTED: Halibut with a browned crusty exterior and moist, flavorful flesh.

With its naturally lean, firm texture and clean, mild flavor, halibut is often preferred braised rather than roasted or sautéed because this moist-heat cooking technique keeps the fish from drying out. The downside, however, is that braising does not develop as much flavor as other methods, producing fish the test kitchen considers lackluster. So we set out to discover a cooking method that not only added flavor but also produced a perfectly cooked, moist, and tender piece of fish.

Before addressing the questions of technique and sauce, we took to the supermarkets and fishmongers to settle on the best cut of halibut with which to proceed. Fillets, we learned, come from smaller fish and are rare, so we ruled them out. By virtue of availability, halibut steaks were a better choice. But steaks vary considerably in size depending on the weight of the particular fish, which typically ranges from 15 to 50 pounds but can reach up to 300 pounds.

After buying more than 40 pounds of halibut, our advice is this: Inspect the steaks in the fish case and choose the two that are closest in size. This approach ensures that the steaks will cook at the same rate, thus avoiding the problem of overcooking the smaller one. We found the best size steak for the home cook to be between 10 and 12 inches in length and roughly 1¼ inches thick (see "Three Kinds of Halibut Steak" on page 157). We did test thinner and thicker steaks, adjusting the cooking time as necessary, and had success on both counts. We also tried halibut steaks that we purchased frozen. The flavor matched that of the fresh fish, but tasters were disappointed in the texture, which they found mushy and fibrous.

Keeping in mind that we wanted to brown the fish to develop flavor, we tested two different techniques: skillet cooking on the stovetop and roasting in the oven at 500 degrees. Neither was ideal. The skillet-seared fish browned nicely but became a little dry. The roasted sample was moist and evenly cooked, but it barely browned and had little flavor; we craved some of the browning from the skillet to intensify the flavor. To achieve this, we chose a common restaurant technique and combined the methods.

First we seared the fish in a heavy-duty, ovenproof skillet on the stovetop, and then we put the whole thing—pan and fish—into the oven to finish cooking. This approach was an improvement, but we still had a problem. Our efforts to brown the fish sufficiently to enhance its flavor usually caused it to overcook.

After much additional testing, we finally hit on the solution. Instead of sautéing the fish on both sides, we seared it on one side only, flipped it in the pan, and then placed it in the oven to finish with the seared side up. This worked beautifully, combining the enhanced flavor of browned fish with the moist interior that came from finishing in the oven's even heat. Finally, moist fish with great sautéed flavor.

Next we explored a few refinements. All home cooks know that fish sticks to the pan, and a nonstick skillet is the common solution to this problem. In this case, however, we feared that many nonstick skillets, even those marked ovensafe, would not be truly oven-worthy at the temperature we'd be using, so we had to solve the sticking problem that came with the use of a traditional skillet. We knew that success would lie in a well-heated pan. In a skillet heated over high heat for just one minute, the fish stuck like crazy. After two minutes, it stuck a little bit. What did the trick was 2½ minutes of heating over high heat, or just until the oil started to smoke.

We also tried searing the halibut in different fats. Butter burned badly, even when combined with oil. The best choice was pure olive oil, the richness of which tasters welcomed over vegetable oil.

Oven temperatures were up next for testing, and we tried four settings: 425, 450, 475, and 500 degrees. Finding no discernible difference in the fish roasted at any of these temperatures, we opted for 425 degrees because it offered the greatest margin for error. (The slower the oven, the longer the window of time for doneness.) Timing is another key to moist, perfectly cooked fish. For the type and thickness of steaks we were using, we found that six minutes of oven time left the fish a bit underdone. At roughly nine minutes the flakes were opaque, but they had not sacrificed any moisture or tenderness.

In addition to timing, we wanted to determine if there were other reliable clues as to when the fish was done properly. Evie Hansen, director of marketing for National Seafood Educators and author of several seafood cookbooks, noted that for health safety reasons, the U.S. Food and Drug Administration suggests a final internal temperature of 140 degrees on an instant-read thermometer. We tested this suggested temperature and concur.

With the fish seared and roasted properly, all we needed was a sauce or two to accompany it. Though we usually think of making an easy sauce from the drippings left in the pan, in this case that was not an option because the pan was overheated from the hot oven. After trying a variety of relishes, salsas, flavored butters, and vinaigrettes, tasters all agreed that they preferred a sauce with some richness (that is, fat) to complement the lean fish. Flavored butters were easy to prepare and fit our requirements in terms of richness, as did vinaigrette because of its olive oil.

WHAT WE LEARNED: Choose steaks of like size so that they all cook at the same rate. Preheat the skillet until the oil is just smoking to prevent the fish from sticking to the pan. For a nice crust and moist interior, sear just one side of the fish on the stovetop and finish cooking the fish in the oven. To determine doneness, use an instant-read thermometer.

PAN-ROASTED HALIBUT STEAKS
Serves 4 to 6

This recipe calls for a heavy ovenproof skillet. If you plan to serve the fish with one of the flavored butters or the vinaigrette that follows (pages 157-158), prepare it before cooking the fish. Even well-dried fish can cause the hot oil in the pan to splatter. You can minimize splattering by laying the halibut steaks in the pan gently and putting the edge closest to you in the pan first so that the far edge falls away from you.

2 tablespoons olive oil
2 (full) halibut steaks (see the photos on page 157), about 1¼ inches thick and 10 to 12 inches long (about 2½ pounds total), gently rinsed, dried well with paper towels, and trimmed of cartilage at both ends (see the illustration below)
   Salt and ground black pepper
   Flavored butter or vinaigrette (recipes follow)

1. Adjust an oven rack to the middle position and heat the oven to 425 degrees. When the oven reaches 425 degrees, heat the oil in a 12-inch heavy-bottomed ovenproof skillet over high heat until the oil just begins to smoke.

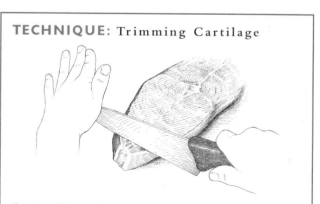

TECHNIQUE: Trimming Cartilage

Cutting off the cartilage at the ends of the steaks ensures that they will fit neatly in the pan and diminishes the likelihood that the small bones located there will wind up on your dinner plate.

2. Meanwhile, sprinkle both sides of both halibut steaks generously with salt and pepper. Reduce the heat to medium-high and swirl the oil in the pan to distribute; carefully lay the steaks in the pan and sear, without moving them, until spotty brown, about 4 minutes. (If the steaks are thinner than 1¼ inches, check browning at 3½ minutes; thicker steaks of 1½ inches may require extra time, so check at 4½ minutes.) Off the heat, flip the steaks over in the pan using two thin-bladed metal spatulas (see the illustration on page 166).

3. Transfer the skillet to the oven and roast until an instant-read thermometer inserted into the steaks reads 140 degrees and the fish flakes loosen and the flesh is opaque when checked with the tip of a paring knife, about 9 minutes (thicker steaks may take up to 10 minutes). Remove the skillet from the oven and, following the illustration on page 158, separate the skin and bones from the fish with a spatula. Transfer the fish to a warm platter and serve immediately with a flavored butter or sauce.

CHIPOTLE-GARLIC BUTTER WITH LIME AND CILANTRO
Makes about ¼ cup

4 tablespoons (½ stick) unsalted butter, softened
1 medium chipotle chile in adobo sauce, seeded and minced, plus 1 teaspoon adobo sauce
2 teaspoons minced fresh cilantro leaves
1 medium garlic clove, minced or pressed through a garlic press (about 1 teaspoon)
1 teaspoon honey
1 teaspoon grated zest from 1 lime
½ teaspoon salt

Beat the butter with a fork until light and fluffy. Stir in the remaining ingredients until thoroughly combined. Dollop a portion of the butter over the pieces of hot cooked fish and allow the butter to melt. Serve immediately.

GETTING IT RIGHT: Three Kinds of Halibut Steak

Most halibut steaks consist of four pieces of meat attached to a central bone (left). It is not uncommon, however, to encounter a steak with just two pieces, both located on the same side of the center bone (center). These steaks were cut from the center of the halibut, adjacent to the belly cavity. The belly, in effect, separates the two halves. We slightly preferred full steaks with four meat sections; each full steak serves two or three people. If you can find only the belly steaks, you will have to purchase four steaks instead of two to make the recipe. Avoid very small, boneless steaks (right) cut entirely free from the bone and each other. Most boneless steaks won't serve even one person.

ANCHOVY-GARLIC BUTTER WITH LEMON AND PARSLEY
Makes about ¼ cup

4	tablespoons (½ stick) unsalted butter, softened
1	anchovy fillet, minced to a paste
2	tablespoons minced fresh parsley leaves
1½	teaspoons juice from 1 lemon
1	medium garlic clove, minced or pressed through a garlic press (about 1 teaspoon)
½	teaspoon salt

Beat the butter with a fork until light and fluffy. Stir in the remaining ingredients until thoroughly combined. Dollop a portion of the butter over the pieces of hot cooked fish and allow the butter to melt. Serve immediately.

CHUNKY CHERRY TOMATO–BASIL VINAIGRETTE
Makes about 1½ cups

½	pint cherry or grape tomatoes, each tomato quartered (about 1 cup)
¼	teaspoon salt
¼	teaspoon ground black pepper
2	medium shallots, minced (about 6 tablespoons)
6	tablespoons extra-virgin olive oil
3	tablespoons juice from 1 lemon
2	tablespoons minced fresh basil leaves

Mix the tomatoes with the salt and pepper in a medium bowl; let stand until juicy and seasoned, about 10 minutes. Whisk the shallots, oil, lemon juice, and basil together in a small mixing bowl, pour the vinaigrette over the tomatoes, and toss to combine. Pour over the pieces of hot cooked fish and serve immediately.

TECHNIQUE: Serving Halibut Steaks

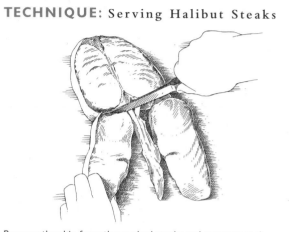

Remove the skin from the cooked steaks and separate each quadrant of meat from the bones by slipping a spatula or knife gently between them. Transfer the pieces of fish to a warm serving platter.

EQUIPMENT CORNER: Oven Mitts

AS EXACTING AS WE GET WHEN SHOPPING FOR SKILLETS (fully clad, stainless steel, 2.6-millimeter-thick sides), such rigor has consistently escaped our oven-mitt-buying decisions (fuzzy, blue). And given the $5 price tags, we've been content to let kitchen décor, not performance, be our guiding light.

Lately, however, oven mitts have turned decidedly more ambitious. Competing with basic terry and cotton are mitts sporting fancy materials and features: leather, "treated" cotton, rubber, silicone, Nomex (a fireproof material used to make race-car-driver gear), and Kevlar (an even stronger synthetic, found in body armor and military helmets). There are flameproof suede gloves meant for welders, and the "melt"-resistant "Ove" Glove (as seen on TV!). These space-age products don't come cheap: The priciest sells for $30—and that's per mitt.

Bells and whistles aside, an oven mitt has two core requirements: enough heat resistance to keep hands from burning and enough pliability to keep cooks from inadvertently smashing food (or dropping pans). Because impressive dexterity is of zero importance if you can't pick up the hot pan in the first place, initial testing focused on heat protection.

We first measured the amount of time testers were able to lift and hold a Dutch oven filled with boiling water before the heat became unbearable. The silicone mitts were the winners, maxing out at an impressive 90 seconds; the Nomex/Kevlar mitts lasted a minute. Most of the rest clocked in at around 45 seconds, the leather model losing with a still-respectable 22 seconds. (How much longer does a Dutch oven need to be held in midair, anyway?)

Clearly, we'd have to brave the oven's high temperatures to separate the best mitt from the worst. But was merely recording how long it took a pan-laden test cook to start trembling nervously an objective enough measure of heat protection? We decided to outfit the interior of each mitt with a thermocouple—a wire probe that feeds temperature data to an attached console—with the probe strategically positioned at the point of contact. Testers would take turns holding a pan of lasagna (heated in a 400-degree oven) for as long as possible. Meanwhile, we would stand nearby duly recording temperature readings from the console.

The sleek lined LamsonSharp leather glove was the first contestant. We barely had time to get our clipboard situated comfortably when the tester emitted a piercing "Owww!" and slammed the bubbling batch of lasagna back onto the oven rack. Luckily, we kept our cool long enough to jot down the data: The LamsonSharp had risen to 109.9 degrees in just four seconds.

The rest of the mitts fared better, screams of pain were rare, and we were making clear progress. First, we had quantified the "ouch" factor: Like clockwork, testers faltered at 110 degrees. What's more, we had established a pecking order based on the number of seconds the mitts kept our hands below that threshold of pain: heavy silicone

(90 seconds); heavy quilted cotton (65); padded Nomex/Kevlar and thin quilted cotton (40); rubber, treated cotton, and quilted terry (30); nonpadded Nomex/Kevlar (the "Ove" Glove) (20); suede (15); and leather (4).

Until now, we had been careful to keep the mitts dry, as per manufacturer warnings. But such a caveat seemed a cop-out for a product meant for settings in which insidious liquids lurk at every turn. So we soaked each mitt for five seconds in room-temperature water, then repeated the Dutch oven lift test. The waterproof silicones and rubbers again kept their cool beyond a minute, but the rest faltered much sooner.

As testers braved the heat-resistance trials, disdain abounded for the Orka mitts, made from heavy silicone. ("I can't even tell the pan handles are there!" complained one panelist.) The thick silicone, so effective for protecting hands, was also inhibiting dexterity. So we devised three new experiments.

First, 12 test kitchen staffers, using each pair of mitts, took turns transferring a baking sheet full of cookies and an empty skillet from the oven to a cooling rack. Afterward, we headed outside to a hot charcoal grill, where we flipped 24 rounds of eggplant with medium-sized tongs. Testers rated each design on how well it negotiated the thin sides of the baking pan, the skinny skillet handle, and the precision movement of the tongs.

Our tests taught us several lessons. First, there's an inverse relationship between heat protection and dexterity. The very attributes that gave some of our mitts such impressive heat resistance (bulky padding, stiff synthetic material) had us chasing eggplant rounds around the grill grate and smashing cookies. By contrast, the highest marks for dexterity went to the leather, the two suedes, and the "Ove" Glove—three of the worst in terms of heat protection. For a satisfactory mitt overall, then, we'd have to choose from above-average but not top-rated performers in both arenas.

During the eggplant trials, we also developed clear mitt-length preferences. The mitt lengths ranged from 8½ inches to 17 inches. The 17-inchers provided more-

than-adequate heat protection—even after several minutes over a hot grill—but smaller testers found this size awkward (there was a tendency for sleeves or elbows to bump the gloves forward). We found 15 inches (12 inches for smaller testers) to be the ideal length for indoors and outdoors.

A constant problem with oven mitts is how to keep them clean—especially when they're used outdoors. So we grabbed a bottle of barbecue sauce and a skillet full of steak grease and returned to our mitts. We spooned a heaping tablespoon of each substance onto the mitts, let them sit overnight, and then washed each according to manufacturer instructions. While most cleaned up beautifully, the leather glove bled dye everywhere and the suedes and the terry were sullied beyond repair.

A common mishap is setting fire to an oven mitt while trying to juggle pans on the stovetop. So we re-created the situation. Armed with safety goggles, fire extinguisher, and galvanized metal bucket, we subjected each mitt to

a five-second flame test over a gas burner turned to high. The terry, cotton, and treated cotton models suffered gaping holes. The rubber glove burned at the seam. The suedes and the leather gave off smelly fumes but remained unharmed. The silicone and Nomex/Kevlar models, however, survived the test without a blemish.

After weeks of testing, then, had we found the perfect mitt? The padded Nomex/Kevlar model, made by Kool-Tek, came pretty close. In addition to providing good heat protection and excellent dexterity, it washed easily and refused to burn. The Kool-Tek's only downfall is price—up to a hefty $24.95 per mitt. After so many years making do with $5 mitts, could we bring ourselves to plunk down that kind of cash for what's really just a souped-up potholder? Skeptics can give our runner-up a try: For eight bucks, the Parvin quilted-cotton mitt handled most tasks well; just keep it out of fire and water. But after this test, we are cheapo-mitt veterans who have seen the light.

Rating Oven Mitts

WE TESTED NINE TYPES OF OVEN MITTS MADE FROM A VARIETY OF MATERIALS. MITTS WERE EVALUATED FOR HEAT protection, ease of manipulation while transferring pans to and from the oven and the stovetop (and while using tongs during grilling), and durability (how well they resisted structural damage and staining). The mitts are listed in order of preference. See www.americastestkitchen.com for up-to-date prices and mail-order sources for top-rated products.

HIGHLY RECOMMENDED
Kool-Tek Protective Apparel
Material: Nomex, Kevlar, treated cotton
$21.95 per mitt (12 inches)
$24.95 per mitt (15 inches)
Everything we want in a mitt—except maybe the price. Mostly Nomex (heat resistant to 450 degrees) with a "racing stripe" of Kevlar (heat resistant to 1,000 degrees), the Kool-Tek won fans for its natural grip, easy dexterity, and stay-cool comfort.

RECOMMENDED
Parvin Flameguard Oven Mitt
Material: Treated cotton exterior with cotton padding
$8.40 per pair (17 inches)
Almost as many fans as the winner—especially for its comfortable dexterity and "just the right amount of padding"—but some found the length "a bit cumbersome." Don't set this one on fire.

RECOMMENDED WITH RESERVATIONS
Duncan's Kitchen Grips
Material: Synthetic rubber
$14.95 per pair (11 inches)
$19.95 per pair (15½ inches)
The "weird flatness" was annoying, and testers with small hands disliked the 2 to 3 inches of useless space at the top. The stylized shape made one tester feel like "a gingerbread man" (and not in a good way).

RECOMMENDED WITH RESERVATIONS
Ritz Quilted Oven Mitt
Material: Padded cotton, with terry interior
$13.95 per mitt (12 inches)
The bulky padding that made for awesome heat protection also made the task of maneuvering pans "a major pain."

NOT RECOMMENDED
Orka Oven Mitt
Material: Silicone
$19.99 per mitt (11 inches)
$29.99 per mitt (17 inches)
The heat-protection champ, but testers hated almost everything else about it. The raised grip on the mitt portion was too bulky, and the interior quickly got sweaty. "Falling! Falling!" warned one tester, who couldn't feel the edges of the cookie sheet and almost dropped it.

NOT RECOMMENDED
Kitchen Supply Mitt Glove
Material: Padded terry, with cotton interior
$13.95 per mitt (12 inches)
Overly insulated finger compartments sapped this design of dexterity. During the washing test, the steak grease stained permanently and some of the padding came out.

NOT RECOMMENDED
Charcoal Companion Suede Gloves
Material: Suede with treated cotton interior
$12.95 per pair (13 inches)
Nice-looking, comfortable, and easy to manipulate, but these gloves got very hot—and quickly. The pair we tested has yet to recover from the barbecue-sauce test.

NOT RECOMMENDED
Lincoln Electric Welder's Gloves
Material: Suede with cotton interior
$14.95 per pair (12 inches)
"Welders must be tougher than I am," said one tester once the heat made it through the suede exterior. The delayed heat penetration gave testers a false sense of comfort—then rudely disturbed it.

NOT RECOMMENDED
The "Ove" Glove Hot Surface Handler
Material: Woven Kevlar/Nomex with cotton/polyester interior
$19.99 per mitt (10 inches)
Everyone was eager to try the famous mitt from the TV ad, but no one trusted it. "It looks like a child's snow glove," said one staffer. And it worked about as well. This Kevlar/Nomex mitt lacked the layer of padding that pushed our winner to the top.

Bridget coats sole fillets in flour, which ensures a delicate, golden brown crust for fish meunière.

SEAFOOD classics

CHAPTER 13

IN THIS CHAPTER

THE RECIPES
Fish Meunière with Browned
    Butter and Lemon
Fish Meunière with Toasted
    Slivered Almonds
Fish Meunière with Capers

Pan-Seared Scallops with Wilted
    Spinach, Watercress, and
    Orange Salad

EQUIPMENT CORNER
Wine Saver Devices

TASTING LAB
Butter Alternatives

Some people are intimidated by the thought of preparing fish, preferring to order it out at restaurants rather than prepare it at home. Classic fish dishes, especially those with sophisticated names like Fish Meunière, can seem even more daunting. But, in reality, you don't need to be wearing a toque to prepare this French classic well.

This chapter also looks at a dish that seems to be on every restaurant menu—a new classic if you will—wilted spinach salad. Many people think of wilted spinach salads as fussy and hard to prepare. Not so. In fact, a wilted spinach salad can easily be transformed into a rich main course with little time or effort. We can show you how. Pan-seared scallops are a natural partner with wilted spinach salad.

These dishes are impressive enough to serve to company, but because they don't involve a lot of work, they can also be prepared on a busy weeknight. That doesn't sound intimidating at all.

FISH MEUNIÈRE

WHAT WE WANTED: Golden brown, delicate fillets served with a rich, nutty butter sauce.

Fish meunière is a deceptively easy French restaurant dish that ought to serve as a model recipe for home cooking. Ideally, fillets are dredged lightly in flour (no need for eggs or bread crumbs) and cooked on the stovetop until a golden crust forms, leaving the inside moist and flavorful. A browned butter sauce seasoned with lemon is then poured over the fish. What could be simpler, more delicious, or better suited to a Tuesday night dinner? That's what we thought, too, before we cooked a few test batches to get a handle on the technique for making this dish. What we got were plates of pale, soggy fillets in pools of greasy sauce; that is, if the fish hadn't stuck to the pan or fallen apart as we tried to plate it. Despite these failures (or maybe because of them), one thing did become clear. The simplicity of this dish makes it imperative that everything be prepared and cooked just so.

Taking a closer look at our initial meunière recipes (the word *meunière* means "miller's wife," a nod to the flour in the recipe), it was no wonder that we had found little success at the stove. Some recipes called for almost two sticks of butter for two pounds of fish—that translates to almost ½ cup butter per 16 ounces of fish. Who wants to eat fish literally swimming in fat? We certainly didn't. Other recipes failed in browning the fish, and the resulting fillets were soggy and pale. It was time to go back to basics.

Whole Dover sole—a variety of white flatfish—is the most authentic choice for preparing à la meunière, but it is hard to come by in the best of fish markets and prohibitively expensive when it can be had. A whole Dover sole, if it can even be found, presents cleaning and filleting issues as well. We decided to look for a filleted white flatfish that would be available in most markets, thinking that sole or flounder would be the options. We soon became aware of a veritable parade of choices—gray sole, lemon sole, yellowtail flounder, southern flounder, summer flounder, winter flounder, petrale sole, rex sole, rock sole, and starry flounder. After cooking 20 pounds of flatfish, we discovered that variety didn't much matter (tasters approved of them all); what counted were the thickness and the freshness of the fillet. If the fillet was thinner than ⅜ inch, it was nearly impossible to brown it without overcooking it. Fillets that were ⅜ inch thick or slightly more were perfect. They weighed five to six ounces each and fit easily in a large skillet. Fillets weighing seven to ten ounces also were acceptable, although they required cutting and trimming.

Small things can make a big difference when it comes to cooking fish. For one, a thin coat of flour speeds up the browning, which is a particularly useful thing to know when you've got thin fillets that cook quickly. Straight from the fishmonger's wrapping paper, fillets are typically wet. They must be patted dry, or the flour will become thick and gluey. Simply dredging the dried fillets in flour presented problems. Excess flour fell off the fish and into the pan, where it burned. Shaking off the extra flour before cooking solved this problem. Still, even after a quick shake, the fillets cooked up with blotchy brown crusts that did nothing for the flavor.

We then tried a technique used by Julia Child, who recommends seasoning the fillets with salt and pepper and letting them sit before dredging. After five minutes, the fillets had begun to glisten with moisture. We dredged them with flour, shook off the excess, and cooked them. "Perfectly seasoned and evenly coated" was the thumbs-up response from tasters. Why does letting the seasoned fish rest for five minutes make such a difference? The salt extracts water from the fish, not so much as to make it wet but just enough to give it a thin coating of moisture that helps to ensure a perfectly even coating of flour. Without "bald spots" in the coating, the fish browns uniformly and tastes better.

The technique of pan-frying necessitates a heavy skillet and a good amount of fat. Food is cooked in a single layer as the cook waits patiently for it to brown, turning it once and then waiting again. The temptation is to lift the food and take a peek, but it is essential to resist the impulse. For maximum browning (and to keep the fish from falling apart), the fish must be left undisturbed as it cooks.

We found that traditional skillets did not work well. No matter how much fat we used, the fish had a tendency to stick. A nonstick skillet, on the other hand, worked well every time, producing beautifully browned fillets and no sticking. A 12-inch skillet is a must, we discovered, and even then only two fillets would fit at a time without overlapping. We wanted our recipe to serve four, but using two skillets side by side seemed unreasonable. Instead, we chose to cook the fish in two batches, using a warmed plate in a preheated 200-degree oven to keep the first batch hot.

Clarified butter (butter with the milk solids removed) is the traditional fat used by the French. Not only does clarified butter lend a rich flavor to the fish, but it has a higher smoking point (and thus burns less easily) than whole butter. Clarifying butter is easy, but it is too lengthy a process for a quick midweek entrée. Would tasters notice its absence? We cooked one batch with canola oil and another with clarified butter, and even the least discerning tasters noticed the difference. Whole butter burned, but a mixture of oil and butter, a classic combination, did the trick.

Next we experimented with the amount of fat. Although recipes ranged from one to six tablespoons (for two fillets), we found that two tablespoons was ample, especially in a nonstick skillet. At this point, because we were using so little fat, we were technically sautéing rather than pan-frying. We began by cooking the fillets over low heat, but the results were mediocre at best; the fillets did not brown but instead poached in the fat, and the taste was lackluster. High heat turned out to be equally problematic. By the time the interior of each fillet had cooked, some of the exterior had scorched, resulting in a bitter and unappealing taste. Our next try was a winner. We heated the pan over high heat, then lowered the heat to medium-high as soon as we added the fish. The exterior browned beautifully, while the inside remained succulent.

For fillets that were the ideal thickness of ⅜ inch, three minutes on the first side and about two minutes on the second side achieved both a flavorful, nutty-tasting exterior and a moist, delicate interior. Because the side that is cooked first is the most attractive, we found it best to stick to the hard-and-fast rule of cooking for three minutes on the first side and then adjusting the time for the second side. (With flatfish, the side of the fillet that you cook first also matters. See "Anatomy of a Flatfish Fillet" on page 167.) The question was, how could we tell when a thin fillet was done? Restaurant chefs press the fillets with their fingers—a reliable technique but one that requires practice. Observation eventually indicated that the fillet was done when opaque. Because the fish continues to cook off the heat of the stovetop (and in the gentle heat of the preheated oven), it is imperative to remove it slightly before it's fully done. Instead of using the tip of a knife, a method that tends to damage the fillet, we found that a toothpick inserted into a thick edge worked well.

One last cooking consideration remained to be resolved. Traditionally, the sauce served with meunière is beurre noisette, or browned butter, with lemon juice and parsley added. Crucial to the flavor of the sauce, which adds a rich nuttiness to the fish, is proper browning of the milk solids in the butter, a task not easily accomplished in a nonstick skillet. The problem is that the dark surface of the pan makes it nearly impossible to judge the color of the butter. The solution was simple: Brown the butter in a medium stainless steel skillet; its shiny bottom makes it easy to monitor the color. We then added lemon juice to the browned butter, sprinkled the fish with parsley, and poured the sauce over the fish.

WHAT WE LEARNED: To prevent the likelihood of overcooking the fish, choose sole or flounder fillets that are no less than ⅜ inch thick. A nonstick skillet is the best pan in which to cook the fish without it breaking apart. Remove the pan from the heat just before the fish is cooked (the fish will continue to cook off the heat). To check the doneness of the fish without marring the flesh, use a toothpick, not a paring knife.

FISH MEUNIÈRE WITH BROWNED BUTTER AND LEMON

Serves 4

Try to purchase fillets that are of similar size, and avoid those that weigh less than 5 ounces because they will cook too quickly. When placing the fillets in the skillet, be sure to place them skin-side up so that the opposite side, which had bones, will brown first. A nonstick skillet ensures that the fillets will release from the pan, but for the sauce a traditional skillet is preferable because its light-colored surface will allow you to monitor the color of the butter as it browns.

fish

½	cup unbleached all-purpose flour
4	sole or flounder fillets, ⅜ inch thick (5 to 6 ounces each), patted dry with paper towels
	Salt and ground black pepper
2	tablespoons vegetable oil
2	tablespoons unsalted butter, cut into 2 pieces

browned butter

4	tablespoons (½ stick) unsalted butter, cut into 4 pieces
1	tablespoon chopped fresh parsley leaves
1½	tablespoons juice from 1 lemon
	Salt
1	lemon, cut into wedges, for serving

1. FOR THE FISH: Adjust an oven rack to the lower-middle position, set 4 heatproof dinner plates on the rack, and heat the oven to 200 degrees. Place the flour in a large baking dish. Season both sides of each fillet generously with salt and pepper; let stand until the fillets are glistening with moisture, about 5 minutes. Coat both sides of the fillets with flour, shake off the excess, and place in a single layer on a baking sheet. Heat 1 tablespoon of the oil in a 12-inch nonstick skillet over high heat until shimmering; add 1 tablespoon of the butter and swirl to coat the pan bottom. When the foaming

subsides, carefully place 2 fillets skin-side up in the skillet (see the photo on page 167). Immediately reduce the heat to medium-high and cook, without moving the fish, until the edges of the fillets are opaque and the bottoms are golden brown, about 3 minutes. Using 2 spatulas, gently flip the fillets (see the illustration below) and cook on the second side until the thickest part of the fillet easily separates into flakes when a toothpick is inserted, about 2 minutes longer. Transfer the fillets to two of the heated dinner plates, keeping them bone-side up, and return the plates to the oven. Wipe out the skillet and repeat with the remaining 1 tablespoon each oil and butter and the remaining fish fillets.

2. FOR THE BROWNED BUTTER: Heat the butter in a 10-inch stainless steel skillet over medium-high heat until the butter melts, 1 to 1½ minutes. Continue to cook, swirling the pan constantly, until the butter is golden brown and has a nutty aroma, 1 to 1½ minutes; remove the skillet from the heat. Remove the plates from the oven and sprinkle the fillets with the parsley. Add the lemon juice to the browned butter and season to taste with salt; spoon the sauce over the fish and serve immediately with the lemon wedges.

TECHNIQUE: Flipping Fish Fillets

To turn fish fillets without breaking them, use two spatulas—a regular model and an extra-wide version especially designed for fish. (In the test kitchen, we use a spatula that is 8 inches wide by 3 inches deep for this job.) Using the regular spatula, gently lift the long side of the fillet. Then, supporting the fillet with the extra-wide spatula, flip it so that the browned side faces up.

VARIATIONS

FISH MEUNIÈRE WITH TOASTED SLIVERED ALMONDS

The toasted almonds provide a pleasant nutty crunch alongside the tender fish.

Follow the recipe for Fish Meunière with Browned Butter and Lemon, adding ¼ cup slivered almonds to the skillet when the butter has melted in step 2.

FISH MEUNIÈRE WITH CAPERS

Capers add a burst of briny freshness in this variation.

Follow the recipe for Fish Meunière with Browned Butter and Lemon, adding 2 tablespoons rinsed capers along with the lemon juice in step 2.

GETTING IT RIGHT: Anatomy of a Flatfish Fillet

"Bone" Side
Rounded indentations run along the length of the fillet on this side.

"Skin" Side
The fillet is darker and flatter.

Flatfish fillets have two distinct sides, and the order in which they are cooked makes a difference. The side of the fillet that was facing the bones in the whole fish browns best and makes the most attractive presentation on the plate. The side of the fillet that was facing the skin is darker and doesn't brown as well. When cooking, start the fillets bone-side down, then flip them once a nice crust has formed. When the fillets are cooked through, slide them, bone-side up, onto heated dinner plates.

TASTING LAB: Butter Alternatives

THE AMERICAN FOOD INDUSTRY LOVES TO REPLACE delicious, natural products (take butter, for example) with substitutes made from cheap ingredients that require processing (margarine) in an effort to increase profit margins and market share. These new products are often sold with dubious claims that they are "healthy," and the strategy has proven enormously successful. In 1909, butter outsold margarine 15 to 1; by 1993, margarine was outselling butter nearly 3 to 1. Here in the test kitchen, we are usually immune to the charms of "new" and "improved" products, but we purchased six new butter substitutes and headed to the test kitchen to see how these products would stack up against the real thing.

Margarine has long been touted as a healthier alternative to butter, which has two to three times as much saturated fat. And until recently, that pitch has been working. But margarine has had a rough time of late. During the 1990s, more and more health experts started to sound the alarm about margarine, especially the solid versions sold in sticks. Margarine is vegetable oil that has been turned into a solid by means of a process called partial hydrogenation, the same process used to make vegetable shortenings such as Crisco. While margarine contains less artery-clogging saturated fat than butter, it does contain much more trans fat, which is a product of partial hydrogenation. Researchers have warned that trans fats may be more dangerous than saturated fat. (Saturated fat is thought to raise total cholesterol, both the "good" kind and the "bad" kind, but trans fats are thought to raise bad cholesterol while lowering good cholesterol—a nutritional double whammy.) In general, the more solid the margarine, the more trans fats it contains.

During the past decade, per capita consumption of margarine has declined by about 25 percent. In contrast, butter consumption has climbed more than 15 percent since 1997. As might be expected, the margarine industry is fighting back. It has responded with a new generation of

"spreads"—sold in tubs, rather than sticks—that don't contain trans fats. (A product qualifies as margarine if it is 80 percent fat, like most butters; it's considered a spread if it's less than 80 percent fat.) Some spreads even contain additives that are supposed to reduce cholesterol. Many health experts, as well as the U.S. Food and Drug Administration, say that these new margarines (all sold in tubs and most containing 25 percent less total fat than regular margarine or butter) are the healthier choice. Because these butter substitutes contain little or no hydrogenated oil, however, gums, emulsifiers, and/or tropical oils (which are naturally solid at room temperature) must be used to make them solid. These products (we tested five of them) are designed for more than just spreading on toast; most manufacturers claim that they can also be used in baking and cooking.

In our tasting, we also included Land O'Lakes Soft Baking Butter with Canola Oil. Although not really a butter substitute, this product doesn't qualify as a true butter, either. The pitch is pretty simple. Any avid baker knows that successful cakes and cookies often start with butter brought to room temperature. Soft Baking Butter is designed for cooks who would rather not wait an hour. We also wanted to see how these new products stacked up against real butter, so we threw two of them into the test: Land O'Lakes and

Land O'Lakes Ultra Creamy, the company's entry into the boutique butter business.

The first taste test was simple enough: We spread each product on toast. The butter substitutes were clear losers. Several spreads tasted like fake movie-theater-popcorn butter, and one reminded us of fish. When choosing a spread for toast, we'll stick with the real thing. Next, we melted the products over green beans and used them to sauté chicken cutlets. To our surprise, Land O'Lakes Soft Baking Butter actually bested the two real butters in both applications. We surmise that the small percentage of canola oil in the baking butter makes it melt better and protects against burning when used for cooking on the stovetop. Two of the butter substitutes, Olivio and Smart Balance, also received decent scores in these tests.

In our final test, making shortbread, our panel had no trouble picking out the two real butters. Tasters thought that the Soft Baking Butter made mediocre shortbread, and the other butter substitutes fared much, much worse. In this test real butter was a slam-dunk.

Overall, our results were decisive: The margarine industry just can't compete with natural, unprocessed, no-additives butter in terms of flavor. It's not nice to fool Mother Nature.

Rating Butter Alternatives

SIXTEEN MEMBERS OF THE AMERICA'S TEST KITCHEN STAFF TASTED SIX BUTTER SUBSTITUTES STRAIGHT FROM THE package, melted over green beans, sautéed with chicken cutlets, and baked into shortbread. We included regular unsalted Land O'Lakes (to represent basic supermarket butters) and unsalted Land O'Lakes Ultra Creamy (to represent high-fat butters) in all four tests. The real butters were the overall winners. The butter substitutes are listed in order of preference based on scores in these four tastings. All brands are available in supermarkets nationwide.

RECOMMENDED
Land O'Lakes Soft Baking Butter with Canola Oil
$4.69 for 16 ounces

Straight from the package, this "pre-softened" butter was "salty," "greasy," and "bland." Despite its labeling as a "baking butter," it showed more promise in savory dishes, besting regular and high-fat Land O'Lakes butter in the green bean and chicken tests.

RECOMMENDED WITH RESERVATIONS
Lee Iacocca's Olivio
$1.69 for 15 ounces

This spread contains olive oil and is endorsed by Lee Iacocca of Chrysler fame. It rivaled butter in the green bean and chicken tests but elicited comments such as "fishy," "oily," and "rancid" when tasted plain.

RECOMMENDED WITH RESERVATIONS
Smart Balance Buttery Spread
$2.29 for 16 ounces

This spread wasn't awful and it actually performed well in the chicken sauté, where it promoted decent browning. But in the plain tasting, panelists complained loudly about its "fake" fruity and vegetable notes and "slippery texture."

NOT RECOMMENDED
Benecol Spread
$4.99 for 8 ounces

According to the label, this spread with plant stanol esters is "proven to significantly reduce cholesterol." But, as one taster said, it tastes "like solidified fryer oil."

NOT RECOMMENDED
Soy Garden Natural Buttery Spread
$2.19 for 16 ounces

This blend of soy, palm, and olive oils as well as crushed soybeans reminded tasters of "rancid mayonnaise." Terrible plain and in shortbread, but deemed less offensive in green bean and chicken tests.

NOT RECOMMENDED
Spectrum Naturals Spread
$2.19 for 10 ounces

This canola oil spread (made with xanthan and guar gums) refused to melt over beans and made awful shortbread. Tasted straight out of tub, it was described as "Jell-O married with fake movie-popcorn butter." Not suitable for cooking.

PAN-SEARED SCALLOPS WITH
WILTED SPINACH SALAD

WHAT WE WANTED: A restaurant-style main course salad of well-dressed greens and crusty caramelized sweet scallops.

Warm spinach salads are often thought of as complicated and difficult to execute, and somehow are perceived as an item you can enjoy only in a restaurant. Most cooks willing to try them at home consider warm spinach salads best suited as the first course at fancy dinner parties. But we found the exact opposite to be true. Warm spinach salads are not only easy to make but also easily transformed into a satisfying meal without expending much effort or time.

Restaurants often feature a protein, such as chicken or shellfish, as part of a main course salad. For our purposes, we decided to focus on scallops—they have a luxurious, creamy texture that pairs well with hearty greens. Also, with virtually no prep involved—trimming, slicing, shelling, or deveining—scallops are just the sort of fuss-free salad centerpiece we were looking for. What we wanted, then, was a union of well-dressed greens and perfectly cooked scallops, hearty and interesting enough to serve as a main course. We'd start from the ground up, focusing on the greens, then moving on to the scallops.

Spinach salad at its finest is a pleasant dish of tender spinach leaves lightly wilted by a warm aromatic dressing. But after several tests in the kitchen, we found this ideal is not automatically achieved. The salads we tried ran the gamut from tough leaves covered with bland, insipid dressing to salads so overdressed they were mushy piles of greens standing in puddles of vinaigrette. To reach the goal of a satisfactory homemade spinach salad, we had to address two major factors: the type of spinach to use and how to dress it.

We tackled spinach type first. There are two categories of spinach: curly leaf and flat leaf. Curly-leaf spinach is probably the variety most people are familiar with; it is usually packaged in cellophane bags and sold at local supermarkets. This type of spinach didn't do well in our tests. Tasters felt the leaves were too dry and chewy, and the remaining stems were fibrous. The leaves also didn't wilt with the addition of the warm vinaigrette, so we decided to reserve this type for recipes in which the spinach is cooked.

Moving on to flat-leaf spinach, our results were more encouraging. We found two types of flat-leaf spinach commonly available at the market. The larger leaf spinach, which was sold in bundles, worked well in our salad; its tender leaves were moist and wilted easily. But the bunches we bought were full of dirt and required several extended periods of soaking to rid them of all the grit. Discouraged by the amount of time it took to wash and prepare the spinach, we bought a bag of the baby spinach sold in the supermarket in the same aisle as the prepared salads-in-a-bag. Baby spinach worked perfectly. We also decided to add watercress in with the spinach; this added a nice spicy contrast of flavor. The watercress also gussied up the salad a bit, giving it something of a restaurant flair. We also experimented with arugula, which has a good bite and can be substituted for the watercress, if desired.

With the base of our salad tested, we could focus on how to make a flavorful dressing that wasn't too heavy. We didn't want it to compete with the richness of the scallops or overwilt the greens. During our tests, we found that the acidic component in the warm dressing should be varied based on the accompanying salad ingredients. Tasters generally preferred wine vinegar or lemon juice, feeling these made a bright salad. We also found that if we added the acidic component of the dressing in the early stages of the cooking process, the flavors were muted. Swirling in the acid at the end, after the pan had been removed from the flame, restored some of the punch.

Another problem with many salads we tested was overdressing. Nothing is worse than limp, soggy salad. So we tried tossing salads with various quantities of dressing and finally settled on about 5 tablespoons of dressing for about 9 cups of greens. This wilted the spinach perfectly; the leaves retained a satisfying crunch without becoming wet and slimy.

Next it was time to move on to the scallops. It's no surprise that restaurants are so successful with scallops. Restaurants cook scallops to order, usually just one serving at a time. At home, however, we're cooking scallops for at least two and usually more, meaning that we're cooking many scallops together in one pan. This isn't a great idea, as the scallops are crowded and don't caramelize properly, if it all. What about cooking the scallops in multiple batches? We tried that, but scallops cool off quickly so that by the time our last batch was done, the first batch was unpalatably cold. It was time for some serious testing

We uncovered a few basic rules. First, you must start with unprocessed scallops. Processed scallops contain more liquid and thus inhibit browning; if you are able to brown processed scallops, rest assured that by that time, the interior of the scallop will be overcooked—tough and chewy. Next we found that a 12-inch skillet provided the best surface area. But even in a 12-inch skillet, 1½ pounds of scallops must be cooked in two batches, or they will steam instead of sear. Somehow, we'd need to develop a technique that neither overcooked the scallops nor let half of them turn cold while the other half finished cooking. To prevent overcooking, we seared the first batch of scallops on one side and then removed them from the pan. We cooked the second batch of scallops on one side, then returned the first batch of scallops to the pan to finish cooking alongside them. This worked like a charm.

To preserve the creamy texture of the flesh, we cooked the scallops to medium-rare, which means the scallop is hot all the way through but the center still retains some translucence. As a scallop cooks, the soft flesh firms and you can see an opaqueness that starts at the bottom of the scallop, where it sits in the pan, and slowly creeps up toward the center. The scallop is medium-rare when the sides have firmed up and all but about the middle third of the scallop

has turned opaque.

We weren't done yet, however. Tasters wanted more than scallops and greens in this dish. Orange chunks were overwhelmingly approved for the burst of citrusy brightness they added to the salad as well as how they offset the richness of the scallops. And for texture, toasted almonds, which are a natural with oranges, added a pleasant crunch. At last, a hearty but elegant main course salad that you can enjoy at home—and not have to worry about someone placing a check on the table afterward.

WHAT WE LEARNED: Choose baby spinach for easy prep and moist, tender greens. Unprocessed scallops are a must for scallops with a crusty exterior. And before cooking, pat the scallops dry to remove any excess moisture, which can prevent the scallops from browning.

PAN-SEARED SCALLOPS WITH WILTED SPINACH, WATERCRESS, AND ORANGE SALAD

Serves 4 as a main course or 8 as an appetizer

Sea scallops can vary dramatically in size from 1 to 1½ ounces each. A dinner portion, therefore, can range from 4 to 6 scallops per person. To ensure that the scallops cook at the same rate, be sure to buy scallops of similar size. To remove the small, firm tendon from the scallop, gently tug at it—it should easily peel away.

salad
- 4 ounces baby spinach (about 5⅓ cups lightly packed)
- 1 small bunch watercress or arugula (about 4 ounces), washed, dried, and stemmed (about 4 cups lightly packed)
- ¾ cup sliced almonds

scallops
- 1½ pounds large sea scallops (16 to 24 scallops) (see note), tendons removed (see note)
  Salt and ground black pepper
- 4 tablespoons vegetable oil

dressing
- 3 tablespoons extra-virgin olive oil
- ½ medium red onion, sliced thin
- 1 teaspoon minced fresh thyme leaves
  Salt
- 2 large oranges, cut into ¼-inch pieces (see illustrations on page 173)
- 2 tablespoons sherry vinegar

1. FOR THE SALAD: Toss the spinach and watercress together in a large bowl; set aside.

2. Toast the almonds in a 12-inch skillet over medium heat, shaking the pan occasionally, until fragrant and lightly browned, about 3 minutes; transfer them to the bowl with the greens. Wipe out the skillet using a wad of paper towels.

3. FOR THE SCALLOPS: Place the scallops on a paper towel–lined plate or baking sheet; season the scallops with salt and pepper. Lay a single layer of paper towels over the scallops; set aside.

4. Add 2 tablespoons of the vegetable oil to the empty skillet and return to high heat until just smoking. Meanwhile, press the paper towel flush to the scallops to dry. Add half of the scallops, dry-side facing down, and cook until evenly golden, 1 to 2 minutes. Using tongs, transfer the scallops, browned side facing up, to a large plate; set aside. Wipe out the skillet using a wad of paper towels. Repeat with the remaining 2 tablespoons oil and the remaining scallops. Once the first side is golden, turn the heat to medium, turn the scallops over with tongs, and return the first batch of scallops to the pan, golden side facing up. Cook until the sides on all the scallops have firmed up and all but the middle third of each scallop is opaque, 30 to 60 seconds longer. Transfer all the scallops to a large plate; set aside.

5. FOR THE DRESSING: Wipe the skillet clean with a wad of paper towels. Add the olive oil, onion, thyme, and ½ teaspoon salt to the skillet and return to medium-high heat; cook until the onions are slightly softened, about 1 minute. Add the oranges and vinegar to the pan and swirl to incorporate. Remove from the heat.

6. TO FINISH THE SALAD: Pour the warm dressing over the salad mixture and gently toss to wilt. Divide the spinach salad among four plates and arrange the scallops on top. Serve immediately.

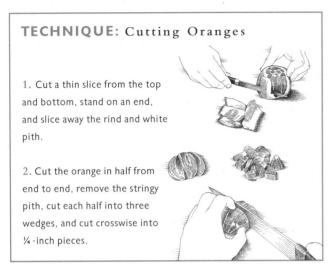
EQUIPMENT CORNER: Wine Saver Devices

A HALF-FINISHED BOTTLE OF WINE MORE THAN A COUPLE of days old is generally relegated to "cooking wine" status. Does that have to be the case? Though you usually want a red wine to breathe a bit before drinking it, too much oxygen can be harmful because it deteriorates the flavor of the wine over time. One expert we consulted said that in his opinion, just three hours of exposure to oxygen is enough to hurt the flavor of a wine.

Fortunately, store shelves are full of tools to help preserve leftover wine. We tried seven wine preservation tools and/or systems, ranging in price from $6 to $110. Two of the devices (the Vacu Vin Vacuum Wine Saver and the EZ Vac Wine Saver) are pumps used to draw the oxygen out of the bottle, thereby creating a vacuum. Haley's Cork is simply a rubber replacement cork. The Private Reserve's Wine Preserver blankets the surface of the leftover wine with inert gas to prevent contact with oxygen; similarly, the Pek Preservation System's method houses a bottle of wine in a cloud of argon gas. The Winekeeper's device acts like a tap on a beer keg, replacing the wine it pumps out of the bottle with nitrogen, again to block contact with oxygen; and the Wine for Later Set is simply a set of small glass decanters to store leftover wine without space in the bottle for oxygen. We also tried two decidedly low-tech, homespun methods—simply shoving the cork back in the partially empty bottle, and pouring the leftover wine into a small plastic soda or water bottle and screwing on the cap.

We took five 25.4-ounce bottles of red wine, removed 10 ounces from each, then "preserved" them using these different methods. Ten days later, we tasted our "preserved" wines alongside a freshly opened bottle from the same case. As expected, our panel of tasters preferred the wine from the new bottle. The wines "protected" by the EZ Vac, the spray, and the rubber replacement cork left tasters puckering. The reused-cork method also produced vinegary results, while the expensive gas systems didn't fare much better. Apparently trapping and replacing gases is an elusive chore. The only two wines that came even close to the fresh bottle in terms of flavor (or absence of off flavors, really) were the wine preserved with the Vacu Vin and the wine stored in a small plastic soda or water bottle.

So, if you don't mind the look of wine in a plastic bottle that was once home to Diet Dr. Pepper, that is the cheapest and most effective solution. If you really want to save the wine in its own bottle, go with the Vacu Vin at only $10.

BEST WINE SAVER DEVICES

For preserving wine in its own bottle, choose the Vacu Vin Vacuum Wine Saver (left), but to save $10, you might want to take the cheap route and transfer the wine to a plastic water or soda bottle with a screw top (right), which did just as well in our tests.

Chris samples less expensive alternatives to Barolo wine and discovers that not all are up to the job for a long-simmered Italian-style pot roast.

ITALIAN classics

CHAPTER 14

IN THIS CHAPTER

THE RECIPES
Fettuccine Alfredo

Beef Braised in Barolo

TASTING LAB
Parmesan Cheese
Substitutes for Barolo

Why is Italian food so popular? Most recipes seem startlingly easy to prepare, requiring just a few simple ingredients. Fettuccine Alfredo is pasta with a simple cheese sauce—basically just cream, butter, and Parmesan cheese. Although the ingredients are minimal, it must be served right away, preferably in preheated serving bowls to prevent this somewhat temperamental dish from cooling off too quickly, thus marring the texture of the silky sauce.

Beef in Barolo is simply pot roast, Italian-style. You get the same juicy, meaty flavor of the beef, but as an added bonus, Barolo wine imparts a lush, sophisticated flavor to the dish, making this pot roast good enough for company. Of course this dish faces the same challenges as any pot roast—the meat is prone to drying out and becoming stringy and chewy. And then there's the choice of wine to consider. Is it necessary to use real Barolo, which can often be pricey, or can another, perhaps less expensive wine be substituted? In this chapter, we demystify these two classic dishes.

FETTUCCINE ALFREDO

WHAT WE WANTED: Foolproof fettuccine Alfredo—tender pasta bathed in a silky, cheese sauce.

Fettuccine Alfredo should be a lovely reminder of what a few ingredients can achieve when handled well. Unfortunately, a trip to Rome, where the dish originated, may be necessary to experience the culinary beauty of these ingredients, as stateside Italian restaurants often produce gargantuan portions of overcooked pasta and a sauce that quickly congeals in the bowl (or the stomach). We wanted a simple recipe that would work at home and also make a worthy tribute to the recipe's creator, Alfredo di Lillo, who developed it back in the 1920s.

Traditional recipes call for homemade fettuccine, but store-bought dried or refrigerated fresh fettuccine has to do for most home cooks. A morning in the test kitchen proved that dried noodles don't "grab" the sauce the way fresh noodles do, instead letting it pool at the bottom of the bowl. Luckily, fresh noodles are widely available in supermarkets and hold on to the sauce perfectly. One 9-ounce package was sufficient for four to six first-course portions. (Alfredo is awfully rich as a main course.)

The sauce consists of cheese, butter, and cream. For the cheese, Parmigiano-Reggiano won for its distinctive flavor, although we quickly discovered that more is not better. Recipes call for anywhere from ½ cup to 2 cups grated cheese. We finally settled on ¾ cup, enough to provide a rich taste of Parmigiano without overwhelming the flavors of the other ingredients. Some recipes use as much as a stick of butter, but we found that a relatively modest 2 tablespoons was fine.

Heavy cream is the foundation for this sauce, and we found it impossible to use less than the standard 1½ cups. Many recipes simmer the cream to give the sauce body. When we simmered the cream until it reduced by half, the sauce was unpalatably thick. After a long series of other tests, we ended up reducing only 1 cup of the cream down to ⅔ cup and then added the remaining ½ cup of cream back into the reduced mixture along with salt and pepper. This not only produced a luxurious texture but also gave the sauce a fresher flavor, as some of the cream remained uncooked. Oh, and there was one other unintended benefit: We could reduce the cup of cream ahead of time because the addition of the uncooked half cup prevented the formation of the skin that would otherwise form on the surface of the cooked cream.

Now we had a supple, velvety sauce, but only if it were consumed in 60 seconds or less! Within minutes—before tasters could finish even a small portion—the sauce congealed, becoming thick and gritty. Restaurant kitchens often solve this problem by adding starch (in the form of flour) to stabilize the sauce, vastly improving its staying power. The downside, of course, is that this produces a thick, weighty sauce that is a continent removed from the delicate marriage of simple ingredients one would find in fettuccine Alfredo's hometown.

Since flour was a no-no, we wondered if there was some other trick we could employ. After some trial and error, we found that adding a little pasta water toward the end of cooking thinned the sauce just enough without compromising its body. Yes, it may appear a bit thin at first, but the sauce thickens as it is served and consumed, virtually before your eyes. Our last discovery was the necessity of heated serving bowls. The warmth significantly prolongs the brief magic of this dish before the clock sounds and the transformation into bad restaurant food begins. Mangia!

WHAT WE LEARNED: Use fresh fettuccine, which holds on to the sauce better than dried. Reduce just part of the cream for body, then add the remaining cream for sauce with a better texture and fresher flavor. Adding a little pasta cooking water to the dish toward the end of cooking helps prevent the pasta from drying out and the sauce from turning gritty. Heated serving bowls are a must for preventing this dish from cooling off too quickly.

FETTUCCINE ALFREDO

Serves 4 to 6 as a first course

Fresh pasta is the best choice for this dish; supermarkets sell 9-ounce containers of fresh pasta in the refrigerator section. Be sure to use the entire 4½ quarts pasta cooking water called for—some of the boiling water is used to warm the serving bowls. When boiling the pasta, undercook it slightly (even shy of al dente) because the pasta cooks an additional minute or two in the sauce just before serving. Note that fettuccine Alfredo must be served immediately; it does not hold or reheat well.

1½	cups heavy cream
2	tablespoons unsalted butter
	Salt
¼	teaspoon ground black pepper
9	ounces fresh fettuccine
1½	ounces Parmigiano-Reggiano, grated (about ¾ cup)
⅛	teaspoon freshly grated nutmeg

1. Bring 1 cup of the heavy cream and the butter to a simmer in a 3- to 4-quart saucepan over medium heat; reduce the heat to low and simmer gently until the mixture reduces to ⅔ cup, 12 to 15 minutes. Off the heat, stir in the remaining ½ cup cream, ½ teaspoon salt, and pepper.

2. While the cream reduces, bring 4½ quarts water to a rolling boil, covered, in a large stockpot or Dutch oven. Using a ladle or heatproof measuring cup, scoop about ½ cup boiling water into each serving bowl; set the bowls aside to warm. Add 1 tablespoon salt and the pasta to the pot of boiling water; cook the pasta until just shy of al dente. Reserve ¼ cup pasta cooking water, then drain the pasta.

3. Meanwhile, return the cream mixture to a simmer over medium-high heat; reduce the heat to low and add the pasta, Parmesan, and nutmeg to the cream mixture. Cook over low heat, tossing the pasta with tongs to combine, until the cheese is melted, the sauce coats the pasta, and the pasta is just al dente, 1 to 2 minutes. Stir in the reserved pasta cooking water; the sauce may look rather thin but will gradually thicken as the pasta is served and eaten. Working quickly, empty the serving bowls of the water; divide the pasta among the bowls, tossing the pasta to coat well with the sauce. Serve immediately.

GETTING IT RIGHT: Time and Temperature Matter

Cold Bowl
Congeals in Just 60 Seconds

Warm Bowl
Still Creamy after 5 Minutes

The texture of the sauce changes dramatically as the dish stands and cools; serving the Alfredo in warmed bowls helps it retain its creamy texture.

TASTING LAB: Parmesan Cheese

WHEN IT COMES TO GRATED PARMESAN CHEESE, THERE'S a wide range of options—everything from the whitish powder in plastic containers to imported cheese that costs $17 a pound. You can buy cheese that has been grated, or you can pick out a whole chunk and grate it yourself. We wondered if the "authentic" Parmigiano-Reggiano imported from Italy would be that much better when tasted side by side with a domestic Parmesan at half the price.

Parmesan is a grana—a hard, grainy cheese. The grana cheese category is composed mostly of Italian grating cheeses. Parmigiano-Reggiano is the most famous (and expensive) of the granas, and its manufacture dates back 800 years. Parmigiano-Reggiano has become an increasingly regulated product; in 1955 it became what is known as a certified name (not a brand name). Since that time the name has indicated that the cheese was made within a specific region of northern Italy and approved by a certifying consortium.

American cheese makers have been making Parmesan only since the beginning of the century and need not abide by any more stringent regulations than basic U.S. Department of Agriculture standards. There is no lack of pregrated products, but only a handful of domestic Parmesans come in wedges. Other granas considered Parmesan types are Grana Padano (from Italy) and Reggianito (from Argentina).

The samples in our tasting included five pregrated Parmesan cheeses (domestic and imported), three wedges of domestic Parmesan, a wedge of Grana Padano, one of Reggianito, and two of Parmigiano-Reggiano. To see if differences in storage and handling could affect the quality of the latter two, we purchased one at a specialty cheese store, where the humidity and temperature of the storage room are controlled and the wedges are cut from the wheel per order, and the other at a large supermarket, where the cheese is sold precut and wrapped in plastic. All of the cheeses were tasted grated, at room temperature.

To get an idea of what tasters might want to look for when tasting the different cheeses, we spoke to a number of cheese experts. All recommended that the tasters rate the cheeses on the basics: aroma, flavor (particularly depth of flavor and saltiness versus sweetness), and overall texture. The experts also said the Parmesans should be left to sit on tasters' tongues to see if they would melt smoothly into creaminess in the mouth. All of the experts we spoke to expressed confidence that Parmigiano-Reggiano would be the hands-down winner. This time the experts were correct. Parmigiano-Reggiano had a depth and complexity of flavor and a smooth, melting texture that none of the others could match.

Parmigiano-Reggiano owes much of its flavor to the unpasteurized milk used to produce it. It is a "controlled-district" cheese, which means not only that it must be made within the boundaries of this zone but also that the milk used to make it and even the grass, hay, and grain fed to the cows that make the milk must come from the district. Consequently, just like good wine, a lot of character comes from the soil and climate where the cheese was made. In the tasting we found that none of the other cheeses had the sweet, nutty, creamy flavor of Parmigiano-Reggiano.

Most of the cheeses in the tasting—except the Parmigiano-Reggiano—were extremely salty. In fact, Parmigiano-Reggiano contains about two-thirds less sodium than the other Parmesans. This is because the wheels of Parmigiano-Reggiano are so large that they do not become as saturated with salt during the brining process that is one of the final steps in making the cheese. (The average wheel is about 9 inches high and 16 to 18 inches in diameter and weighs 75 to 90 pounds; domestic Parmesan wheels average 24 pounds.)

The low salt content of Parmigiano-Reggiano makes it more perishable than other cheeses once cut from the wheel. Once cut, the cheese will also begin to dry out. This was evident in the Parmigiano-Reggiano sample purchased at the grocery store. Tasters rated this a few tenths of a point lower than the sample purchased at the specialty cheese store because of a chalky finish. This drying effect was even more glaring with the chalky pregrated products, which received consistently poor ratings.

Another benefit of the larger wheel is that it gives the cheese more time to age. Parmigiano-Reggiano ages for about 24 months, while domestic Parmesan ages for about 10 months. The longer aging allows more complex flavors and aromas to develop. The aging also makes a difference in texture, creating a distinctive component that tasters

described as "crystal crunch." The crunch stems from proteins breaking down into free amino acid crystals during the latter half of the aging process. The crystals are visible, appearing as white dots in the cheese. No other Parmesan showed this effect.

Other textural differences are created by the fact that the curds for Parmigiano-Reggiano are cut into fragments the size of wheat grains, which are much finer than the fragments cut in the manufacture of domestic Parmesan. The benefit of smaller curds is that they drain more effectively. Domestic Parmesans are mechanically pressed to rid them of excess moisture. The consequence, as our tasting panel discovered with several domestic Parmesans that were not pregrated, is a cheese that is much more dense. Tasters characterized these cheeses as "rubbery," "tough," and "squeaky."

One domestic Parmesan scored well enough to be recommended. This was Wisconsin-made DiGiorno. The other less expensive options paled in comparison with the real thing. The pregrated cheeses received especially low ratings and harsh comments from our panel. Most were much too salty and marred by odd off flavors. Most everyone agreed that these poor imitations could actually ruin a dish.

THE BEST PARMESANS

Nothing compares with real Parmigiano-Reggiano (left). If you can, buy a piece freshly cut from a large wheel. Expect to spend $12 to $17 per pound. However, a good alternative is domestically made DiGiorno Parmesan (right), priced at just $8 per pound, which is surprisingly good and is our best buy.

BEEF IN BAROLO

WHAT WE WANTED: The ultimate pot roast—tender meat in a rich, savory sauce.

As cashmere cannot be confused with acrylic, neither can beef in Barolo be mistaken for the standard workaday pot roast. Featuring tender, moist beef enveloped in a rich, silky red wine sauce—rather than the beefy gravy and vegetable bits characteristic of its down-home American cousin—beef in Barolo appears in countless Italian cookbooks. Most recipes utilize a tough cut of meat that is slowly braised in the famed Piedmontese wine. So what's the problem? For starters, Barolo isn't Chianti; most bottles start at a whopping $30. For that kind of investment, we wanted a lot more than a glorified pot roast. Cheap meat cooked in expensive wine? We had our doubts, but given that Italian cooking is usually about practical home cooking, not silly showmanship, we put them aside.

Prior test kitchen efforts to perfect pot roast revealed chuck roast as the overwhelming favorite cut of meat for its moistness and flavor. Initial tests of several beef in Barolo recipes confirmed these results. In contrast, a boneless sirloin yielded what one taster called "insanely dry" meat and a watery, raw-tasting wine sauce. Perhaps it would be wiser to stick with a chuck roast after all. But which one?

In a side-by-side comparison of three classic chuck roasts—a boneless chuck-eye roast, a seven-bone roast, and a top-blade roast—tasters praised each for being moist, tender, and beefy. In the end, the decision boiled down to aesthetics and convenience. The center of the top-blade roast sported an unappealing strip of partially melted connective tissue that was reminiscent of meat-flavored gummy bears. The seven-bone roast was hard to carve and even harder to find in the supermarket. The chuck-eye roast won by default. (For more information, see "Chuck Roasts" on page 183.)

Our recipe was beginning to take shape, but after four long hours of braising, the meat was precariously close to being shredded and overdone and contained unsightly pockets of squishy fat and connective tissue. While this might be acceptable in a more rustic pot roast, beef in Barolo demands a more refined presentation. The fat would have to go.

We wondered what would happen if we split the large cylindrical roast into two sleeker halves. Dividing the roast into two fairly equal pieces was easy, as the seam of fat that runs down the center of the roast acts as a built-in guide. We trimmed out the obvious wads of fat from each lobe, leaving a thin layer of fat cap, and seasoned and tied each piece to keep it from falling apart during braising. With less extraneous fat and a shortened cooking time to boot (the meat was now done in three hours), these two roasts were definitely better than one.

Following Italian custom, we began this recipe by searing the roasts in olive oil, but the sauce needed pizzazz. We remembered seeing pancetta in some recipes and decided to brown the meat in the fat rendered from this Italian bacon instead. This helped immensely in developing flavor. Putting the browned roast aside, we then sautéed onions, carrots, and celery, adding a tablespoon of tomato paste to create a deep roasted flavor. After stirring in minced garlic, a bit of sugar, and a tablespoon of flour to help thicken the sauce during the final reduction, we were ready to add the wine.

Made from Nebbiolo grapes grown in the northern region of Piedmont, Barolo is a bold, full-bodied, often tannic and acidic red wine that is hailed as Italy's "king of wines and wine of kings." The price alone makes it the "wine of kings." Unlike its lighter, fruitier Italian counterparts, such as Chianti, which are often better off quaffed from a glass than used in vigorous cooking, Barolo is very hearty and can carry the day, even after being simmered for hours. But we found that in a pinch, two other, cheaper "big reds" can be substituted (see page 183).

Unfortunately, the robust flavor also added unexpected difficulties. Big red wines can be harsh. First, we focused on how and when to add the wine. Should it be reduced first to concentrate its flavors, added in two parts (at the beginning and the end), or simply dumped in with the meat? Much to our surprise and delight, dumping the whole bottle into the pot won out.

But we still needed to find an ingredient to counterbalance the harsh flavors in this big wine. Broth did not work; neither did water. Eventually, we discovered that drained diced tomatoes did the trick. The meatiness of the tomatoes produced the balance of sweet, salty, and hearty flavors this dish needed.

We then gently placed the browned roasts back into the pot along with a few fresh herbs, brought everything back up to a simmer, covered the pot with foil to prevent moisture loss, replaced the lid, and let the beef braise in a 300-degree oven for three hours. (When given less time, the meat was too resilient; given more, it fell apart.) Flipping the meat every 45 minutes helped to achieve perfect tenderness without dry patches.

Once the meat was tender, we removed it from the pot to rest while we concentrated on the sauce, which we felt ought to be a far cry from the typical pot roast liquid. After all, why use Barolo to start with if the sauce isn't grand? After skimming off the top layer of fat to remove as much grease as possible, we reduced the liquid over high heat to concentrate and intensify the multiple layers of flavor. Pureeing the liquid, vegetables, and herbs yielded a weak sauce that eventually separated into watery and mealy components. Straining out the vegetables proved to be key. Boiled down to 1½ cups, the sauce was dark and lustrous, with the body and finesse of something you might serve over a fine steak.

Better than workaday pot roast? You bet. And you don't need to dip into a trust fund to put this dish on the table.

WHAT WE LEARNED: Chuck-eye roast is the best cut for tender meat that doesn't dry out. Separating the roast into two pieces, trimming the connecting fat, and tying the two pieces results in nicer presentation, easier carving, and reduced cooking time. Browning the roast in rendered pancetta adds a rich layer of flavor. And the addition of canned diced tomatoes tempers the harshness of the wine.

BEEF BRAISED IN BAROLO

Serves 6

Don't skip tying the roast—it keeps the roast intact during the long cooking time. Purchase pancetta that is cut to order, about ¼ inch thick. If pancetta is not available, substitute an equal amount of salt pork (find the meatiest piece possible), cut it into ¼-inch cubes, and boil it in 3 cups of water for about 2 minutes to remove excess salt. After draining, use it as you would pancetta.

This braise can be prepared up to 2 days in advance; complete the recipe through step 2. When you're ready to serve, skim off the fat congealed on the surface and gently warm until the meat is heated through. Continue with the recipe from step 3.

1   boneless chuck-eye roast (about 3½ pounds)
     Salt and ground black pepper
4   ounces pancetta, cut into ¼-inch cubes (see note)
2   medium onions, chopped medium
2   medium carrots, chopped medium
2   medium celery ribs, chopped medium
1   tablespoon tomato paste
3   medium garlic cloves, minced or pressed through a garlic press (about 1 tablespoon)
½   teaspoon sugar
1   tablespoon unbleached all-purpose flour
1   (750-milliliter) bottle Barolo wine
1   (14.5-ounce) can diced tomatoes, drained
1   sprig fresh thyme plus 1 teaspoon minced leaves
1   sprig fresh rosemary
10   sprigs fresh parsley

1. Adjust an oven rack to the middle position; heat the oven to 300 degrees. Pull the roast apart at its major seams (delineated by lines of fat) into two halves. Use a knife as necessary. With the knife, remove the large knobs of fat from each piece, leaving a thin layer of fat on the meat. Tie three pieces

of kitchen twine around each piece of meat. Thoroughly pat the beef dry with paper towels; sprinkle generously with salt and pepper. Place the pancetta in an 8-quart heavy-bottomed Dutch oven; cook over medium heat, stirring occasionally, until browned and crisp, about 8 minutes. Using a slotted spoon, transfer the pancetta to a paper towel–lined plate and reserve. Pour off all but 2 tablespoons of fat; set the Dutch oven over medium-high heat and heat the fat until beginning to smoke. Add the beef to the pot and cook until well browned on all sides, about 8 minutes total. Transfer the beef to a large plate; set aside.

2. Reduce the heat to medium; add the onions, carrots, celery, and tomato paste to the pot and cook, stirring occasionally, until the vegetables begin to soften and brown, about 6 minutes. Add the garlic, sugar, flour, and reserved pancetta; cook, stirring constantly, until combined and fragrant, about 30 seconds. Add the wine and tomatoes, scraping the bottom of the pan with a wooden spoon to loosen the browned bits; add the thyme sprig, rosemary, and parsley. Return the roast and any accumulated juices to the pot; increase the heat to high and bring the liquid to a boil, then place a large sheet of foil over the pot and cover tightly with the lid. Set the pot in the oven and cook, using tongs to turn the beef every 45 minutes, until a dinner fork easily slips in and out of the meat, about 3 hours.

3. Transfer the beef to a cutting board; tent with foil to keep warm. Allow the braising liquid to settle about 5 minutes then, using a wide shallow spoon, skim the fat off the surface. Add the minced thyme, bring the liquid to a boil over high heat, and cook, whisking vigorously to help the vegetables break down, until the mixture is thickened and reduced to about 3½ cups, about 18 minutes. Strain the liquid through a large fine-mesh strainer, pressing on the solids with a spatula to extract as much liquid as possible; you should have 1½ cups strained sauce (if necessary, return the strained sauce to the Dutch oven and reduce to 1½ cups). Discard the solids in the strainer. Season the sauce to taste with salt and pepper.

4. Remove the kitchen twine from the meat and discard. Using a chef's knife or carving knife, cut the meat against the grain into ½-inch-thick slices. Divide the meat between warmed bowls or plates; pour about ¼ cup sauce over each portion and serve immediately.

TASTING LAB: Substitutes for Barolo

NOT EVERYONE HAS A BOTTLE OF BAROLO LYING AROUND the house. Could a moderately priced wine-cabinet staple take the place of this king of wines? We tested our Beef Braised in Barolo recipe using five inexpensive red wines to see which was best suited to wear the crown. We found that it takes a potent wine to withstand three hours in the oven and still have much character. Our one Italian entrant, the Chianti, fell flat, as did the Merlot and Côtes du Rhône, the other medium-bodied wines in our tasting. These fruity wines lacked the potency of a heady Barolo. We had better luck with Zinfandel, but Cabernet Sauvignon was the most commanding and was, therefore, the best substitute.

GOOD STAND-INS:
Cabernet Sauvignon, Zinfandel

NOT SUITED FOR THE JOB:
Merlot, Côtes du Rhône, Chianti

GETTING IT RIGHT: Chuck Roasts

Seven-Bone Pot Roast

Top-Blade Pot Roast

Chuck-Eye Roast

The seven-bone pot roast (left) is a well-marbled cut with an incredibly beefy flavor. It gets its name from the bone found in the roast, which is shaped like the number seven. Because it is only 2 inches thick, less liquid and less time are needed to braise this roast. Do not buy a seven-bone pot roast that weighs more than 3½ pounds, as it will not fit into a Dutch oven. This roast is also sometimes referred to as a seven-bone steak.

The top-blade pot roast (middle) is also well marbled with fat and connective tissue, which makes this roast very juicy and flavorful. Even after thorough braising, this roast retains a distinctive strip of connective tissue, which is not unpleasant to eat. This roast may also be sold as a blade roast.

The chuck-eye roast (right) is the fattiest of the three roasts and the most commonly available. Its high proportion of fat gives pot roast great flavor and tenderness. Because of its thicker size, this roast takes the longest to cook, though in our recipe for Beef Braised in Barolo (page 181) we separate the roast into two halves, thus shaving about an hour off the braising time.

Chris and Bridget learn they can enjoy spicy curry without calling for take-out.

TWO CURRY *traditions*

CHAPTER 15

In this chapter, we look at two styles of curry: rich and exotically spicy Indian curry and the more herbaceous and somewhat lighter Thai curry. Our goal in developing these curry recipes was to translate the many dishes that earn this name into a basic formula that could be easily adapted to a variety of ingredients.

The spices in Indian curry should blend harmoniously but sometimes they can become muddied and heavy tasting. Traditional recipes for Indian curry also contain many steps, which involve hours of preparation and time at the stove. We wanted to develop a rich, well-balanced curry with authentic complexity in a more manageable time frame.

Thai curries are just as intriguing as Indian curries. Coconut milk provides the rich backbone to Thai curries, which are fragrant with herbs. Thai curries, however, contain a plethora of hard-to-find ingredients, such as kaffir lime leaves, Thai basil, coriander roots, and dried Thai chiles. We'd need to find reasonable substitutes for these ingredients, or ways to approximate their flavors.

We hope the next time you crave curry, whether Indian or Thai, you'll turn to this chapter instead of a take-out menu.

IN THIS CHAPTER

THE RECIPES
Indian Curry
Beef Curry with Crushed Spices
    and Channa Dal

Thai Green Curry with Chicken,
    Broccoli, and Mushrooms
Green Curry Paste
Thai Red Curry with Shrimp,
    Pineapple, and Peanuts
Red Curry Paste

EQUIPMENT CORNER
Mini Food Processors

TASTING LAB
Coconut Milk

INDIAN CURRY

WHAT WE WANTED: A complex but not heavy-flavored curry that won't take all day to prepare.

Indian curry is a mysterious, complex, and highly personal dance of spice, flavor, and fragrance. We wanted to develop a curry with bold, intense, bright flavors, each bite exploding in layers of distinct, individual tastes of sweet and sour, bitter, salty, and fragrant.

To begin our quest for the ultimate Indian curry, we studied a recipe for meat curry from a favorite Indian cookbook. The dish was essentially a meat stew, flavored with onion, garlic, fresh ginger, ground coriander, cumin, turmeric, and cayenne and simmered in water with chopped tomato. It used familiar enough techniques, following the predictable route of browning the meat, browning the onions, adding the spices, then cooking for a couple of hours with the liquid. The dish was nicely spiced, hearty and satisfying, but complex? Not really. We went on to check out other books.

In our research, we found recipes that used less familiar techniques: Spices were added and cooked at different points depending on whether they were dry or wet, whole or ground, and the meat was added to the mixture partway through the cooking process with no preliminary browning. At a loss, we went to locate an Indian cook we could talk to.

We spoke with several Indian home cooks and ate the food they prepared for us. The food was astonishingly complex—just what we were looking for and exactly what was lacking in the cookbook recipes we tried. The only problem was, the time it took to prepare these dishes seemed too long and the techniques too involved for the typical American home cook. We sought to find a compromise.

We found that compromise in Samia, an Indian cook we spoke with from a local restaurant. Presumably because her own restaurant work had required her to shuttle regularly between the cooking of two cultures, she had managed to translate the heady sensibility that inspired the home cooks' cuisine into a simple, accessible formula that invited endless variation. And she'd vastly condensed traditional technique as well.

Samia made us a curry, preparing all of her ingredients completely before cooking them. She started by pureeing the garlic and ginger. While every Indian household would have a grinding stone to grind spices daily, she pureed the garlic and ginger with a little water in an electric minichopper until smooth. This choice was in part based on speed and convenience. In addition, experience had shown her that puree cooked more evenly than a mince and melted into the sauce for a smooth finish. And because a puree is wet where a mince is dry, this method gave her a cushion against burning. She sliced onion for convenience—chopping the onion takes longer, she pointed out. She also ground her own cumin and coriander seed.

Samia began cooking by frying the sliced onion in oil until translucent. Then, to our surprise, she added most of the rest of her ingredients: all of the spices she had prepared as well as a pound of boneless cubed meat, salt, and ½ cup of chopped tomato. She cooked the mixture, stirring until the oil separated (about five minutes), and then cooked another 30 seconds to cook the spices completely. She told us that this cooking of the spices was the heart of the dish. Then she added 2 cups of water and a halved chile pepper (she liked the flavor of the fresh chile better than that of cayenne) and simmered the dish until tender, about 40 minutes.

We asked Samia how she got away with condensing all these steps, which completely contradicted what the Indian home cooks had taught us. She explained that contrary to traditional technique, her experience was that as long as the oil separated, allowing the spices to fry in the oil for about 30 seconds, there was no need for long cooking. She further explained that her formula could be used as the base for many, many flavor combinations. We could add any number of cubed vegetables. We could cook beef, lamb, chicken,

fish, or shrimp this way. We could reduce the recipe to its bare roots—a very simple stew of protein, onion, garlic, ginger, turmeric (for some reason she always uses turmeric, she said), and water—or embellish it with more spices, vegetables, or legumes. That day, for example, she made a chicken variation using browned onion for deeper flavor and ½ cup yogurt instead of the tomato, and flavored the curry with double the amount of coriander, but no cumin. The technique was exactly the same, but the richness of the yogurt and the browned onion produced a different result altogether. Now it was time to go into the test kitchen and cook our curries based on what we'd learned.

We ran several experiments with spices. We compared a curry made with only ground spices with a curry using ground and whole spices. The comparison showed us that preground spices formed a kind of background wash; left whole, they came through as bright, individual flavors. (Thus, the cook can use the same spices with different effects.)

Then we cooked three curries to determine how long the combined ground spices needed to cook to develop their flavor. We tried 30 seconds, 5 minutes, and 10 minutes after the oil had separated. We found that 30 seconds was all it took. We also determined that the heavy, muddy taste of our early curries probably resulted from spices that had burned and turned bitter when they stuck to the bottom of the skillet. The spices were less likely to stick when cooked quickly, and the addition of yogurt or tomato obviated the need to make a paste.

Next we made a curry in which we added the stewing liquid before the oil had separated. Indeed, the curry tasted raw. We learned to use our ears to help us recognize when the spices are frying in pure oil. The sound changes from the gentle sound of a simmer to the loud, staccato sound of frying.

Finally, we played around with the amount of spice. It seems that the quantity is a matter more of personal preference than of rule, more spice resulting in heavier flavor. For the master recipe that follows, we chose quantities that fell in between those given us by the home cooks and Samia simply

because we liked that flavor. Precise quantities of wet spices are even less critical than of dry because their flavor is weaker, but we like equal quantities of garlic and ginger. In any event, the beauty of the formula is that it invites experimentation.

The method of the recipe that follows is largely the same as the one Samia demonstrated for us. As in standard French technique, it begins by heating the oil to provide a cooking medium. After that, however, it diverges completely from French style. Rather than browning the meat in the oil, we first sauté the whole spices, then the onions. The wet spices (ginger and garlic) are then added, along with the meat or fowl and the moistening agent, either tomatoes or yogurt. All of these are cooked until the liquid evaporates, the oil separates, and the spices begin to fry and become fully aromatic. Greens in the form of either spinach or cilantro are then added, along with water and chile peppers, and the whole is cooked until the meat is tender, at which point the vegetables are added and cooked until tender.

The ingredients in the recipe are completely interchangeable, depending on what result you're looking for. The whole spice combination (cinnamon, cloves, cardamom, peppercorns, and bay leaf) can be abbreviated to cinnamon and cloves or to cinnamon, cloves, and cardamom, if you like. The cumin and the coriander can also be used crushed, as in the Beef Curry with Crushed Spices and Channa Dal variation.

WHAT WE LEARNED: Allow the spices to cook completely to fully release their flavor. Garlic and ginger pureed with a bit of water in a minichopper yields a smooth curry that is less likely to scorch when cooked.

INDIAN CURRY

Serves 4 to 6

Gather and prepare all of your ingredients before you begin. You may substitute a scant ½ teaspoon of cayenne pepper for the jalapeño, adding it to the skillet with the other ground dried spices. If you don't have a minichopper for pureeing the garlic and ginger, use a microplane grater. As for choosing combinations of meat or fish with vegetables, we like the following: top sirloin or lamb with potatoes, chicken with zucchini, and shrimp with peas, but feel free to create your own pairings. Serve this curry with basmati rice.

whole spice blend (optional)

1½	cinnamon sticks
4	ground cloves
4	green cardamom pods
8	black peppercorns
1	bay leaf

curry

¼	cup vegetable or canola oil
1	recipe Whole Spice Blend
1	medium onion, sliced thin
4	large garlic cloves, pureed in a minichopper with 1 tablespoon water (about 2 tablespoons)
1	tablespoon fresh ginger, pureed in a minichopper with 1 to 2 teaspoons water
1½	pounds top sirloin or boneless leg of lamb, trimmed and cut into ¾-inch cubes, or 6 chicken thighs, skinned, or 1½ pounds shrimp, peeled and deveined
2	teaspoons ground cumin
2	teaspoons ground coriander
1	teaspoon ground turmeric
	Salt
3	canned plum tomatoes, chopped, plus 1 tablespoon juice or ⅔ cup crushed tomato or ½ cup plain low-fat yogurt
2	bunches (1½ pounds) spinach, stemmed, washed, and chopped coarse (optional)
½	cup chopped fresh cilantro leaves (optional)
2	cups water
1	jalapeño chile, stemmed and cut in half through the stem end
½	cup channa dal (Indian split peas) or 4 medium boiling potatoes, peeled and cut into ¾-inch cubes, or 4 medium zucchini, cut into ½-inch cubes, or 1 cup green peas
2–4	tablespoons chopped fresh cilantro leaves (use the lesser amount if you've already added the optional cilantro)

1. Heat the oil in a large deep skillet or soup kettle, preferably nonstick, over medium-high heat until hot but not smoking. If using the Whole Spice Blend, add it to the oil and cook, stirring with a wooden spoon until the cinnamon stick unfurls and the cloves pop, about 5 seconds. Otherwise, simply add the onion to the skillet; sauté until softened, 3 to 4 minutes, or browned, 5 to 7 minutes.

2. Stir in the garlic, ginger, selected meat (except shrimp), ground spices, ½ teaspoon salt, and the tomatoes or yogurt; cook, stirring almost constantly, until the liquid evaporates, the oil separates and turns orange, and the spices begin to fry, 5 to 7 minutes, depending on the skillet or kettle size. Continue to cook, stirring constantly, until the spices smell cooked, about 30 seconds longer.

3. Stir in the optional spinach and/or cilantro. Add the water and the jalapeño and season to taste with salt; bring to a simmer. Reduce the heat; cover and simmer until the meat is tender, 20 to 30 minutes for chicken, 30 to 40 minutes for beef or lamb.

4. Add the selected vegetable (except green peas); cook until tender, about 15 minutes. Stir in the cilantro. Add the shrimp and/or peas if using. Simmer 3 minutes longer and serve.

BEEF CURRY WITH CRUSHED SPICES AND CHANNA DAL

Regular green split peas may be substituted for the channa dal, or you can use 4 medium red potatoes, peeled and cut into ¾-inch pieces. Gather and prepare all of your ingredients before you begin. You may substitute a scant ½ teaspoon of cayenne pepper for the jalapeño, adding it to the skillet with the other ground dried spices. Feel free to increase the wet (garlic, ginger, jalapeños, and onions) or dry spice quantities. Serve this curry with basmati rice.

¼	cup vegetable or canola oil
2	teaspoons coriander seeds
1	teaspoon cumin seeds
1	medium onion, sliced thin
4	large garlic cloves, pureed in a minichopper with 1 tablespoon water (about 2 tablespoons)
1	tablespoon fresh ginger, pureed in a minichopper with 1 to 2 teaspoons water
1½	pounds top sirloin, trimmed and cut into ¾-inch cubes
1	teaspoon ground turmeric
	Salt
3	canned plum tomatoes, chopped, plus 1 tablespoon juice or ⅔ cup crushed tomatoes
2	cups water
1	jalapeño chile, stemmed and cut in half through the stem end
½	cup channa dal (Indian split peas)
2–4	tablespoons chopped fresh cilantro leaves

1. Heat the oil in a large deep skillet or soup kettle, preferably nonstick, over medium-high heat until hot but not smoking. Crush the coriander and cumin seeds in a mortar and pestle or minichopper and add to the skillet. Almost immediately add the onion to the skillet; sauté until softened, 3 to 4 minutes.

2. Stir the garlic, ginger, beef, ground turmeric, ½ teaspoon salt, and tomatoes into the skillet with the onion and spices. Cook, stirring almost constantly, until the liquid evaporates, the oil separates and turns orange, and the spices begin to fry, 5 to 7 minutes, depending on the skillet or kettle size. Continue to cook, stirring constantly, until the spices smell cooked, about 30 seconds longer.

3. Add the water and jalapeño and season to taste with salt; bring to a simmer. Reduce the heat; cover and simmer until the meat is tender, 30 to 40 minutes.

4. Add the channa dal; cook until tender, about 15 minutes. Stir in the cilantro. Simmer 3 minutes longer and serve.

THAI CURRY

WHAT WE WANTED: An authentic Thai curry perfumed with lemon grass, hot chiles, and coconut milk, not second-rate greasy take-out fare.

Like most Thai food, Thai curries embrace a delicate balance of tastes, textures, temperatures, and color that come together to create a harmonious whole. Thai curries (basically any spicy stew is called a curry in Thailand) are considered signature dishes of this cuisine, although they have their antecedents in India. As with their Indian counterparts, Thai curries simmer spices and liquid together to create a sauce, to which protein and vegetables are added (there's no browning of meat or deglazing of pans). However, there are several major differences between Indian and Thai curries.

Thai curries almost always contain coconut milk, which not only blends and carries flavors but also forms the backbone of the sauce. Thai curries also tilt the spice balance toward fresh aromatics. The aromatics are added in the form of a paste, which usually consists of garlic, ginger, shallots, lemon grass, kaffir lime leaves, shrimp paste, and chiles. These pastes can be quite involved and may require an hour of preparation. The curries themselves come together rather quickly and simmer gently for far less time than Indian curries.

With these differences in mind, we set out to explore the two most common types of Thai curries: green curry and red curry. We wanted to understand the basic structure of these dishes and figure out ways to simplify the process of making them. In doing so, we would need to find substitutes for some ingredients, such as kaffir lime leaves and shrimp paste, which are not readily available in most American supermarkets. We would start with the pastes.

Thai curry pastes are intensely flavored. Traditionally, ingredients are pounded together in a mortar and pestle to form a smooth paste. Since this process can take up to an hour, we wanted to develop paste recipes that could be assembled by other means. We tested a blender and a food processor.

With its narrow base, a blender isn't the best tool for this job. The lack of liquid in the curry paste also presented a problem when we tried using a blender. Large chunks just sat on top of each other as the blade went round and round.

The food processor—though not perfect—did a much better job. You must make a lot of curry paste (2 cups, enough for four curry recipes) when using the food processor. (Curry paste holds for a long time, so there's some logic to buying and preparing ingredients once and then enjoying curry on four different occasions.) With smaller batches, the blade simply wouldn't engage the ingredients. Even with more ingredients in the workbowl, we found that a little oil was needed to help bring the ingredients together. We also had the best results when we minced or cut the aromatics fairly small before adding them to the food processor. Note, however, that curry paste prepared in a food processor will be a tad grainy, not silky smooth like one ground in a mortar and pestle.

In further testing, we found that a minichopper works just as well as a food processor. Owing to its smaller bowl size, the minichopper will produce about half as much curry paste as the food processor—enough for two of our curry recipes, not four.

It was time to test the ingredients themselves. We started with green curry paste. Hot Thai chiles, sometimes called bird chiles, are the basis for most green curry pastes. These tiny chiles are less than an inch long and offer an intriguing balance of heat and floral flavors. We tested several substitutions and found that a combination of serranos and jalapeños provided the right amount of heat and flavor.

Shallots, garlic, and ginger are constants in most Thai curry pastes. After testing various ratios, we concluded that 2 parts shallots to 1 part each garlic and ginger lends pungency to the herbaceous green curry paste.

Toasted and ground coriander seeds, as well as fresh coriander roots, are other common additions to curry pastes. We found that cilantro leaves are too moist and floral to use as a substitute for the roots but that cilantro stems are fine. The stems are fairly dry and have a pungent, earthy flavor that's similar to the roots. We also liked the effect that ground cumin and pepper had on the pastes.

Lemon grass is an essential ingredient. We tried to prepare curry pastes without it, and tasters uniformly panned them. However, we did find a substitute for galangal, a rhizome related to ginger that's both peppery and sour: A combination of fresh ginger and lime juice added the necessary hot and sour notes. We found that the flavor of the lime juice is best preserved by adding it directly to the curry rather than to the curry paste.

Kaffir lime leaves have a clean, floral aroma, which many tasters compare with lemon verbena. We found that lime zest approximates this flavor.

Shrimp paste—a puree of salted, fermented shrimp and other seasonings—adds a salty, fishy note to Thai curry pastes. Since this ingredient is very hard to find, we searched for substitutes. Anchovy paste was a reasonable solution, but adding fish sauce directly to the curry is traditional and adds the same kind of subtle briny flavor. We decided to make anchovy paste an optional ingredient in our curry pastes. It adds another layer of flavor but is not essential.

Red chile paste relies on a similar alignment of ingredients except it uses equal parts of shallot, garlic, and ginger and, of course, includes different chiles. Traditional recipes call for dried red chiles, soaked in hot water until softened. We found that pastes made with dried chiles alone seemed thin, lacking the body we were looking for. A combination of soaked dried chiles and fresh red jalapeños provided a more satisfying combination of flavor and body. We found that any small hot dried red chile worked in our recipe. Dried red Thai chiles, also called bird chiles, are traditional, but japonés and de árbol chiles are equally hot and delicious.

Happy with our chile pastes, we shifted gears and started to test ways to cook them. Our goal was to figure out

the best way to unlock the flavors of the pastes. Given our experience with Indian Curry (see page 188), we figured that frying the curry paste in fat would be key.

In our research, we ran across three different methods for cooking the curry paste: sautéing in oil, simmering in coconut milk, and cooking with the thick coconut cream that floats to the top of cans of coconut milk.

For our first test, we sautéed curry paste in peanut oil and then added the coconut milk. The aroma was good, but the sauce seemed thin and not as flavorful as we wanted. For our second test, we stirred curry paste into coconut milk, then brought the mixture to a simmer and let it cook until it thickened considerably, but this method just didn't deliver. For our last test, we spooned off 1 cup of thick coconut cream from the top of a can of coconut milk. We mixed this cream with curry paste in a pan and then turned on the heat. After about 10 minutes, the fat in the coconut cream separated out, and the paste began to fry in the oil. We let the curry paste fry in the oil until it was very aromatic, a process that took just one to two minutes. We added the remaining liquid ingredients, following with the protein and vegetables. The finished curry was thick and flavorful, with a glorious sheen.

Cooking the moisture out of the coconut cream is a

somewhat magical process. At first the cream is bubbling away, but then it begins to separate into a solid mass that comes together like soft dough, and a liquid oil (the color of the curry paste) emerges. Listen for the change that takes place as the gentle sound of liquid simmering becomes the louder, more staccato sound of oil frying.

The fat separates from the solids in the coconut cream at different rates, depending on the thickness of the coconut cream, how much is being cooked, and the amount of moisture in the curry paste. The thicker the cream, or the more cream in the pan, the longer the process takes. Dry store-bought curry pastes speed up the process, while moist homemade pastes slow it down.

Once the coconut oil separates out from the cream, the curry paste need only fry in the oil for a minute or two. The remaining coconut milk, fish sauce, and brown sugar are then added to the pot. We found that simmering the sauce for five minutes allowed the flavors to blend.

At this point, the protein and vegetables are added to the abundant liquid and cooked directly in the sauce. Aside from gauging the timing so that slow-cooking items, such as potatoes, go into the pot before quick-cooking items, such as snow peas, the process is very simple. Once the protein and vegetables are cooked, a final garnish of fresh herbs (we found that a combination of basil and mint best approximates the flavor of Thai basil) finishes the dish.

Thai curries are saucy and hot and require a nice cushion of rice. Jasmine rice is the most traditional option, but regular long-grain rice works fine. Rice noodles are another good idea, and pickled vegetables or cucumber relish round out the meal.

WHAT WE LEARNED: A food processor or minichopper makes quick work of blending together the curry pastes. Serrano chiles can be substituted for the sometimes hard-to-find Thai (bird) chiles. Likewise, grated lime zest approximates the flavor of kaffir lime leaves. Cooking the moisture out of the coconut cream gives the curry silky body and intense, rich flavor.

THAI GREEN CURRY WITH CHICKEN, BROCCOLI, AND MUSHROOMS

Herbaceous green curry is a perfect partner to the chicken and vegetables. Freeze the chicken for 15 minutes to make it easier to cut.

    2 (14-ounce) cans unsweetened coconut milk, not
       shaken
    ½ cup Green Curry Paste (recipe follows) or
       2 tablespoons store-bought green curry paste
    2 tablespoons fish sauce
    2 tablespoons brown sugar
   1½ pounds boneless, skinless chicken breasts,
       trimmed of excess fat and sliced thin
       Salt
   2½ cups broccoli florets (about 6 ounces)
    4 ounces white or shiitake mushrooms, stems
       discarded and mushrooms quartered (about
       2 cups)
    1 medium red bell pepper, stemmed, seeded, and
       cut into thin strips
    1 fresh hot chile, stemmed, seeded, and quartered
       lengthwise (optional)
    1 tablespoon juice from 1 lime
    ½ cup whole basil leaves
    ½ cup whole mint leaves

1. Carefully spoon off about 1 cup of the top layer of cream from one can of coconut milk—this layer will be thick and possibly solid. Place the coconut cream and curry paste in a large Dutch oven and bring to a simmer over high heat, whisking to blend, about 2 minutes. Maintain this brisk simmer and whisk frequently until almost all of the liquid evaporates, 3 to 5 minutes. Reduce the heat to medium-high and whisk constantly until the cream separates into a puddle of colored oil and coconut solids, 3 to 8 minutes. (You should hear the curry paste starting to fry in the oil.) Continue cooking until the curry paste is very aromatic, 1 to 2 minutes.

2. Whisk in the remaining coconut milk, the fish sauce, and brown sugar. Bring back to a brisk simmer and cook until the flavors meld and the sauce thickens, about 5 minutes. Season the chicken with salt and add it to the pot, stirring until the pieces are separated and evenly coated with the sauce, about 1 minute. Stir in the broccoli and mushrooms and bring back to a brisk simmer over medium heat. Cook until the vegetables are almost tender, about 5 minutes. Stir in the bell pepper and fresh chile, if using, and cook until these vegetables are crisp-tender, about 2 minutes. Off the heat, stir in the lime juice, basil, and mint. Serve immediately.

GREEN CURRY PASTE

Makes about 2 cups, enough to prepare 4 curries

Thai green curry paste uses fresh green chiles and is prized for its herbaceous, aromatic flavor. It is most often used in poultry, seafood, and vegetable curries. Small green Thai chiles, also called bird chiles, are less than an inch long and provide the most authentic heat and herbal flavor. This recipe is designed to be prepared in a food processor. Cut the quantities in half if using a minichopper. See the illustrations on page 194 for tips on handling lemon grass. Although you can store curry paste in a plastic container, the container will absorb the flavor and color of the paste and cannot be reused (even after washing) for other purposes. A glass container is a better option.

30	green Thai chiles or 15 green serranos, stemmed, seeded, and chopped coarse (about ¾ cup)
4	large or 6 medium green jalapeño chiles, stemmed, seeded, and chopped coarse (about ¾ cup)
3–4	stalks lemon grass, outer sheath removed, bottom 3 inches trimmed and minced (about ½ cup)
2	medium shallots, chopped coarse (about 6 tablespoons)
20	medium garlic cloves, minced or pressed through a garlic press (about ⅓ cup)
¼	cup minced cilantro stems
3	tablespoons minced fresh ginger
2	tablespoons ground coriander

TECHNIQUE: Cutting Chicken Breast into Strips

Starting with chicken that has been frozen for 15 minutes will make it easier to slice.

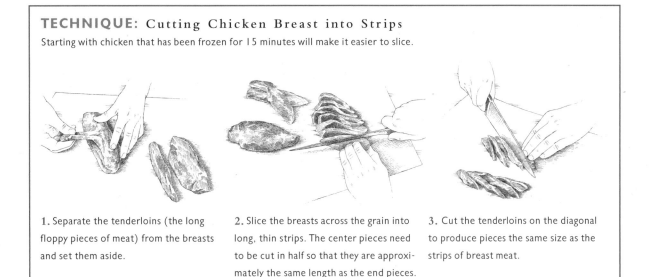

1. Separate the tenderloins (the long floppy pieces of meat) from the breasts and set them aside.

2. Slice the breasts across the grain into long, thin strips. The center pieces need to be cut in half so that they are approximately the same length as the end pieces.

3. Cut the tenderloins on the diagonal to produce pieces the same size as the strips of breast meat.

TECHNIQUE: Mincing Lemon Grass

Because of its tough outer leaves, lemon grass can be difficult to mince. We like this method, which relies on a sharp knife.

1. Trim all but the bottom 3 to 4 inches of the lemon grass stalk.

2. Remove the tough outer sheath from the trimmed lemon grass. If the lemon grass is particularly thick or tough, you may need to remove several layers to reveal the tender inner portion of the stalk.

3. Cut the trimmed and peeled lemon grass in half lengthwise, then mince fine.

2 tablespoons peanut or canola oil
4 teaspoons grated zest from 4 limes
2 teaspoons ground cumin
1 teaspoon salt
½ teaspoon ground white pepper
½ teaspoon shrimp paste or anchovy paste (optional)

Place all the ingredients in a food processor and pulse 10 times, each pulse lasting 4 to 5 seconds; stop and use a spatula to push down the ingredients every few pulses. Once the ingredients begin to form a paste, process until smooth, stopping occasionally to push down the ingredients, about 3 minutes. Store in a covered glass container or bowl in the refrigerator for up to 1 month or in the freezer for several months. (If freezing, divide the curry paste into ½-cup amounts, so that one portion will make one recipe, and freeze individually.)

THAI RED CURRY WITH SHRIMP, PINEAPPLE, AND PEANUTS

Fiery red curry paste is delectable with shrimp, sweet pineapple, and peanuts. Red peppers and snow peas add some crunch and bright color to this classic combination. If desired, try cashews instead of peanuts. For a more authentic appearance, leave the shells on the shrimp tails.

2 (14-ounce) cans coconut milk, not shaken
½ cup Red Curry Paste (recipe follows) or 2 tablespoons store-bought red curry paste
2 tablespoons fish sauce
2 tablespoons brown sugar
1½ pounds medium shrimp, shelled (40 to 50 per pound)
    Salt
3 cups pineapple chunks (preferably 1-inch cubes)
4 ounces snow peas, trimmed
1 medium red bell pepper, stemmed, seeded, and cut into thin strips

1   fresh hot chile, stemmed, seeded, and quartered
     lengthwise (optional)
1   tablespoon juice from 1 lime
½   cup whole fresh basil leaves
½   cup whole fresh mint leaves
½   cup unsalted dry-roasted peanuts, chopped
     coarse

1. Carefully spoon off about 1 cup of the top layer of cream from one can of coconut milk—this layer will be thick and possibly solid. Place the coconut cream and curry paste in a large Dutch oven and bring to a simmer over high heat, whisking to blend, about 2 minutes. Maintain this brisk simmer and whisk frequently until almost all of the liquid evaporates, 3 to 5 minutes. Reduce the heat to medium-high and whisk constantly until the cream separates into a puddle of colored oil and coconut solids, 3 to 8 minutes. (You should hear the curry paste starting to fry in the oil.) Continue cooking until the curry paste is very aromatic, 1 to 2 minutes.

2. Whisk in the remaining coconut milk, the fish sauce, and brown sugar. Bring back to a brisk simmer and cook until the flavors meld and the sauce thickens, about 5 minutes. Season the shrimp with salt and add the shrimp and pineapple to the pot, stirring until the pieces are separated and evenly coated with the sauce, about 1 minute. Bring back to a brisk simmer over medium heat. Cook until the shrimp is almost done, about 4 minutes. Stir in the snow peas, bell pepper, and fresh chile, if using, and cook until the vegetables are crisp-tender, about 2 minutes. Off the heat, stir in the lime juice, basil, and mint. Garnish with the peanuts and serve immediately.

RED CURRY PASTE

Makes about 2 cups, enough to prepare 4 curries

This paste is hotter and even more versatile than green curry paste. Dried red chiles are traditionally used, but we found a combination of dried and fresh red chiles created a better texture. Red curry is delicious paired with beef, pork, duck, chicken, and all types of seafood. This recipe is designed to be prepared in a food processor. Cut the quantities in half if using a minichopper. See the illustrations on page 194 for tips on handling lemon grass.

½   ounce dried small red chiles (Thai, japonés, or
     de árbol), stems snapped off, chiles broken in
     half, and seeds shaken out (about ½ cup)
4   large or 6 medium fresh red jalapeño chiles,
     stemmed, seeded, and chopped coarse (about
     ¾ cup)
3–4 stalks lemon grass, outer sheath removed,
     bottom 3 inches trimmed and minced (about
     ½ cup)
20   medium garlic cloves, minced or pressed
     through a garlic press (about ⅓ cup)
3   tablespoons minced fresh ginger
1   medium shallot, chopped coarse (about
     3 tablespoons)
2   tablespoons minced cilantro stems
2   tablespoons ground coriander
2   tablespoons peanut or canola oil
4   teaspoons grated zest from 4 limes
2   teaspoons ground cumin
1   teaspoon salt
½   teaspoon ground black pepper
½   teaspoon shrimp paste or anchovy paste
     (optional)

1. Place the dried red chiles in a small bowl and pour hot water over to cover. Let stand until soft and rehydrated, about 30 minutes. Remove the chiles, discarding the liquid. Dry the chiles with paper towels.

2. Place all the ingredients in a food processor and pulse 10 times, each pulse lasting 4 to 5 seconds; stop and use a spatula to push down the ingredients every few pulses. Once the ingredients begin to form a paste, process until smooth, stopping occasionally to push down the ingredients, about 3 minutes. Store in a covered glass container or bowl in the refrigerator for up to 1 month or in the freezer for several months. (If freezing, divide the curry paste into ½-cup amounts, so that one portion will make one recipe, and freeze individually.)

TASTING LAB: Coconut Milk

COCONUT MILK IS NOT THE THIN LIQUID FOUND INSIDE the coconut itself; that is called coconut water. Coconut milk is a product made by steeping equal parts shredded coconut meat and either warm milk or water. The meat is pressed or mashed to release as much liquid as possible, the mixture is strained, and the result is coconut milk.

The same method is used to make coconut cream, but the ratio of coconut meat to liquid is higher, about 4 to 1. (The cream that rises to the top of coconut milk after it sits awhile is also referred to as coconut cream.) Finally, cream of coconut—not to be confused with coconut cream—is a sweetened product based on coconut milk that also contains thickeners and emulsifiers. Cream of coconut and coconut cream are not interchangeable in recipes, as the former is heavily sweetened (it is used in piña coladas and other mixed drinks) and the latter is not.

Coconut milk is probably the most useful of these products (unless you're a bartender). It can be used in puddings, rice dishes, and curries. We sampled eight brands and found that fat content is the most important factor to

consider when shopping. The fat content in the six "regular" coconut milks ranged from 12.2 to 17.5 percent. All of these products were acceptable. The fat content in the two "lite" coconut milks tested was around 6 percent and both of these brands landed at the bottom of the rankings. The light coconut milks were especially problematic in our curry tests, where they made particularly thin sauces.

Among the six regular brands, tasters gravitated to those with more solid cream at the top of the can. These brands also had a much stronger coconut flavor. Lower-rated brands were lacking that coconut punch tasters wanted.

Rating Coconut Milks

SIXTEEN MEMBERS OF THE AMERICA'S TEST KITCHEN STAFF TASTED EIGHT BRANDS OF COCONUT MILK IN COCONUT PUDDING, coconut rice, and green chicken curry. The coconut milks are listed below in order of preference based on their scores in these tastings. All brands are available in supermarkets and Asian markets nationwide.

HIGHLY RECOMMENDED
KA-ME Coconut Milk
$1.79 for 14 ounces

The most complex milk—tasters mentioned tropical fruits and lemongrass—also had a rich, velvety texture.

HIGHLY RECOMMENDED
Chaokoh Coconut Milk
$1.79 for 13.5 ounces

This coconut milk lacked the complexity of KA-ME, but made up for it with its superior smooth texture. Voted "the creamiest" brand.

RECOMMENDED
Goya Coconut Milk
$1.50 for 13.5 ounces

The only brand not made in Thailand (it's from the Dominican Republic) wasn't as rich as the top milks, but it had a good, honest coconut flavor.

RECOMMENDED
Thai Kitchen Premium Coconut Milk
$1.99 for 14 ounces

Although this brand lacked the solid cream that rises to the top of the can, it had an assertive coconut flavor.

RECOMMENDED WITH RESERVATIONS
A Taste of Thai Coconut Milk
$1.99 for 13.5 ounces

A few tasters likened this brand to "toasted coconut," but most found it to be unusually tart and sour.

RECOMMENDED WITH RESERVATIONS
Oriental King Coconut Milk
$.99 for 14 ounces

This milk's bland flavor had tasters wondering, "Where's the coconut?" Its relatively low fat content and no added emulsifiers also led to a broken curry sauce.

RECOMMENDED WITH RESERVATIONS
A Taste of Thai Lite Coconut Milk
$1.59 for 13.5 ounces

The coconut flavor in this brand played second fiddle to an overwhelming sweetness that didn't work well in the curry sauce—but at least it didn't break.

NOT RECOMMENDED
Thai Kitchen Lite Coconut Milk
$1.79 for 14 ounces

This milk only offered a fleeting coconut flavor and seemed "watered down."

EQUIPMENT CORNER: Mini Food Processors

FULL-SIZE FOOD PROCESSORS ARE NOT SUITED FOR chopping small amounts of food. Everyone has tried to mince two or three cloves of garlic or a handful of nuts in a full-size food processor (usually in recipes where the processor is used for other tasks as well) only to see the nuts get chipped and dented as they fly around the huge bowl or the garlic get squished, bruised, and stuck under the blade.

Perhaps a mini food processor (aka food chopper or minichopper) is the answer for those mid-sized jobs—amounts too small to be chopped efficiently in a full-size unit, but bigger than you care to do by hand. To find out, we tested eight food choppers, each with a 3-cup capacity (or as close to that as we could get, depending on the manufacturer). Prices ranged between $19.99 and $49.99.

Tests included chopping dry ingredients (1 cup of almonds, 1½ ounces of Parmesan cheese, and fresh garlic cloves, two at a time and six at a time), mincing herbs (1 cup parsley), and processing a mixture of dry and wet ingredients (a single recipe of green curry paste with 10 cloves garlic, 15 green Thai chiles, 2 large jalapenos, 1½ tablespoons fresh ginger, 2 stalks lemon grass, 1 small shallot, oil, and numerous herbs and spices).

The KitchenAid and both the Cuisinart models managed to do a decent job with the almonds, producing mostly ¼-inch pieces, but each left behind 2 to 3 tablespoons of unusable powder. Lower-rated models either left large chunks of almonds or proved difficult to adjust (as did the Ultimate Chopper) before breaking the nuts down into powder.

All of the models handled the Parmesan fairly well, although the cheese grated in the Hamilton Beach, the General Electric, and the Black & Decker was too coarse. The Ultimate Chopper grated the cheese very unevenly, with some powder so fine that it was gummy and some powder

that was very course. Both Cuisinarts, the KitchenAid, and the Bosch did a good job, breaking down the cheese quickly into an even grind. All of the models except for the Ultimate Chopper did a good job mincing both two and six cloves of garlic.

Every single one of the choppers failed to produce acceptable minced parsley. The best of the bunch (the KitchenAid) managed only a fair rating (bruised, unevenly cut leaves with a fair number of whole, intact leaves left). You're better off mincing parsley by hand.

Green Curry Paste was our final test. We started with all of the ingredients chopped into ½-inch pieces. One full recipe was too large a quantity for the minis to produce a suitably smooth paste; all of the pastes except for the one made in the Bosch were too rough and/or chunky for our tastes. We had more success with making a smaller batch of curry paste (a full-size food processor can handle the whole recipe).

There were some design factors to take into consideration as well. None of the models we tested had slicing or shredding attachments, or one-touch "on" buttons (we had to hold their buttons down for the motor to run). On the Bosch we appreciated the sealed workbowl and sealed motor unit (which kept the motor itself from getting dirty). However, the top-mounted motor made it difficult to see what was going on in the workbowl, which was a major pain because you have to monitor the food in the bowl visually to see how broken down it is. All of the models except for the Bosch, Ultimate Chopper, and Black & Decker included drip holes in their feed tubes, to ease the process of making mayo or other emulsified sauces.

So what should you buy? If you already own a full-size food processor with a mini-bowl attachment, the attachment will work just fine for smaller jobs. But if you have the counter space, a mini food processor can be a good addition to your kitchen. The KitchenAid Chef's Chopper would be our first choice because it performed most of the tasks with relative ease.

Rating Mini Food Processors

WE ROUNDED UP EIGHT MINI FOOD PROCESSORS AND PUT THEM THROUGH A VARIETY OF TASKS (CHOPPING almonds, grating Parmesan, mincing garlic and parsley, and processing a curry paste) to determine if any of them could handle these jobs with ease. The processors are listed in order of preference. See www.americastestkitchen.com for up-to-date prices and mail-order sources for top-rated products.

RECOMMENDED
KitchenAid Chef's Chopper (KFC3100)
Capacity: 3 cups
$39.99

The best of the bunch managed the curry and made short work of the chopped almonds. Mincing parsley was beyond its—and every other chopper's—ability, but the motor-on-bottom design gives the cook a good view of what's going on and easy access to the bowl.

RECOMMENDED WITH RESERVATIONS
Cuisinart Mini-Prep Plus Processor (DLC-2A)
Capacity: 3 cups
$39.99

Its results rivaled that of the KitchenAid, but this "jumpy" machine needed a hand to keep it from processing itself off the counter.

RECOMMENDED WITH RESERVATIONS
Cuisinart Mini-Prep Processor (DLC-1)
Capacity: about 2.5 cups
$29.95

This model produced decent results, but its cramped work bowl kept it from rivaling the larger Cuisinart.

RECOMMENDED WITH RESERVATIONS
Bosch Universal Chopper (MMR0800UC)
Capacity 3.5 cups
$49.99

A champ with the tough-to-process green curry, this chopper has a few design issues. It has a large workbowl with a user-friendly on-off mechanism, but the huge top-mounted motor overshadows its good performance, literally.

NOT RECOMMENDED
Ultimate Chopper
Capacity: 2¾ cups
$39.50

This brutish machine pulverized almonds into powder before we had a chance to stop at "chopped." The largest chopper, in terms of counter space occupation, has a puny plastic workbowl and couldn't lure parsley to its blades.

NOT RECOMMENDED
General Electric Deluxe Chopper (106848)
Capacity: 3 cups
$14.95

This extremely loud machine's bark is much worse than its bite. Food had trouble working down the tall, narrow workbowl into the blades.

NOT RECOMMENDED
Hamilton Beach Fresh Chop Food Chopper (72600)
Capacity: 3 cups
$19.99

Like the GE Deluxe Chopper, this model is extremely loud, and food tends to float above the blades rather than fall into them.

NOT RECOMMENDED
Black & Decker Chopper (EHC650)
Capacity: 3 cups
$24.99

Parsley just took many harmless spins around the workbowl of this model and almonds were merely roughed up. The top-mounted motor gets messy and is tough to clean.

A long-handled spider makes it easy to retrieve deep-fried chunks of orange-flavored chicken from hot oil.

ASIAN CHICKEN classics

CHAPTER 16

IN THIS CHAPTER

THE RECIPES
Orange-Flavored Chicken

Chicken Teriyaki

EQUIPMENT CORNER
Electric Deep Fryers

TASTING LAB
Store-Bought Teriyaki Sauce

When you eat chicken frequently, as many of us do, it pays to have a number of preparations and flavor ideas on hand. In this chapter, we turn to two Asian dishes—one a popular offering on Chinese restaurant menus, orange-flavored chicken, and the other a classic standby by at Japanese restaurants, chicken teriyaki.

Orange-flavored chicken can be a guilty pleasure. Deep-fried chunks of tender white meat chicken are slathered in a sweet and tangy orange glaze. Surveying takeout orders of this dish from Chinese restaurants, we were faced with plate after plate of greasy chicken covered with a sickeningly sweet, gloppy sauce. We decided to rescue this dish.

Teriyaki chicken, often a safe bet at Japanese restaurants, has unfortunately also become a frequent offering at mall food courts, sports bars, and family-style chain restaurants, where it's been corrupted into another dish entirely. The sticky and sweet glaze often masks strips of poor-quality chicken. We wanted to bring this dish back to its authentic Japanese roots.

With these recipes added to your repertoire, chicken for dinner won't be so boring after all.

ORANGE-FLAVORED CHICKEN

WHAT WE WANTED: Tender chunks of crispy, fried chicken in a fresh-tasting orange sauce.

When Americans order Chinese takeout, a container of orange-flavored chicken is often delivered with the egg rolls, fried rice, and egg drop soup. While it's far from authentic Chinese fare, it's not difficult to understand why this dish is so popular: The chicken is deep-fried, and the sauce is sticky and sweet. Sounds like a winning, if decadent, combination. But, while a quick taste of a candy-coated chicken nugget might have some appeal, our culinary satisfaction goes sharply downhill with successive bites.

Never was this more apparent than during the afternoon we spent strolling the neighborhoods surrounding the test kitchen (where there are a number of Chinese restaurants), ordering orange chicken at every turn. Faced with mouthful after mouthful of ultra-thick breading wrapped around scraps of greasy, gristly, tasteless chicken bathed in "orange" sauce (perhaps a mixture of corn syrup and orange food coloring?), our appetites waned. But our interest in this dish was not entirely squelched. Pushing back the last plate of subpar chicken in favor of a steaming cup of black tea, we dreamed wistfully about the possibilities.

We wanted chicken that we could actually swallow—and that meant substantial, well-seasoned chunks with a crisp, golden brown crust. Puny scraps of chicken and heavy globs of breading need not apply. A perfect coating would be moderately crunchy and maintain its texture beneath a blanket of sauce. As for the sauce, we'd have to modulate the typical Chinese American sweet-tart flavor profile, which generally leans much too far to the sweet side. But above all we wanted the sauce to offer a clear hit of fresh orange flavor, with balanced sweet, sour, and spicy background notes, plus a pleasing consistency.

Back in the test kitchen, we decided to tackle the chicken coating first, jotting down every coating or breading possibility we could think of, then ticking them off our list after kitchen tests. A fried chicken coating (a buttermilk dip followed by a flour and baking powder dip) was somewhat tough and shatteringly crisp. Panko (Japanese bread crumbs) tasted great but weren't right for this recipe, a cake flour batter slipped off the chicken once fried, and a beer batter coating turned spongy and doughy beneath the sauce. We kept going and tried flour and a whole egg, flour and egg whites, cornstarch and sherry, and even flour and seltzer water. All failed.

Some of the recipes we tested early on called for

GETTING IT RIGHT: Secrets to Great Orange Chicken

1. Soy-orange marinade keeps the chicken juicy.

2. Patting the marinated chicken dry helps the coating adhere.

3. Beaten egg whites act as "glue," securing the coating to the chicken.

4. The cornstarch and baking soda coating fries up golden and crisp.

5. Frying in peanut oil produces chicken with fresh, clean flavor.

"velveting" the chicken, a process used in some stir-fries, in which the chicken is coated in a thin batter of foamy egg whites mixed with some cornstarch. While this approach wasn't quite the ticket when it came to deep-frying (the coating was insubstantial and turned soggy), when we separated the ingredients and dunked the chicken first in egg white, then in cornstarch, it worked. This chicken was perfect! We cornered our science editor to find out why. He explained that when egg whites and cornstarch are combined, the starch absorbs water from the whites and creates a sort of glue that, not surprisingly, turns soggy after frying. Our successful two-step (egg white and then cornstarch) coating created a thin sheath of protein (the egg white) beneath plenty of dry cornstarch, which never got the opportunity to swell and absorb water. This dry coating browned and crisped much more readily than a wet, gluey one.

So we had a coating that was tender and yielding in some spots and delicately crunchy in others, falling somewhere between fast-food fried chicken and tempura. Tasters couldn't get enough and gobbled the chicken down, unsauced.

We made some minor refinements. A pinch of cayenne gave the chicken some zip, and baking soda was called in to help develop a golden color. (In baking and frying, baking soda aids in browning.) The contest between light and dark meat was easily decided—thigh meat has richer flavor and is more apt to remain moist when deep-fried (or cooked just about any other way) than drier breast meat. (Surprisingly, not one of the published recipes we found suggested dark meat for this dish, while every restaurant version we tried was made with boneless chicken thighs.) We also wondered if oil choice mattered much and ran a quick test, pitting peanut oil against vegetable oil. Peanut oil was unanimously preferred, producing chicken that was noticeably cleaner and fresher tasting than chicken fried in vegetable oil.

Having selected the oil, we fiddled with frying temperatures between 325 and 375 degrees and settled right in the middle. At 350 degrees, the chicken was crisp but not greasy in just 5 minutes, requiring one quick flip halfway through cooking.

We know from developing stir-fry recipes that a salty marinade works wonders toward developing flavor and maintaining juiciness in chicken. To marinate chicken for this recipe, soy sauce was a natural choice; it would serve as a brine, seasoning the meat and locking in moisture. Garlic, ginger, sugar (brown, for its gentle sweetness) and vinegar (white, for its unobtrusive acidity), plus plenty of orange juice and some chicken broth rounded out the recipe.

We also decided to make extra marinade, putting some in service as a sauce for the deep-fried chicken. We added some cornstarch to the extra marinade and then tasted it as a sauce. Truth be told, it had not even a hint of orange flavor. Luckily, we had other ideas for infusing orange flavor into the marinade: orange marmalade, frozen orange juice concentrate, reduced fresh orange juice, fresh orange zest, and dried orange zest. The marmalade was bitter, orange juice concentrate and reduced orange juice tasted "fake" and "exceedingly bright," and bottled dried zest was gritty and pithy. In the end, a combination of fresh orange juice and fresh zest lent deep, pronounced orange flavor. The slightly bitter, floral taste of the zest plus a healthy dose of cayenne helped the sauce to grow up in a hurry, transforming it from sweetly one-dimensional and boring to complex, spicy, and savory.

Finishing the dish was a snap: we just tossed the fried chicken into the sauce and garnished with strips of orange peel and whole dried red chiles. Left whole, the chiles don't lend much flavor, but they almost always show up in this dish for visual appeal. Now we can look forward to savoring an entire serving (maybe even two) of orange-flavored chicken rather than forcing down just one bite.

WHAT WE LEARNED: Marinate the chicken for well-seasoned meat. For a crisp, golden crust, coat the chicken first in beaten egg white, then in cornstarch. Peanut oil works best for frying the chicken. Use a combination of orange juice and grated zest for a not-too-sweet sauce with vibrant orange flavor. A bit of cayenne gives the sauce a spicy kick.

ORANGE-FLAVORED CHICKEN

Serves 4

We prefer the flavor and texture of thigh meat for this recipe, though an equal amount of boneless skinless chicken breasts can be used. It is easiest to grate the orange zest and remove the strips of orange peel before juicing the oranges; use a sharp vegetable peeler to remove the strips. For extra spiciness, increase the cayenne added to the sauce to ½ teaspoon. The whole dried chiles are added for appearance, not for flavor, and can be omitted. To fry the chicken, use a Dutch oven or a straight-sided sauté pan (with at least a 3-quart capacity); do not use a 12-inch skillet with sloped sides, as it will be too small to contain the oil once the chicken is added. White rice and steamed broccoli are good accompaniments.

marinade and sauce

1½	pounds boneless, skinless chicken thighs, trimmed and cut into 1½-inch pieces
¾	cup low-sodium chicken broth
¾	cup juice, 1½ teaspoons grated zest, and 8 strips orange peel (each about 2 inches long by ½ inch wide) from 2 oranges (see note)
6	tablespoons distilled white vinegar
¼	cup soy sauce
½	cup packed dark brown sugar
3	medium garlic cloves, minced or pressed through garlic press (about 1 tablespoon)
1	tablespoon grated fresh ginger
¼	teaspoon cayenne
1	tablespoon plus 2 teaspoons cornstarch
2	tablespoons cold water
8	small whole dried red chiles (optional)

coating and frying oil

3	large egg whites
1	cup cornstarch
½	teaspoon baking soda
¼	teaspoon cayenne
3	cups peanut oil

1. FOR THE MARINADE AND SAUCE: Place the chicken in a 1-gallon zipper-lock bag; set aside. Combine the chicken broth, orange juice, grated zest, vinegar, soy sauce, brown sugar, garlic, ginger, and cayenne in a large saucepan (with at least a 3-quart capacity); whisk until the sugar is fully dissolved. Measure out ¾ cup of the mixture and pour into the bag with the chicken; press out as much air as possible and seal the bag, making sure that all the pieces are coated with the marinade. Refrigerate 30 to 60 minutes, but no longer.

2. Bring the remaining mixture in the saucepan to a boil over high heat. In a small bowl, stir together the cornstarch and cold water; whisk the cornstarch mixture into the sauce. Simmer, stirring occasionally, until thick and translucent, about 1 minute. Off the heat, stir in the orange peel and chiles, if using (the sauce should measure 1½ cups); set the sauce aside.

3. FOR THE COATING: Place the egg whites in a pie plate; using a fork, beat until frothy. In a second pie plate, whisk the cornstarch, baking soda, and cayenne until combined. Drain the chicken in a colander or large mesh strainer; thoroughly pat the chicken dry with paper towels. Place half of the chicken pieces in the egg whites and turn to coat; transfer the pieces to the cornstarch mixture and coat thoroughly. Place the dredged chicken pieces on a wire rack set over a baking sheet; repeat with the remaining chicken.

4. TO FRY THE CHICKEN: Heat the oil in an 11- to 12-inch Dutch oven or straight-sided sauté pan with at least a 3-quart capacity over high heat until the oil registers 350 degrees on an instant-read or deep-fry thermometer. Carefully place half of the chicken in the oil; fry until golden brown, about 5 minutes, turning each piece with tongs halfway through cooking. Transfer to a paper towel–lined plate. Return the oil to 350 degrees and repeat with the remaining chicken.

5. TO SERVE: Reheat the sauce over medium heat until simmering, about 2 minutes. Add the chicken and gently toss until evenly coated and heated through. Serve immediately.

EQUIPMENT CORNER: Electric Deep Fryers

ELECTRIC DEEP FRYERS ARE APPEALING FOR SEVERAL reasons. Because the hot oil is away from lit stovetop burners, they add a significant measure of safety to what can be a dangerous operation. Lids promise to reduce the mess and subdue the stink. Finally, built-in thermostats mean no more fussing with clip-on thermometers, which always seem to drop into the oil at the least opportune moment.

We ordered nine deep fryers, all priced under $65 (who wants to spend more on an infrequently used kitchen item?), and noticed that they fell into two distinct camps. In the first were the traditional round models. In the second were some newer models styled in the fashion of the sleek stainless steel fryers you might see in a fast-food restaurant. These professional-style models also have a larger capacity.

For our first test, we noted how long each fryer took to heat the oil to 375 degrees. We then measured heat loss when we dumped frozen fries into the heated oil. Whereas the temperature in the top-rated Oster, a professional-style model, dropped just 40 degrees, the temperature in the Black & Decker, a home-style fryer, plummeted more than 130 degrees. What does this mean in practical terms? It means that the Oster produced super-crisp fries, while the fries cooked in the Black & Decker absorbed a lot of oil and emerged pale, limp, and soggy.

We also measured the time it took the oil to recover between batches of fries. Ultimately, we ignored the thermostats and fried two batches of chicken tenders back to back, without waiting for the oil to reheat (something you might do when kids are begging for more food, fast). Only the professional-style models could manage this daunting task successfully.

Ten gallons of oil later, what had we learned? The "professional" fryers, with their powerful heating elements, were best able to keep the oil up to temperature, especially in the frozen french fry test, which some of the home-style models failed. The latter hide the electric heating coil inside a stay-cool plastic housing, whereas in professional-style models the heating coil sits at the bottom of the cooking chamber and is in direct contact with the oil. But there's a price to pay for this performance. Professional models are real oil hogs, calling for an extra quart or so.

So which model should you buy? On points, the professional-style fryer from Oster was the champ. If you'd like to save money on oil, though, the Rival Cool Touch is our favorite home-style fryer. It holds on to heat nearly as well as the "professional" models—and, more important, it turns out fried foods every bit as addictive.

TECHNIQUE: Disposing of Oil Neatly

Fried foods, such as Orange-Flavored Chicken (page 204), are a real treat, but cleaning up after frying is not. Disposing of the spent oil neatly and safely is a particular challenge. Here's how we do it. First we allow the oil to cool completely. Then we make a quadruple- or quintuple-layered bag using four or five leftover plastic grocery bags. With someone holding the layered bags open over a sink or in an outdoor area, we carefully pour the cooled frying oil from the pot into the innermost bag. We tie the bag handles shut and dispose of the oil in the garbage.

Rating Electric Deep Fryers

WE TESTED NINE DEEP FRYERS—SIX HOME-STYLE AND THREE PROFESSIONAL-STYLE. RATINGS ARE BASED ON HOW LONG it took each fryer to heat the oil to 375 degrees and its subsequent heat loss when frozen fries were added. We then measured the amount of time it took the oil to recover between batches. Fryers are divided into home-style and professional-style and are listed in order of preference. See www.americastestkitchen.com for up-to-date prices and mail-order sources for top-rated products.

HOME-STYLE DEEP FRYERS

RECOMMENDED
Rival Cool Touch Deep Fryer CF275
Capacity: 2.5 liters
$49.99

This model maintained heat as well as the "professional" fryers. The only model with a window in the lid that did not steam over. Because the built-in timer will turn off the heat when the set time expires, use the "stay on" setting and rely on a separate timer.

RECOMMENDED
Aroma Cool Fry Deep Fryer ADF-172D
Capacity: 2 quarts
$59.99

The body and lid remained the coolest of any fryer tested. Results equaled the top-rated Rival and Oster fryers, but the fry basket is smallish and the window fogs immediately.

RECOMMENDED WITH RESERVATIONS
DeLonghi Cool Touch Deluxe Fryer D650-UX
Capacity: 2 quarts
$62.99

A drain allows for easy oil removal, but to clean the bowl and lid (which are not removable) we had to lug the fryer to the sink. The lack of a thermostat is a serious shortcoming.

RECOMMENDED WITH RESERVATIONS
Presto Dual Daddy Electric Deep Fryer 05450
Capacity: 2 quarts
$37.70

This rudimentary fryer lacks all bells and whistles. No basket, no thermostat, and no lid to control the mess, but it cranks out intense heat.

NOT RECOMMENDED
Presto Cool Daddy Cool-Touch Electric Deep Fryer 05444
Capacity: 2 liters
$49.99

This model failed our heat loss test, and both preheat and recovery times exceeded acceptable limits. The shallow bowl made it impossible to submerge chicken.

NOT RECOMMENDED
Black & Decker Fry Mate DF200
Capacity: 2 liters
$54.99

Painfully slow to preheat and recover temperature between batches. The oil temperature plummeted 130 degrees during the frozen food test, leading to greasy, pale fries.

PROFESSIONAL-STYLE DEEP FRYERS

RECOMMENDED
Oster Immersion Deep Fryer ODF540
Capacity: 3 liters
$59.99

The top performer among the sleek restaurant-style fryers. Excels at maintaining heat, but not everyone will want to deal with 3 liters of used oil. On the bright side, only the heating element and control box are not dishwasher-safe.

RECOMMENDED
General Electric Professional Style Deep Fryer 106770
Capacity: 3.5 liters
$54.85

The huge basket matches the excessive capacity of this fryer. Only for the serious deep-fry enthusiast. Identical results can be achieved with other fryers that use much less oil.

RECOMMENDED WITH RESERVATIONS
Rival Commercial-Style Deep Fryer CZF610
Capacity: 3 liters
$59.99

Preheating and recovery times are excellent. However, the too-smart-for-its-own-good timing system cuts the heat once the set time has expired, and there is no way to bypass this safety system.

CHICKEN TERIYAKI

WHAT WE WANTED: Authentic chicken teriyaki—moist tender chicken in a well-seasoned sauce—not a food court rip-off.

When the fish isn't so fresh and the soba's just so-so, you can usually count on chicken teriyaki as a reliable standby at most Japanese restaurants. But with so many lackluster Americanized adaptations out there—including everything from skewered chicken chunks shellacked in a corn-syrupy sauce to over-marinated, preformed chicken breast patties—what is the real deal? Traditionally, chicken teriyaki is pan-fried, grilled, or broiled, with the sauce added during the last stages of cooking. In fact, the Japanese term "teriyaki" can be translated as *teri*, meaning "shine" or "luster"—referring to the glossy sauce—and *yaki*, meaning "to broil."

The chicken is most often served off the bone and cut into thin strips. The sauce itself (unlike most bottled versions) consists of just three basic ingredients: soy sauce, sugar, and either mirin (a sweet Japanese rice wine) or sake.

The half-dozen test recipes we assembled were, for the most part, disappointing. The most promising recipes had one thing in common: The skin was left on. Despite minor complaints about the sauce being too watery, tasters seemed to like a marinated and broiled version best, followed by one in which the chicken was pan-fried and simmered in sauce during the final minutes of cooking. While the skin kept the meat tender and moist, it also had a major flaw: its chewing-gum-like texture. We had to come up with a way to keep the skin crisp, even with the addition of sauce. A skillet or broiler, or perhaps a tag-team effort employing both, would be integral to getting us there.

Chicken thighs were clearly preferred by tasters over chicken breasts. The deeper, meatier taste of the thighs stood up nicely to the salty profile of the teriyaki sauce. But questions remained. Bone-in or bone-out, skin-on or skin-off? The skin seemed to create a protective barrier against the heat source, keeping the meat moist, so it would have to be left on. Because most skin-on chicken thighs are sold with the bone attached, we would have to bone them ourselves if we wanted to serve the meat in easy-to-eat strips. Even with a sharp paring knife and a straightforward technique, it took kitchen novices a few tries before they felt completely comfortable with the procedure. But the effort was well worth it. Not only did boning the chicken thighs allow the meat to cook faster, it also made cutting the pieces of hot chicken into strips much easier (and less messy). If you want to skip the knife work, you can cook and serve the chicken with the bone in, but the presentation is not nearly as nice and everyone will have to work harder at the table.

Because most of the recipes we came across in our research called for marinating the meat to infuse it with as much flavor as possible, all of our initial efforts began with this step. But whether we pricked the skin with a fork or slashed it with a knife, marinating the thighs in the teriyaki sauce caused the skin to become unattractively flabby. A combination of searing the thighs and then finishing them under the broiler yielded the most promising results, but once the meat received its final dredge in a reduced portion of the marinade (which we now referred to as a sauce) to get that glazy shine, the skin always slipped back into sogginess.

Exhausted at the thought of having to refine a lengthy process of boning, marinating, searing, reducing, and broiling that didn't seem to work, one test kitchen colleague suggested something so simple, so obvious, that we wondered why we hadn't thought of it sooner. "Why not just broil the chicken without marinating it and spoon the sauce on at the end?" she asked. We had gotten so caught up with trying to infuse the meat with flavor that we had all but forgotten a main principle of traditional teriyaki: applying the sauce at the end.

After playing musical racks with the oven broiler to get the thighs up to the requisite 175-degree temperature without burning the skin or leaving it pale and fatty, we found that placing the rack in the middle (about 8 inches from the heat source) provided the most consistent level of browning and crispness for the lightly salt-and-peppered thighs. On the middle rack, the skin turned almost as crispy as a potato chip, but there were still some spots where the fat didn't render completely. To remedy this problem, we slashed the skin, thus allowing the heat to penetrate more easily, and tucked the exposed edges of meat underneath the skin while smoothing out the tops, thus reducing the occurrence of dips and bumps where small pockets of fat had gotten trapped.

With the chicken taken care of, it was time to concentrate on the sauce. Bottled teriyaki sauce (see the tasting on page 209) was uniformly rejected in favor of a homemade sauce, which took just five minutes to prepare. Working with various amounts of soy sauce, sugar, and mirin (which tasters preferred to sake), we found that the best balance of sweetness and saltiness was achieved with equal amounts of soy sauce and sugar (½ cup) and with a smaller amount of mirin (2 tablespoons), which added a slightly sweet wine flavor. In terms of consistency, getting the sauce glaze-like (but neither as thick as molasses nor as thin as water) was difficult. No matter how carefully we watched the sauce simmer, it either was too thin or became tacky while the soy sauce burned, producing what one person called a "strangely bologna-like" flavor. A minimal amount of cornstarch (½ teaspoon) quickly solved this problem. Although the sauce was now clean and balanced, it needed more depth, which was achieved through the addition of some grated ginger and minced garlic. With at-once crisp and moist, sweet and salty glazed chicken now available at home, we would never have to eat food-court teriyaki again.

WHAT WE LEARNED: Use chicken thighs, which cook up tender and moist under the high heat of the broiler. Slash the skin, which allows the heat to penetrate more easily. Tuck the exposed meat underneath to evenly render the fat. Skip store-bought teriyaki sauces and make your own.

TECHNIQUE: Preparing Chicken Thighs

1. After trimming excess skin and fat (leave enough to cover the meat), cut a slit along the white line of fat from one joint to the other joint to expose the bone.

2. Using the tip of a knife, cut or scrape the meat from the bone at both joints.

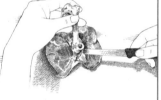

3. Slip the knife under the bone to separate the meat completely from the bone.

4. Discard the bone. Trim any remaining cartilage from the thigh.

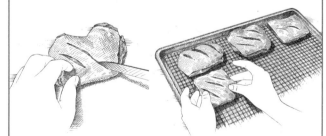

5. Cut three diagonal slashes in the skin. Do not cut into the meat.

6. Tuck the meat under the skin and lightly flatten the thigh to an even thickness.

CHICKEN TERIYAKI

Serves 4 to 6

If you prefer to serve whole bone-in thighs and thereby skip the step of boning the chicken, trim the thighs of excess skin and fat, position the oven rack about 12 inches from the heat source, and increase the broiling time to 20 to 26 minutes, rotating the pan once halfway through the cooking time. This recipe was developed to work in an in-oven broiler, not the drawer-type broiler typical of older gas ovens. Mirin, a sweet Japanese rice wine, is a key component of teriyaki; it can be found in the international section of most major supermarkets and in most Asian markets. If you cannot find it, use 2 tablespoons white wine and an extra teaspoon of sugar. Serve with steamed rice, preferably short grain.

8	bone-in, skin-on chicken thighs (about 5 ounces each), trimmed, boned, and skin slashed (see illustrations 1 through 5 on page 208)
	Salt and ground black pepper
½	cup soy sauce
½	cup sugar
½	teaspoon grated fresh ginger
1	medium garlic clove, minced or pressed through a garlic press (about 1 teaspoon)
2	tablespoons mirin
½	teaspoon cornstarch

1. Position an oven rack about 8 inches from the heat source; heat the broiler. Season the chicken thighs with salt and pepper; set the thighs skin-side up on a broiler pan (or foil-lined rimmed baking sheet fitted with a flat wire rack), tucking the exposed meat under the skin and lightly flattening the thighs to be of relatively even thickness (see illustration 6). Broil until the skin is crisp and golden brown and the thickest parts of the thighs register 175 degrees on an instant-read thermometer, 8 to 14 minutes, rotating the pan halfway through the cooking time for even browning.

2. While the chicken cooks, combine the soy sauce, sugar, ginger, and garlic in a small saucepan; stir together the mirin and cornstarch in a small bowl until no lumps remain, then stir the mirin mixture into the saucepan. Bring the sauce to a boil over medium-high heat, stirring occasionally; reduce the heat to medium-low and simmer, stirring occasionally, until the sauce is reduced to ¾ cup and forms a syrupy glaze, about 4 minutes. Cover to keep warm.

3. Transfer the chicken to a cutting board; let rest 2 to 3 minutes. Cut the meat crosswise into ½-inch-wide strips. Transfer the chicken to a serving platter; stir the teriyaki sauce to recombine, then drizzle to taste over the chicken. Serve immediately, passing the remaining sauce separately.

TASTING LAB: Store-Bought Teriyaki Sauce

CONSIDERING THAT A GREAT TERIYAKI SAUCE CAN BE prepared quickly with just six ingredients, bottled sauces can hardly boast convenience. But how do bottled teriyaki sauces taste? We sampled seven leading brands to find out. Our tasters had difficulty identifying many of these sauces as teriyaki. Several brands resembled hoisin, oyster, or even barbecue sauce. Of the three that met tasters' standards for teriyaki, Annie Chun's All Natural received top marks, having a "smooth, rich texture" and indisputable teriyaki flavor. A second tasting pitted Annie Chun's against our homemade teriyaki sauce. Our judges deemed Annie Chun's harsh in comparison to the brighter-tasting and better-balanced teriyaki we made fresh, so we suggest taking a few extra minutes to make it yourself.

THE BEST STORE-BOUGHT TERIYAKI SAUCE
Annie Chun's All Natural Teriyaki Sauce

Grilled Tomato and Cheese Pizza **page 224**

Black Bean Soup **page 30**

Beef Tacos **page 24**

Onion-Braised Beef Brisket **page 88** and Buttermilk Mashed Potatoes **page 56**

Pan-Roasted Halibut Steaks **page 156** with Chipotle-Garlic Butter with Lime and Cilantro **page 157**

Pan-Roasted Asparagus with Toasted Garlic and Parmesan **page 104**

234

French Potato Salad with Radishes, Cornichons, and Capers **page 254**

235

Boston Baked Beans **page 81**

All-Purpose Cornbread **page 269**

Spritz Cookies **page 320**

Chocolate-Chunk Oatmeal Cookies with Pecans and Dried Cherries **page 315**

239

German Chocolate Cake with Coconut-Pecan Filling **page 336**

Deep-Dish Apple Pie **page 300**

Blueberry Cobbler **page 287**

Free-Form Summer Fruit Tart **page 291**

Grill-Roasted Pork Loin **page 247**

GRILL-ROASTED
pork loin

CHAPTER 19

IN THIS CHAPTER

THE RECIPES

Grill-Roasted Pork Loin for a
    Charcoal Grill
Grill-Roasted Pork Loin for a Gas
    Grill
Chili-Mustard Spice Rub
Sweet and Savory Spice Rub

French Potato Salad
French Potato Salad with Arugula,
    Roquefort, and Walnuts
French Potato Salad with
    Radishes, Cornichons, and
    Capers
French Potato Salad with Hard
    Salami and Gruyère

EQUIPMENT CORNER

Kitchen Twine

TASTING LAB

Dijon Mustards

When you're entertaining at the grill, it pays to have a
few tricks up your sleeve in addition to the usual offerings of hamburgers,
steaks, and barbecued chicken. Take pork loin, for example. Sure, this cut
is delicious roasted in the oven, but it takes on a whole new character
when cooked on the grill. The fire imparts a delicate smokiness to the
meat and the intense heat creates a handsome crust. But as with most
cuts of pork, pork loin is prone to drying out and can become quite
tasteless. We decided to fine-tune grilled pork loin, and knew we'd need
to take measures to keep the meat moist and succulent.

You don't want to serve a mayo-based American potato salad with
pork loin (too heavy) nor do you want a bacony German potato salad
(too much pork). French potato salad—sliced red potatoes dressed
with a zippy herb-infused vinaigrette—is a perfect counterpoint to the
pork recipe. This potato salad is also great served with a wide variety of
warm-weather dishes such as grilled salmon and grilled chicken.

GRILL-ROASTED PORK LOIN

WHAT WE WANTED: A roasted pork loin with a deep brown, peppery crust and moist, smoky meat.

The affordable and widely available pork loin roast is a popular cut to grill. The obvious problem, however, is that today's leaner pork dries out considerably when cooked with this dry-heat method. Salsa is the culinary scoundrel's solution, but we wanted to investigate the heart of the matter and produce an aromatic roast with a deep brown crust and succulent, smoke-flavored meat.

What is a loin roast? Two muscles run along the back of a pig. The larger, longer muscle is simply referred to as the loin and the smaller, shorter one is called the tenderloin, which is more tender and less flavorful.

Butchers typically cut and merchandise a loin roast in three sections. Closest to the shoulder is the blade end (*blade* refers to the shoulder blade). Moving down the back of the pig you find the center cut, which is the most expensive—comparable to a beef prime rib when sold bone-in. The third and last section is called the sirloin. Here the loin muscle tapers off and rests above the tenderloin. When the sirloin section is cut into roasts or chops, part of the tenderloin is included. The tenderloin muscle can be purchased separately as a boneless roast, but it should not be confused with the larger loin roast—the roast that is the subject of this article.

We wondered if one of these three roasts—the blade end, the center cut, or the sirloin—was better suited to grilling than the others, so we bought all three cuts and put them to the test. The sirloin roast was quickly eliminated. Its two relatively large muscles cooked at vastly different speeds. We thought the center-cut roast, with its one attractive large muscle, would be the favorite, but tasters found its meat pale, dry, and bland, especially when compared with the meat from the blade roast, which was richer in flavor and relatively moist. Containing small parts of various shoulder muscles that are redder and more fibrous than the center cut, the blade roast was favorably likened to the dark meat of chicken. The fatty pockets that separate the different muscles added moistness and flavor. It was the hands-down winner.

First we tried to grill a blade roast directly over a hot fire, but the outside scorched before the inside was cooked through. The result was the same when we tried to grill the meat directly over a moderate fire. We quickly moved on to grill-roasting, an indirect-heat approach in which a covered grill creates an oven-like environment. We built a modified two-level fire by banking the lit coals on one side of the kettle, leaving the other side empty, then placed the loin roast over the empty side, covered the grill, and left the roast to cook. Now it lacked a crisp crust, and the side closest to the coals cooked faster.

We tried again, this time searing all sides directly over the hot coals before moving the roast to the coal-free side of the grill. Then, halfway through cooking, we flipped it so that both long sides of the loin spent time close to the coals. Forty minutes into cooking, the crust was well browned and the meat was done.

We were well on our way to success, but tasters kept complaining about dry meat, a common problem with today's lean pork. In the test kitchen, we find that lean pork roasts and chops should display a hint of pink when sliced. A final internal temperature of 150 degrees is ideal. Because the temperature continues to climb as a roast rests, we found it best to take the meat off the grill when it hit 140 degrees. This step helped to alleviate the dryness—but still not enough to satisfy our tastes.

We tried the test kitchen's favorite approach to improving texture: brining. Sure enough, brined roasts produced rave reviews. The meat was juicy, moist, and even more flavorful.

GRILL-ROASTED PORK LOIN FOR A CHARCOAL GRILL

Serves 4 to 6

If only "enhanced" pork is available (it will be stated on the label), do not brine the roast. Instead, simply add 2 tablespoons kosher salt to the black pepper seasoning. If you are brining, you can use either table or kosher salt, but note that fine-grained table salt measures differently from the larger crystals of kosher salt and that brands of kosher salt measure differently too, which is why we provide measurements for the two most common brands.

With minor recipe adjustments, a roast larger than the one called for can be cooked using the same method. For each additional pound of meat over 3 pounds (do not use a roast larger than 6 pounds), increase the salt in the brine by ¼ cup and the water by 1 quart; also increase the oil and pepper by 1 teaspoon each (if using a spice rub, increase the recipe by one-third). Because the cooking time depends more on the diameter of the loin than its length, the cooking time for a larger roast will not increase significantly. After rotating the roast in step 5, begin checking the internal temperature after 30 minutes of cooking. Note that the recipe for a charcoal grill uses wood chunks and the variation for a gas grill uses wood chips. Wood chunks and chips impart a delicious smoky flavor to the pork loin.

¾ cup table salt, 1½ cups Diamond Crystal
  Kosher salt, or 1 cup plus 2 tablespoons
  Morton Kosher salt (see note)
1 boneless blade-end pork loin roast,
  2½ to 3 pounds, tied with kitchen twine
  at 1½-inch intervals
2 tablespoons olive oil
1 tablespoon coarsely ground black pepper
  or 1 recipe spice rub (recipes follow)
2 (3-inch) wood chunks

1. Dissolve the salt in 3 quarts water in a large container; submerge the roast, cover with plastic wrap, and refrigerate until fully seasoned, 3 to 4 hours. Rinse the roast under cold water and dry thoroughly with paper towels.

Up until now, we had been simply seasoning the out-side of the roast with pepper (the brine contributed enough salt), but perhaps we could up the ante a bit. Keeping things simple, we tried using a coarser grind to create a pepper crust. (We also developed two spice rub variations on this theme.) Finally, we had found the grill-roasted pork loin we were searching for.

WHAT WE LEARNED: For optimal moistness and flavor, buy a blade roast. A modified two-level fire allows the roast to cook for an extended period of time while still developing a nice crust. Brine the pork to improve its texture and flavor and to prevent it from becoming too dry.

2. Rub the roast with the oil; sprinkle with the pepper and press the pepper into the meat. Let the roast stand at room temperature 1 hour.

3. Meanwhile, soak the wood chunks in water to cover for 1 hour; drain. About 25 minutes before grilling, open the bottom grill vents. Using a large chimney starter, light about 5 quarts charcoal, or about 80 individual briquettes; allow to burn until all the charcoal is covered with a layer of fine gray ash, 15 to 20 minutes. Empty the coals into the grill; build a modified two-level fire by arranging the coals to cover one half of the grill, piling them about 3 briquettes high. Place the soaked wood chunks on the coals. Position the cooking grate over the coals, cover the grill, and heat until hot, about 5 minutes (you can hold your hand 5 inches above the cooking grate for 2 seconds). Scrape the cooking grate clean with a grill brush.

4. Grill the pork directly over the fire until browned, about 2 minutes; using tongs, rotate one quarter turn and repeat until all the sides are well browned, about 8 minutes total. Move the loin to a cooler side of the grill, positioning the roast parallel with and as close as possible to the fire. Open the grill lid vents halfway; cover the grill so that the vents are opposite the fire and draw the smoke through the grill. (The internal grill temperature should be about 425 degrees.) Cook 20 minutes.

5. Remove the cover; using tongs, rotate the roast 180 degrees so that the side facing the fire now faces away. Replace the cover and continue cooking until an instant-read thermometer inserted into the thickest part of the roast registers 140 degrees, 10 to 30 minutes longer, depending on the thickness.

6. Transfer the roast to a cutting board; tent loosely with foil and let rest 15 minutes. The internal temperature should rise to 150 degrees. Remove the twine; cut the roast into ½-inch-thick slices and serve.

Q&A

What's the best way to light a charcoal fire?

We find that a chimney starter, also called a flue starter, is your best bet. A chimney starter is foolproof and it eliminates the need for lighter fluid, which can impart harsh, acrid flavors to food. We strongly recommend that you visit a hardware store (or other shop that sells grilling equipment) and purchase this indispensable device (or see the illustrations on page 249 on how to make your own).

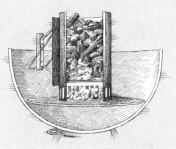

To use a chimney starter, place several sheets of crumpled newspaper in the lower chamber and set the starter on the bottom grate of a kettle grill (where the charcoal will eventually go); the top cooking grate should not be in place. Fill the upper chamber with as much charcoal as directed. Light the newspaper through the holes in the side of the chimney starter and wait until the coals at the top of the pile are covered with fine gray ash. (This will take about 20 minutes.) Dump the lit charcoal in the bottom of the grill and arrange as directed. (For additional firepower, add more unlit charcoal and wait until it has caught fire before grilling.) You can then set the cooking grate in place, allow it to heat up, and then clean it. After that, you are ready to grill.

Note that after you empty the lit charcoal into the grill, the starter will still be very hot. Don't put it down on the lawn—it will burn the grass. Instead, set the starter on a concrete or stone surface away from any flammable objects and allow it to cool off for at least half an hour. Make sure you choose a spot away from children and pets.

TECHNIQUE: Making Your Own Chimney Starter

Although a chimney starter is relatively inexpensive (about $15 to $25), you may want to save money and improvise with an empty 39-ounce coffee can that has had both ends removed with a can opener. Note that there are two drawbacks to this method. Because the improvised starter has no handles, you must maneuver it with long-handled tongs. Also, because of its size, this improvised starter can't light enough charcoal for most grilling jobs; you will need to add unlit coals once the lit coals have been dumped onto the charcoal grate.

1. Using a church-key can opener, punch six holes along the lower circumference of the can.

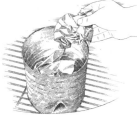

2. Set the can on the charcoal grate with the triangular holes at the bottom. Load the can about one-half full with crumpled newspaper and top it off with charcoal.

3. Insert a long match through one of the triangular holes at the bottom to set the crumpled paper on fire.

4. When the coals are lit (after about 20 minutes), use tongs to grasp the top of the starter and dump its contents onto the charcoal grate. Place more coals loosely around and on top of the burning coals to build up a cooking fire.

VARIATIONS

GRILL-ROASTED PORK LOIN FOR A GAS GRILL

1. Follow the recipe for Grill-Roasted Pork Loin for a Charcoal Grill through step 2. Instead of using wood chunks, soak 2 cups wood chips in cold water to cover for 30 minutes; drain. Place the chips in a small disposable aluminum pan.

2. About 20 minutes before grilling, place the wood-chip pan on the primary burner (the burner that will remain on during cooking); position the cooking grate. Ignite the grill, turn all the burners to high, cover, and heat until very hot and the chips are smoking, about 15 minutes. (If the chips ignite, use a water-filled squirt bottle to extinguish them.) Scrape the cooking grate clean with a grill brush.

3. Continue with the recipe from step 4, turning off all the burners except the primary burner after browning the pork.

CHILI-MUSTARD SPICE RUB

Makes about 2 tablespoons

This rub packs some heat, so use the lesser amount of cayenne if you want a milder rub.

2	teaspoons chili powder
2	teaspoons powdered mustard
1	teaspoon ground cumin
½–1	teaspoon cayenne

Combine all the ingredients in a small bowl.

SWEET AND SAVORY SPICE RUB

Makes about 2 tablespoons

Toasting the spice seeds before grinding them intensifies their flavors.

1	tablespoon cumin seeds
1½	teaspoons coriander seeds
1	teaspoon fennel seeds
½	teaspoon ground cinnamon
¼	teaspoon ground allspice

Combine the cumin, coriander, and fennel in a small skillet; toast over medium heat until fragrant, about 2 minutes, shaking the skillet occasionally. Cool to room temperature and grind coarse. Transfer to a small bowl; stir in the cinnamon and allspice.

EQUIPMENT CORNER: Kitchen Twine

A RECIPE CALLS FOR KITCHEN TWINE, BUT THE ONLY twine you have is a skein from the hardware store. Should you use it? Probably not. Because it's not intended for use with food, it's probably not food-safe. Still, we thought we'd give it a try, pressing into service some nylon twine from the hardware store. Although it didn't melt or burn, the Day-Glo yellow colorant leached onto the pork roast we had tied with it.

A common recommended alternative to kitchen twine is unwaxed dental floss, but it is so thin that while being tied on to a piece of meat it often cuts through it. After cooking, this whitish, almost translucent filament is all but invisible and so can be difficult to remove. We also found that dental floss is particularly ill suited to grilling because it easily singes and then breaks. You can also forget about butchers' netting, which is a pain to apply and which brought most of the crust with it when we cut it off the cooked meat.

As for bona fide kitchen twine, you can buy cotton or linen. Though linen twine is thin, it did not cut into the meat and our testers liked it because it held the beginnings of a knot especially well and was therefore very easy to tie. In addition, it pulled away from the cooked meat easily, taking a minimum amount of seared crust with it. That said, cotton twine worked nearly as well as linen and is a more economical choice. Look for a midweight cotton twine. The thin, 4-ply twine cut into the meat much like the dental floss, and the heavy, 30-ply twine inhibited crust formation on the grill, then pulled off big bits of crust when we removed it. Of the four weights we tested, we liked 16-ply best.

Rating Kitchen Twine

WE TESTED EIGHT DIFFERENT TYPES OF TWINE (FIVE WERE ACTUALLY KITCHEN TWINE AND THREE WERE alternatives) to see which performed best when used to tie a roast. The twines are listed in order of preference. See www.americastestkitchen.com for up-to-date prices and mail-order sources for top-rated products.

RECOMMENDED
Linen Kitchen Twine with Dispenser (3,000 feet)
$5.99
This twine resisted taking crust with it when removed, but it's more expensive per foot than poly/cotton twine.

RECOMMENDED
16-ply Polyester/Cotton Kitchen Twine (medium thickness)
$6.85 for 1-lb. cone
This was strong, easy to handle, economical, and caused a minimal loss of crust when removed.

RECOMMENDED
All Cotton Kitchen Twine
$3.49
This medium-thickness twine was fine.

NOT RECOMMENDED
18-ply Twisted Nylon Household String (colored)
$4.49
The nylon didn't melt, but the coloring did leach into the meat. It's not necessarily food-safe.

NOT RECOMMENDED
30-ply Polyester/Cotton Kitchen Twine (thick)
$6.85
This was too thick and inhibited browning.

NOT RECOMMENDED
Unflavored, Unwaxed Dental Floss
$1.79
So thin that it can cut into the meat when you tie it on. Also, it's not strong enough for the grill—if it doesn't dissolve or break while it's on the grill, then it's very difficult to remove from the cooked roast because it becomes nearly invisible.

NOT RECOMMENDED
4-ply Polyester/Cotton Kitchen Twine (thin)
$6.85
Like the floss, this began to cut into the meat.

NOT RECOMMENDED
Elastic String Butcher's Netting (30-inch length, small size)
$1.30
Available in five sizes and we tried the smallest. Stuffing the beef tenderloin into this netting was a major pain. Then, when we removed the netting after the meat was cooked, almost every bit of our lovely crust came with it.

FRENCH POTATO SALAD

WHAT WE WANTED: Tender sliced potatoes in a well-balanced vinaigrette rich with garlic and herbs.

Having little in common with its American counterpart, French potato salad is served warm or at room temperature and is composed of sliced potatoes glistening with olive oil, white wine vinegar, and plenty of fresh herbs. We knew we wanted to go the traditional route and use red potatoes for our salad. Red potatoes don't crumble when cut into slices and are therefore more aesthetically pleasing for a composed salad.

We expected quick success with this seemingly simple recipe—how hard could it be to boil a few potatoes and toss them in vinaigrette? We sliced the potatoes, dressed them while they were still warm (warm potatoes are more absorbent than cool ones), and served them up. Our confidence plummeted as taster after taster remarked on how dull and bland our salad was.

We shifted our focus toward the vinaigrette ingredients, all traditional components of French potato salad: olive oil, white wine vinegar, herbs, mustard, minced onion, chicken stock, and white wine. We decided to experiment with each component until we found a surefire way to pump up the flavor.

The first improvement came by using slightly more vinegar than is called for in the test kitchen's standard formula for vinaigrette, 4 parts oil to 1 part vinegar. These bland potatoes could handle extra acid. We loved the sharp flavor notes added by champagne vinegar but found that white wine vinegar worked well, too. As for the olive oil, extra-virgin or pure olive oil made an equally good base for the dressing; tasters found little distinction between the two (the former being more flavorful than the latter), presumably because of the other potent ingredients in the vinaigrette. However, expensive fruity olive oils were rejected for their overpowering nature—we didn't want it masking the other flavors.

We liked the extra moisture and layer of complexity that chicken stock (or broth) and wine added (salads made strictly with oil and vinegar were a tad dry), but it seemed wasteful to uncork a bottle or open a can to use only a few tablespoons.

We found a solution to this problem and a revelation when we consulted Julia Child's *The Way to Cook* (Knopf, 1989). She suggests adding some of the potato cooking water to the vinaigrette, a quick and frugal solution that also added plenty of potato flavor and a nice touch of saltiness. Two teaspoons of Dijon mustard and a sprinkle of ground black pepper perked things up, while the gentle assertiveness of minced shallot and a partially blanched garlic clove (raw garlic was too harsh) added even more depth. As for the fresh herbs, we made salads with all manner of them, including chives, dill, basil, parsley, tarragon, and chervil. But an inherently French fines herbes mixture seemed appropriate in theory and was heavenly in reality. Chives, parsley, tarragon, and chervil make up this classic quartet with its anise undertones.

The last but not least fine point: How to toss the cooked, warm potatoes with the vinaigrette without damaging the slices? The solution was simple. We carefully laid the potatoes in a single layer on a rimmed baking sheet, then poured the vinaigrette over them. Spreading out the potatoes in this way also allowed them to cool off a bit, preventing residual cooking and potential mushiness. While we let the vinaigrette soak into the potatoes, we had just enough time to chop the herbs and shallot before sprinkling them on the finished salad.

WHAT WE LEARNED: A little extra vinegar—more than we would normally call for in a vinaigrette—adds a pleasing sharpness, while some reserved potato water adds just the right amount of moisture and saltiness to the salad. Pour the vinaigrette over the potatoes rather than tossing the two together to keep the potato slices intact.

FRENCH POTATO SALAD

Serves 4 to 6

If fresh chervil isn't available, substitute an additional ½ table-spoon of minced parsley and an additional ½ teaspoon of minced tarragon. For best flavor, serve the salad warm, but to make ahead, follow the recipe through step 2, cover with plastic wrap, and refrigerate. Before serving, bring the salad to room temperature, then add the shallot and herbs.

- 2 pounds (about 6 medium or 18 small) red potatoes, scrubbed and cut into ¼-inch-thick slices
- 2 tablespoons salt
- 1 medium garlic clove, peeled and threaded on a skewer
- 1½ tablespoons champagne vinegar or white wine vinegar
- 2 teaspoons Dijon mustard
- ¼ cup olive oil
- ½ teaspoon ground black pepper
- 1 small shallot, minced (about 2 tablespoons)
- 1 tablespoon minced fresh chervil leaves
- 1 tablespoon minced fresh parsley leaves
- 1 tablespoon minced fresh chives
- 1 teaspoon minced fresh tarragon leaves

1. Place the potatoes, 6 cups cold water, and the salt in a large saucepan. Bring to a boil over high heat, then reduce the heat to medium. Lower the skewered garlic into the simmering water and blanch, about 45 seconds. Immediately run the garlic under cold tap water to stop the cooking process; remove the garlic from the skewer and set aside. Simmer the potatoes, uncovered, until tender but still firm (a thin-bladed paring knife can be slipped into and out of the center of a potato slice with no resistance), about 5 minutes. Drain the potatoes, reserving ¼ cup cooking water. Arrange the hot potatoes close together in a single layer on a rimmed baking sheet.

2. Press the garlic through a garlic press or mince by hand. Whisk the garlic, reserved potato cooking water, vinegar, mustard, oil, and pepper together in a small bowl until combined. Drizzle the dressing evenly over the warm potato slices; let stand 10 minutes.

3. Meanwhile, toss the shallot and herbs gently together in a small bowl. Transfer the potatoes to a large serving bowl. Add the shallot-herb mixture and mix lightly with a rubber spatula to combine. Serve immediately.

VARIATIONS

FRENCH POTATO SALAD WITH ARUGULA, ROQUEFORT, AND WALNUTS

Follow the recipe for French Potato Salad, omitting the herbs and tossing the dressed potatoes with ½ cup walnuts, toasted and chopped coarse, 4 ounces Roquefort cheese, crumbled, and 1 small bunch arugula, washed, dried, stemmed, and torn into bite-sized pieces (about 3 cups), along with the minced shallot in step 3.

FRENCH POTATO SALAD WITH RADISHES, CORNICHONS, AND CAPERS

Follow the recipe for French Potato Salad, omitting the herbs and substituting 2 tablespoons minced red onion for the shallot. Toss the dressed potatoes with 2 medium red radishes, thinly sliced (about ⅓ cup), ¼ cup capers, rinsed and drained, and ¼ cup cornichons, thinly sliced, along with the red onion in step 3.

FRENCH POTATO SALAD WITH HARD SALAMI AND GRUYÈRE

Follow the recipe for French Potato Salad, omitting the herbs and substituting 2 teaspoons whole-grain mustard for the Dijon mustard and 2 tablespoons minced red onion for the shallot. Toss the dressed potatoes with 3 ounces hard salami, cut into ¼-inch matchsticks, 2 ounces Gruyère, very thinly sliced or shaved with a vegetable peeler, and 1 tablespoon minced fresh thyme leaves along with the red onion in step 3.

GETTING IT RIGHT: Label Sleuthing

Freshness matters when buying mustard, especially if you want a spread with heat. Some labels clearly indicate a use-by date, while others rely on cryptic manufacture dates or lot numbers. Eventually, we cracked these codes, but our advice is to buy one of the recommended brands on page 257 with a use-by date, choosing a jar with the most distant date.

TASTING LAB: Dijon Mustards

ASK MOST AMERICANS HOW THEY USE MUSTARD, AND THEY will report smearing it on a ballpark or backyard barbecue hot dog—a pretty humble application. Dijon mustard from France, however, is considered anything but humble. A lofty version of a common condiment, real Dijon mustard has culinary clout, and some are as revered as a great wine.

Many Dijon mustards, however, are actually manufactured here in the United States. (Grey Poupon, for example, is produced in this country by Nabisco.) Conventional wisdom has it that real French mustard must be superior to its made-in-America brethren, a notion that we set out to confirm or deny. We placed a call to Barry Levenson, founder and curator of the Mount Horeb Mustard Museum, who helped us assemble samples of eight popular Dijon mustards from France and America to taste—twice, by the end of our saga—in blind tests. The results were, to say the least, an education in the mysteries of mustard.

First, a word about how mustard is made. Mustard comes by its characteristic heat naturally. The plant that produces mustard seeds, the basis of all mustard, belongs to the Cruciferae family, in the genus *Brassica*. So do horseradish, turnips, radishes, cabbage, and watercress, all noted in varying degrees for their sharp flavor.

Three types of mustard seeds are used to make mustard: yellow (*Brassica hirta*), black (*Brassica nigra*), and brown (*Brassica juncea*). Black and brown seeds are hotter, so they produce spicier condiments. Real Dijon mustard is based on brown, or sometimes black, seeds, which are almost identical chemically. Milder yellow seeds are used to make American, or ballpark-style, yellow mustard.

While mustard preferences are largely subjective (some like it hot and some don't), tasters did agree on the importance of several characteristics. With regard to flavor, we all thought that pungency, acidity, and saltiness should be well balanced and that any aftertaste should be clean, melodious, and free of any off flavors that tasters could perceive

as musty, plasticky, metallic, artificial, or fishy. Tasters also sought a smooth texture that was neither too thick nor too thin. In terms of heat, even the most sensitive palates sought a moderate to assertive level. According to our tasters, insufficient or excessive spiciness was grounds for poor ratings.

Now to answer our initial question about whether real Dijon mustard—the stuff that is made in France—is better than American products such as Nabisco's Grey Poupon. The answer is an unequivocal no. After tallying our results we found that we could recommend five brands, and only two of them, Roland Extra Strong and Delouis Fils, were French. The other three—Grey Poupon (maybe the guys in the limos in the Grey Poupon ads know something after all), French's Napa Valley Style Dijon, and Barhyte—were American-made. Of the three brands that we could not recommend, one was French and two were American.

To explain this bizarre outcome, we turned to our food lab, which analyzed all of the samples for heat level by measuring the quantity of allyl isothiocyanate, the active ingredient in mustard that gives it heat. Two of the three lowest-rated mustards—Maille and Plochman's—lost points for lack of bite, and their allyl isothiocyanate content gauged fewer than 20 milligrams per kilogram (mg/kg). The third, Inglehoffer, offered more spice (although still less than the top-rated mustards) at 120 mg/kg, but it was downgraded for excessive sweetness (oddly, this American brand contains sugar and balsamic vinegar). The recommended brands were spicier: All but one had allyl isothiocyanate levels between 210 and 420 mg/kg (fourth-place French's Napa brand had a modest heat level of 100 mg/kg).

Shortly after this tasting, we learned that spiciness—a key variable in a mustard's rating—diminishes with age. That means that two jars of the same product, one manufactured last month and the other manufactured last year, will have different levels of spice. Because we did not allow for the relative age of the mustards in our initial tasting, we went back to square one, where we took a crash course in how to decode mustard labels to determine date of manufacture.

Our first step was to call the companies, and we found that the shelf life of mustard is roughly six to 18 months, depending on the packaging material and storage conditions. Delouis Fils prints a lot number on its labels. Barhyte, Maille, and Grey Poupon print a "best if used by" date, and the remaining three brands—French's, Inglehoffer, and Plochman's—include codes designating the date of manufacture. Reviewing the jars from our taste test, we immediately discovered that one of the "not recommended" brands near the bottom of the heat scale, Plochman's, was indeed well past its recommended shelf life. At the time of our tasting, it was nearly two years old.

It seemed that in ignoring freshness, we may have invalidated our tasting results. The obvious remedy was to purchase fresh mustards and do a second tasting and heat analysis. This is exactly what we did and found that the fresher samples were, for the most part, spicier. Two brands, Barhyte and Plochman's, remained consistent from the first sample to the second, while the Delouis Fils, the only brand whose manufacture dates we could not accurately determine, slipped a little in terms of heat. The allyl isothiocyanate levels in the remaining brands, however, increased from the first sample to the second. The most dramatic example was the Inglehoffer, which skyrocketed from a tame 120 mg/kg to an explosive 1,690 mg/kg.

Did the changes in heat level have a significant effect on our recommendations? Interestingly, no. Despite increased spiciness in all of the "not recommended" brands but one (Plochman's), flavor and/or texture flaws kept them at the bottom of the ratings in both tastings. (Plochman's was consistently perceived as too mild to recommend.) All of the recommended mustards retained their rank from the first tasting to the second, largely by dint of their good balance of flavors and favorable texture.

What should you look for, then, when purchasing Dijon mustard? First of all, forget about American versus French. Both our "recommended" and "not recommended" mustards include both French and American products. Second, because mustard quickly loses its heat, a fresher product is always better. Although reading labels is confusing at best, Grey Poupon, the number two mustard in our tasting, does include a "best if used by" date on the label, which gives you a fighting chance at finding the freshest sample on the shelf.

No matter what mustard you choose, though, try not to store it at home for long periods (even our test cooks have been known to store jars of Dijon for years in the refrigerator). Purchase small jars, and replace them frequently.

Rating Dijon Mustards

TWENTY MEMBERS OF THE AMERICA'S TEST KITCHEN STAFF TASTED EIGHT DIJON MUSTARDS, ON PLAIN WHITE BREAD, ON two different occasions. Tasted first were samples purchased at local supermarkets or ordered online (just as any consumer would) without regard to freshness. The second tasting comprised fresher samples, ordered directly from the manufacturer whenever possible. The mustards are listed in order of preference based on their scores in the second tasting. All brands are available in supermarkets nationwide.

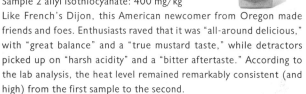

RECOMMENDED
Roland Extra Strong Dijon Mustard
$2.25 for 7 ounces

Sample 1 allyl isothiocyanate: Unavailable
Sample 2 allyl isothiocyanate: 420 mg/kg

An American brand manufactured in France, this cross-national hybrid was widely praised for its excellent flavor balance, having acidity, salt, and heat in pleasing proportions. The heat level was moderate, with the mustard displaying "a nice horseradish flavor."

RECOMMENDED
Grey Poupon Dijon Mustard
$2.69 for 10 ounces

Sample 1 allyl isothiocyanate: 240 mg/kg
Sample 2 allyl isothiocyanate: 840 mg/kg

This mustard is manufactured stateside by Nabisco in accordance with the original recipe from Dijon. Tasters praised its "well-rounded flavor," "nice balance," and "smooth," "creamy" texture. The flavor was "tangy," with a "slight bitterness" and "bite" recalling horseradish. Generally regarded as spicy, the second sample was indeed hotter than the original sample purchased at a supermarket.

RECOMMENDED
Delouis Fils Moutarde de Dijon
$4.50 for 7 ounces

Sample 1 allyl isothiocyanate: 210 mg/kg
Sample 2 allyl isothiocyanate: 110 mg/kg

This French mustard exhibited a multidimensional, deep, well-balanced flavor. Tasters detected sufficient heat, with salt and acidity at levels that pleased them, using phrases such as "straightforward," "pungent," and "tangy." Oddly, some tasters picked up a mild sweetness, while others observed the texture to be slightly "chalky."

RECOMMENDED
French's Napa Valley Style Dijon Mustard
$3.29 for 12 ounces

Sample 1 allyl isothiocyanate: 100 mg/kg
Sample 2 allyl isothiocyanate: 360 mg/kg

Somewhere between powerhouse and wimp when it came to heat, this self-described "truly American Dijon" was indeed deemed friendly to American palates. The majority of tasters received it well, noting its "mild" flavor, "slowly developing heat," and smooth texture.

RECOMMENDED
Barhyte Select Dijon Mustard
$4 for 9 ounces

Sample 1 allyl isothiocyanate: 410 mg/kg
Sample 2 allyl isothiocyanate: 400 mg/kg

Like French's Dijon, this American newcomer from Oregon made friends and foes. Enthusiasts raved that it was "all-around delicious," with "great balance" and a "true mustard taste," while detractors picked up on "harsh acidity" and a "bitter aftertaste." According to the lab analysis, the heat level remained remarkably consistent (and high) from the first sample to the second.

NOT RECOMMENDED
Maille Dijon Originale
$2.99 for 13.4 ounces

Sample 1 allyl isothiocyanate: 20 mg/kg
Sample 2 allyl isothiocyanate: 160 mg/kg

Several tasters swore by this highly esteemed French mustard before stepping into the tasting room, but opinions changed quickly, evidenced by comments such as "dull," "no depth," "pasty," and "soapy aftertaste." A few defenders countered with descriptors such as "smooth," "creamy," "rounded," and "fresh."

NOT RECOMMENDED
Plochman's Premium Dijon
$2.89 for 9 ounces

Sample 1 allyl isothiocyanate: <20 mg/kg
Sample 2 allyl isothiocyanate: <20 mg/kg

Definitely the mildest sample of the bunch, with tasters repeatedly likening this American mustard to plain yellow "ballpark" or "hot dog" mustard. Many tasters picked up on a "fruity sweetness" like that of "cider vinegar" as well as a lingering "pickle" flavor.

NOT RECOMMENDED
Inglehoffer Hot Dijon Mustard
$2.49 for 8 ounces

Sample 1 allyl isothiocyanate: 120 mg/kg
Sample 2 allyl isothiocyanate: 1,690 mg/kg

The overbearing heat of the second sample (hottest of all, according to the lab) was variously described as "crazy," "wicked," "searing," and "painful." Also overbearing was the sweetness (in both samples), attributed to the sugar and balsamic vinegar listed among the ingredients.

Bridget piles tender shreds of pulled pork onto a bun, while Chris cuts squares of cornbread for a classic barbecue meal.

PULLED PORK
CHAPTER 20
& cornbread

IN THIS CHAPTER

THE RECIPES

Barbecued Pulled Pork on a
Charcoal Grill
Barbecued Pulled Pork on a Gas
Grill
Eastern North Carolina Barbecue
Sauce
Mid–South Carolina Mustard
Sauce
Cuban-Style Barbecued Pulled
Pork with Mojo Sauce
Dry Rub for Barbecue

All-Purpose Cornbread
Spicy Jalapeño-Cheddar
Cornbread

EQUIPMENT CORNER

Liquid Measuring Cups
Plastic Wrap

Pulled pork, also called pulled pig and sometimes just plain barbecue, is slow-cooked pork roast that is shredded, seasoned, and then served on a hamburger bun (or sliced white bread) with just enough of your favorite barbecue sauce, a couple of dill pickle chips, and a topping of coleslaw. We wanted to develop a recipe for pulled pork that would rival that found in the best barbecue joints, but not be an all-day affair—or require a trip down South to apprentice with a barbecue pit master.

Cornbread is another barbecue classic, but it goes with many other foods as well. Cornbread may be southern in origin, but as it migrated north, it was translated into a sweeter, cakier bread. We wondered if we could create an all-purpose cornbread that would be a compromise between the two styles. We also wanted to address a shortcoming found in many, regardless of style—weak corn flavor.

With these recipes in tow, you can satisfy barbecue cravings all summer long.

PULLED PORK

Our goal was to devise a procedure for cooking this classic Southern dish that was both doable and delicious. The meat should be tender, not tough, and moist but not too fatty. Most barbecue joints use a special smoker. We wanted to adapt the technique for the grill. We also set out to reduce the hands-on cooking time, which in some recipes can stretch to eight hours of constant fire tending.

There are two pork roasts commonly associated with pulled pork sandwiches: the shoulder roast and the fresh ham. In their whole state, both are massive roasts, anywhere from 14 to 20 pounds. Because they are so large, most butchers and supermarket meat departments cut both the front and back leg roasts into more manageable sizes. The part of the front leg containing the shoulder blade is usually sold as either a pork shoulder roast or a Boston butt and runs from 6 to 8 pounds. The meat from the upper portion of the front leg is marketed as a picnic roast and runs about the same size. The meat from the rear leg is often segmented into three or four separate boneless roasts called a fresh ham or boneless fresh ham roast.

For barbecue, we find it best to choose a cut of meat with a fair amount of fat, which helps keep the meat moist and succulent during long cooking and adds considerably to the flavor. For this reason, we think the pork shoulder roast, or Boston butt, is the best choice. We found that picnic roasts and fresh hams will also produce excellent results, but they are our second choice.

To set our benchmark for quality, we first cooked a Boston butt using the traditional low-and-slow barbecue method. Using a standard 22-inch kettle grill, we lit about two quarts of coals and cooked the roast over indirect heat (with the coals on one side of the grill and the roast on the other), adding about eight coals every half hour or so. It took seven hours to cook a 7-pound roast. While the meat was delicious, tending a grill fire for seven hours is not something many people want to do.

In our next test we tried a much bigger initial fire, with about six quarts of charcoal. After the coals were lit, we placed the pork in a disposable aluminum pan and set it on the grate. The trick to this more intense method is not to remove the lid for any reason until the fire is out three hours later. Because you start with so many coals, it is not necessary to add charcoal during the cooking time.

Unfortunately, the high initial heat charred the exterior of the roast, while the interior was still tough and not nearly fork-tender when we took it off the grill. So we tried a combination approach: a moderate amount of charcoal (more than in the low-and-slow method but less than in the no-peek procedure), cooking the pork roast for three hours on the grill and adding more charcoal four times. We then finished the roast in a 325-degree oven for two hours. This method produced almost the same results as the traditional barbecue, but in considerably less time and with nine fewer additions of charcoal.

We found it helpful to let the finished roast rest wrapped in foil in a sealed paper bag for an hour to allow the meat to reabsorb the flavorful juices. In addition, the sealed bag produces a steaming effect that helps break down any remaining tough collagen. The result is a much more savory and succulent roast. Don't omit this step; it's the difference between good pulled pork and great pulled pork. As with most barbecue, pork roast benefits from being rubbed with a ground spice mixture. However, because the roast is so thick, we find it best to let the rubbed roast "marinate" in the refrigerator for at least three hours and preferably overnight. The salt in the rub is slowly absorbed by the meat and carries some of the spices with it. The result is a more evenly flavored piece of meat.

WHAT WE LEARNED: Use pork shoulder (or Boston butt)—its high fat content keeps the meat moist during the extended cooking process. For extremely tender meat in less time, start the roast on the grill and then transfer it to the oven. Finish by placing the roast in a sealed bag to steam the meat and break down any remaining collagen.

TECHNIQUE: Key Steps to Pulled Pork

1. If using a fresh ham or picnic roast, cut through the skin with the tip of a chef's knife. Slide the blade just under the skin and work around to loosen it while pulling it off with your other hand. Boston butt, or shoulder roast, does not need to be trimmed.

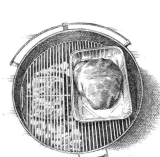

2. Set the unwrapped roast, which has been placed in a disposable aluminum pan barely larger than the meat itself, on the cooking grate opposite the coals and the wood.

3. After cooking, as soon as the meat is cool enough to handle, remove the meat from the bones and separate the major muscle sections with your hands.

4. Remove as much fat as desired and tear the meat into thin shreds.

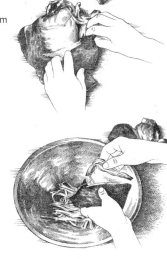

TECHNIQUE: Using a Charcoal Grill for Indirect Cooking

1. Pile the lit coals on one half of the grill and leave the other half free of coals.

2. Place soaked and drained wood chunks or a foil packet filled with wood chips on top of the coals. Set the top grate in position, heat briefly, and then scrape the grate clean with a grill brush. You are now ready to cook over the cooler part of the fire. Put the food on the grill and set the lid in place. Open the air vents as directed in individual recipes.

3. A grill thermometer inserted through the vents on the lid can tell you if the fire is too hot or if the fire is getting too cool and you need to add more charcoal. You will get different readings depending on where the lid vents are and thus where the thermometer is in relation to the coals. Because you want to know the temperature where the food is being cooked, rotate the lid so that the thermometer is close to the food. Make sure, however, that the thermometer stem does not touch the food.

BARBECUED PULLED PORK ON A CHARCOAL GRILL

Serves 8

Pulled pork can be made with a fresh ham or picnic roast, although our preference is for Boston butt. If using a fresh ham or picnic roast, remove the skin (see illustration 1 on page 261). Preparing pulled pork requires little effort but lots of time. Plan on 10 hours from start to finish: 3 hours with the spice rub, 1 hour to come to room temperature, 3 hours on the grill, 2 hours in the oven, and 1 hour to rest. Wood chunks help flavor the meat; hickory is the traditional choice with pork, although mesquite can be used if desired. Serve the pulled pork on plain white bread or warmed buns with the classic accompaniments of dill pickle chips and coleslaw. You will need a disposable aluminum roasting pan that measures about 10 inches by 8 inches as well as heavy-duty aluminum foil and a brown paper grocery bag.

¾ cup Dry Rub for Barbecue (page 265)
1 bone-in pork roast, preferably Boston butt (6 to 8 pounds)
4 (3-inch) wood chunks
2 cups barbecue sauce (see pages 263–264)

1. Massage the dry rub into the meat. Wrap the meat tightly in a double layer of plastic wrap and refrigerate for at least 3 hours. (For stronger flavor, the roast can be refrigerated for up to 3 days.)

2. At least 1 hour prior to cooking, remove the roast from the refrigerator, unwrap, and let it come to room temperature. Soak the wood chunks in cold water to cover for 1 hour and drain.

3. Meanwhile, light a large chimney starter filled a bit less than halfway with charcoal briquettes (about 2½ quarts, or about 40 briquettes) and allow to burn until all the charcoal is covered with a layer of fine gray ash. Empty the coals into the grill; build a modified two-level fire by spreading the coals onto one side of the grill, piling them up in a mound

2 or 3 briquettes high, leaving the other half with no coals. Open the bottom vents completely. Place the soaked wood chunks on the coals. Position the cooking grate over the coals, cover the grill, and heat until hot, about 5 minutes (you can hold your hand 5 inches above the coals for 2 seconds). Use a grill brush to scrape the cooking grate clean.

4. Set the unwrapped roast in a disposable aluminum pan (see note) and place it on the grate opposite the fire (see illustration 2 on page 261). Open the grill lid vents three-quarters of the way and cover, turning the lid so that the vents are opposite the wood chunks to draw smoke through the grill. Cook, adding about 8 briquettes every hour or so to maintain an average temperature of 275 degrees, for 3 hours.

5. Adjust an oven rack to the middle position and heat the oven to 325 degrees. Wrap the pan holding the roast with heavy-duty foil to cover completely. Place the pan in the oven and cook until the meat is fork-tender, about 2 hours.

6. Slide the foil-wrapped pan with the roast into a brown paper bag. Crimp the end shut. Let the roast rest for 1 hour.

TECHNIQUE: Using a Gas Grill for Indirect Cooking

Remove part or all of the cooking grate. Place a foil tray with soaked wood chips on top of the primary burner. Make sure the tray is resting securely on the burner so that it will not tip. Replace the cooking grate. Light all the burners and cover the grill. When you see a lot of smoke (after about 20 minutes), turn off the burner (or burners) without chips and place the food over it (or them). If the chips start to flame, douse the fire with water from a squirt bottle. Cover the grill.

7. Transfer the roast to a cutting board and unwrap. When cool enough to handle, "pull" the pork by separating the roast into muscle sections, removing the fat, if desired, and tearing the meat into thin shreds with your fingers (see illustrations 3 and 4 on page 261). Place the shredded meat in a large bowl. Toss with 1 cup of the barbecue sauce, adding more to taste. Serve, passing the remaining sauce separately.

VARIATIONS
BARBECUED PULLED PORK ON A GAS GRILL

1. Follow the recipe for Barbecued Pulled Pork on a Charcoal Grill through step 2. Soak 4 cups wood chips in cold water to cover for 30 minutes; drain. Place the wood chips in a small disposable aluminum pan.

2. Place the wood-chip pan on the primary burner (the burner that will remain on during cooking). (See the illustration at left.) Ignite the grill, turn all the burners to high, cover, and heat until very hot and the chips are smoking heavily, about 20 minutes. (If the chips ignite, use a water-filled squirt bottle to extinguish them.) Turn the primary burner down to medium and turn off the other burner(s). Set the unwrapped roast in the disposable pan, position the pan over the cooler part of the grill, and close the lid. Barbecue for 3 hours. (The temperature inside the grill should be a constant 275 degrees; adjust the lit burner as necessary.) Proceed as directed from step 5 of the recipe.

EASTERN NORTH CAROLINA BARBECUE SAUCE

Makes about 2 cups
This sauce contains no tomato but is rich with heat and vinegar.

- 1 cup distilled white vinegar
- 1 cup cider vinegar
- 1 tablespoon sugar
- 1 tablespoon red pepper flakes
- 1 tablespoon hot pepper sauce, such as Tabasco
  Salt and ground black pepper

Mix all of the ingredients, including salt and pepper to taste, together in a medium bowl. (The sauce can be refrigerated in an airtight container for several days.)

MID–SOUTH CAROLINA MUSTARD SAUCE

Makes about 2½ cups

- 1   cup cider vinegar
- 1   cup vegetable oil
- 6   tablespoons Dijon mustard
- 2   tablespoons maple syrup or honey
- 4   teaspoons Worcestershire sauce
- 2   teaspoons salt
- 1   teaspoon hot pepper sauce, such as Tabasco
     Ground black pepper

Mix all of the ingredients, including black pepper to taste, together in a medium bowl. (The sauce can be refrigerated in an airtight container for several days.)

CUBAN-STYLE BARBECUED PULLED PORK WITH MOJO SAUCE

Mojo sauce (recipe follows) is a citrus-flavored Cuban sauce served with pork. Rice with black beans is an excellent accompaniment to this dish. The use of wood for flavoring is not traditional in this dish and can be omitted if you prefer to keep the emphasis on the pork and seasonings.

Mix 9 medium garlic cloves, minced or pressed through a garlic press (about 3 tablespoons), 3 tablespoons extra-virgin olive oil, 1 tablespoon ground cumin, 1 tablespoon dried oregano, 1 tablespoon salt, 2 teaspoons brown sugar, and 1½ teaspoons ground black pepper together in a small bowl. Follow the recipe for Barbecued Pulled Pork (charcoal or gas), replacing the Dry Rub for Barbecue with the garlic mixture. Proceed with the recipe, omitting the barbecue sauce. To serve, pass Mojo Sauce separately with the pulled pork.

MOJO SAUCE

Makes 1 generous cup

This citrusy Cuban sauce is delicious with pork.

- ½   cup extra-virgin olive oil
- 6   medium garlic cloves, minced or pressed through a garlic press (about 2 tablespoons)
- ½   teaspoon ground cumin
- ½   cup orange juice
- ¼   cup juice from 4 limes
- 1   teaspoon salt
- ½   teaspoon ground black pepper

1. Heat the oil in a small, deep saucepan over medium heat until shimmering. Add the garlic and cumin and cook until fragrant but not browned, 30 to 45 seconds.

2. Remove the pan from the heat and add the orange juice, lime juice, salt, and pepper carefully, as the mixture may splatter. Place the pan back on the heat, bring to a simmer, and cook for 1 minute. Remove the pan from the heat and cool the sauce to room temperature. (The sauce can be refrigerated in an airtight container for up to 3 days.)

DRY RUB FOR BARBECUE

Makes about 1 cup

You can adjust the proportions of spices in this all-purpose rub or add or subtract a spice, as you wish. For instance, if you don't like spicy foods, reduce the cayenne. Or, if you are using hot chili powder, eliminate the cayenne entirely.

4	tablespoons sweet paprika
2	tablespoons chili powder
2	tablespoons ground cumin
2	tablespoons dark brown sugar
2	tablespoons salt
1	tablespoon dried oregano
1	tablespoon sugar
1	tablespoon ground black pepper
1	tablespoon ground white pepper
1–2	teaspoons cayenne pepper

Mix all of the ingredients together in a small bowl.

EQUIPMENT CORNER: Liquid Measuring Cups

FOR YEARS, THE TERM "LIQUID MEASURING CUP" MEANT one thing: a flared, graded cup with a handle, usually made from Pyrex-brand glass. No longer. Nowadays, the ubiquitous Pyrex shares retail shelf space with cups sporting a dizzying array of newfangled options, including gleaming metals, angled consoles, laboratory-style beaker shapes, and gradations broken down to number of teaspoons.

Do these innovations go beyond bells and whistles? Is it finally time to upgrade from the classic Pyrex? We brought 11 models into the test kitchen to find out.

There's a clear distinction between liquid measuring cups and dry. A liquid measuring cup has multiple gradation lines. Dry measuring cups have none—there's a different cup for every amount.

Dry ingredients and wet ingredients are also measured differently. The test kitchen measures the dry sort by dipping the cup into the ingredient, scooping a heaping cupful, then sweeping across the cup with a spatula (or the flat side of a knife) until the contents are level with the top of the cup—a method referred to as "dip and sweep."

We measure liquids by filling the cup until the surface of the liquid is even with the correct gradation line when viewed at eye level (which means stooping down to look). So far, so good—but be careful which part of the surface you're looking at. Liquids in a container have a tendency to form a meniscus, a slight curving of the surface. (The meniscus forms because water molecules are more attracted to the cup material than to one another, so they creep up the sides a bit.) When viewed from the side of the cup, the meniscus looks like a "cord" around the top of the liquid. To maximize accuracy, simply measure from the bottom of the cord, not the top.

As we began our tests, it became obvious that metal is absolutely the wrong choice of material for liquid measuring cups: There's no way to view the gradation lines at eye level, much less spot the bottom of the meniscus. Was it fair to dismiss metal cups based solely on our meniscus-reading theory? Not, we reasoned, if accuracy were only negligibly affected. So we had 12 test-kitchen staffers measure 1 cup of water from the sink with each model, then pour the water into a waiting bowl. As testers focused on making comments about each model's design (ease of pouring, handle shape, etc.), we were busy weighing the amount of water they'd managed to transfer to the bowl. Now we had proof. The only two cups off by more than half an ounce were made of metal: All-Clad, which was an average of 0.73 ounce over, and Polder, which averaged a whopping 1.1 ounces over—that's 6.6 extra teaspoons per cup!

As we watched panelists measure water with each model, another pattern emerged: They seemed to be filling the plastic cups at a faster pace. Puzzled, we pored through the testing sheets. Comments of "nice, flat water line" and "easy-to-read meniscus" popped up repeatedly for the plastic cups but never for the glass. Additional research uncovered an interesting bit of physics: Water molecules are more attracted to glass than to plastic, so less surface curvature occurs with plastic cups—an enhanced clarity testers appreciated.

Sometimes lack of clarity affected accuracy; other times, it was simply irritating. For instance, testers were annoyed by the sheer number of markings on some of the models, with column after column obsessively delineating useless equivalent measures in cups, third-cups, quarter-cups, milliliters, cubic centimeters, tablespoons, and more. As one tester put it, "I've never made a recipe that calls for 78 teaspoons of anything."

Less may be more, but not if it's ridiculously less. The All-Clad had just three gradation lines (¼ cup, ½ cup, ¾ cup); nowhere except for the discarded packaging was there an indication that its full capacity was 1 cup. Other models, which performed well in every test, inexplicably had no ⅓-cup gradation markings.

The most innovative cup of the bunch, the Oxo Angled, represents an attempt to eliminate stooping altogether. The gradation lines, printed both on the sides and on a diagonal plane that juts through the cup, are designed to be read from above rather than at eye level. However, the multiple planes created an awkward optical effect: The meniscus line on the interior of the cup seemed out of phase with the one on the side, as though they were at different levels.

To minimize spillage, liquid measures should feature extra space between the uppermost gradation marking and the rim. Two of our models lacked this buffer zone, making liquid transfer a daunting task.

Measuring, then transferring, cups of honey with each model convinced us of the virtues of roomy, rounded interiors. The skinnier designs had us reaching for our smallest spatulas, while the wider models made honey transfer quick work even with a standard-size spatula. The Oxo Angled was the loser in this round: Its multiple planes provided numerous edges where honey could take refuge.

In the test kitchen, we often ladle hot chicken broth into a measuring cup before adding it to a simmering saucepan. It's a task that doesn't go so smoothly with a narrow-mouthed cup. Broth dribbled down the sides of the three narrowest cups: the Norpro Measuring Glass, the Catamount Flameware, and the All-Clad.

The broth test earned plastic cups some new fans by staying noticeably cooler than the glass. That said, many staffers still weren't ready to give up on the classic Pyrex, even though the plastic matched the glass in the dishwasher and microwave challenges. But little did we know that the plastic cups would soon win over a few more testers.

One afternoon, toward the end of testing, we were engrossed in a spirited debate of our tentative chart order, and that's when the Catamount Flameware bit the dust. There it lay, glass shards strewn across the test kitchen's slip-resistant floors. A moment of shocked silence. Then eerie calm: "I think the Pyrex would have survived," one of us said, resuming the original debate.

That's all it took. We quickly cleared out a section of the test kitchen, donned safety goggles, and lined up the surviving models along the countertop. In front of a rapt crowd of onlookers ("I can't not look!" exclaimed one wide-eyed test cook), we dropped each cup three times from a height of 3 feet by tipping it off the countertop. The cups made of metal or plastic survived with mere scratches. The Norpro Measuring Glass lasted one drop before exploding into hundreds of pieces. The thick-glass Pyrex and Anchor Hocking? Three drops, no mess.

The rubber surface victories were impressive, but how would these invincible glass cups fare with a tile kitchen floor? We moved our experiment to a tile-floored restroom. Using a 2½-foot-high shelf as a stand-in for the countertop, we dropped our nine intact cups once again. The metals and the plastics got a bit more banged up (the Polder suffered a dent). And, yes, the Pyrex and the Anchor Hocking met their demise with a smash.

At the end of the day, then, which cup do we recommend? The fancy, stylish pretenders to the Pyrex throne failed to overthrow the king. But as we swept up the king's remains from the tile floor, we crowned the not-so-fancy Rubbermaid—with its wide mouth, flat meniscus, and stay-cool, sturdy plastic—as a worthy successor.

Rating Liquid Measuring Cups

WE TESTED 11 LIQUID MEASURING CUPS AND RATED THEM BASED ON ACCURACY, DESIGN (DIMENSIONS, SHAPE, GRADATION markings, and material) and durability (whether or not they could withstand repeated dishwasher cycles and a drop to the floor from the counter). The measuring cups are listed in order of preference. See www.americastestkitchen.com for up-to-date prices and mail-order sources for top-rated products.

RECOMMENDED
Rubbermaid Measuring Cup
Plastic $3.79

The roomy, rounded interior made quick work of honey transfer, the wide mouth was optimal for ladling broth, and the plastic kept cool, survived our stress tests, and boasted a flat meniscus. Buy the model with ⅓-cup markings.

RECOMMENDED
Pyrex Measuring Cup
Glass $4.95

Wide mouth, comfortable handle, and readable markings. Residual honey was removed with one swipe of the spatula. A bit heavy, and not for klutzes with tile floors.

RECOMMENDED
Emsa Perfect Beaker
Plastic $4.95

A spacious design with an excellent pour and a nice, shallow meniscus. On the downside, the concave base is a trap for dirty dishwasher water, and some testers complained about units-of-measure overkill.

RECOMMENDED
Anchor Hocking Liquid Measuring Cup
Glass $6.75

The model we tested has raised, see-through markings that testers found hard to read, but the company does make one with flat, colored markings. "This is just like the Pyrex but less balanced," said one panelist, referring to the heavy cup's disproportionately light handle.

RECOMMENDED WITH RESERVATIONS
Cambro Camwear 1-Pint
Plastic $6.90

Thin gradation lines, raised and painted numbers, clean cylindrical shape, and shallow meniscus almost put this cup on top. Not until late in the testing did we notice a flaw: no ⅓-cup markings.

RECOMMENDED WITH RESERVATIONS
Oxo Angled Measuring Cup
Plastic with rubber $7.99

Testers questioned the merits of angled markings: "How much effort does it really save?" Having numbers both on the sides and down the diagonal was distracting, and the multiple planes created an irritating phasing effect—and wasted plenty of honey. Best pour of the bunch.

RECOMMENDED WITH RESERVATIONS
Catamount Flameware Liquid Measuring Cup
Glass $9.95

Flame-safe, ovensafe, dishwasher-safe, microwave-safe—but linoleum-floor-safe would have been a nice touch. The laboratory-style beaker handled most tasks well, but testers didn't trust its sturdiness. The narrow mouth made ladling broth a chore.

NOT RECOMMENDED
Amco See Thru Measuring Cup
Stainless steel with plastic window $11.25

Why make a liquid measure that's only partially see-through? To read the numbers, you must position the handle directly away from you, and there are spouts on every side but the useful one (opposite the handle).

NOT RECOMMENDED
Norpro Measuring Glass
Glass $11.50

Testers were unimpressed with the narrow, spoutless mouth, sloppy pour, and "shimmery" cursive markings. We needed a potholder to finish the hot broth test. Its relative accuracy saved this model from last place.

NOT RECOMMENDED
All-Clad 1-Cup Liquid Measure
Stainless steel $19.99

The packaging says "liquid measure," but testers weren't convinced. Major spillage, sloppy pouring, and unclear markings were this cup's downfalls—not to mention the quick-heating material it's made from.

NOT RECOMMENDED
Polder 4-Cup Measure Cup
Stainless steel $10.00

The 1-cup line was so deep down in this "clunky" behemoth that testers had trouble judging when to stop filling. During the broth test, excess steam made the task even harder, and the metal got piping hot.

CORNBREAD

WHAT WE WANTED: Cornbread with serious corn flavor, a deeply browned crust, and a texture somewhere in between that of the dense skillet bread of the South and its cakey northern counterpart.

Deeply rooted in American culture, cornbread has been around long enough to take on a distinctly different character depending on where it is made. In the South, it has become a squat, savory skillet bread. In cooler northern regions, where it has become more cake than bread, it is light, tender, and generously sweetened. Despite these regional variations in texture and appearance, however, cornbread has remained unfortunately constant in one respect: It often lacks convincing corn flavor.

Wanting to avoid a regional food fight, we figured that everyone north and south of the Mason-Dixon line could agree on one simple notion: Cornbread ought to be rich with the flavor of corn. A deeply browned crust also seemed far from controversial, and when it came to texture, we attempted a reasonable regional compromise: moist and somewhat fluffy but neither cakey nor heavy.

We started out with a northern-style recipe calling for equal amounts of flour and cornmeal. (It is customary for southern-style recipes to minimize or eliminate the flour altogether.) Our first tests involved the cornmeal. The different brands ran the gamut from fine and powdery to coarse and uneven, yielding wild variations in texture, from dry and cottony to downright crunchy, but not one produced very much corn flavor. We quickly came to the conclusion that our recipe, like it or not, would have to call for a national brand of cornmeal to avoid these huge textural swings. The obvious option was Quaker yellow cornmeal, which is available in every supermarket from New Orleans to Portland, Maine. Although our choice may rightfully be considered heretical by many cornbread mavens, it was the only way we could be sure our recipe would deliver consistent results.

Reliable though it is, Quaker cornmeal is degerminated—robbed of the germ (the heart of the kernel) during processing. It is thus also robbed of flavor. (In whole-grain cornmeal, the germ is left intact.) By using degerminated cornmeal, we were now taking a step backward in our quest to build more corn flavor. Increasing the amount of cornmeal to compensate caused the cornbread to lose its lightness. And tasters didn't care for the abundance of hard, crunchy grains. Our next move was to soak the cornmeal in boiling water before mixing it with the other ingredients (a common recipe directive), reasoning that this would both soften the cornmeal and extract more of its flavor. But the added moisture made the cornbread even heavier and slightly rubbery, while contributing not a bit of extra corn flavor. Relenting, we reduced the cornmeal (we now had more flour than cornmeal), which produced the best texture so far and alleviated any grittiness or heaviness.

To boost corn flavor, a few recipes added fresh corn to the batter. While appreciating the sweet corn taste, tasters objected to the tough, chewy kernels. Chopping the corn by hand was time-consuming. Pureeing the corn in the food processor was much quicker and broke down the kernels more efficiently. With pureed corn, our recipe was finally starting to develop a fuller flavor.

The dairy component up until now had been whole milk. To compensate for the extra liquid exuded by the pureed corn, we reduced the amount, but this just made the cornbread bland. We tried substituting a modest amount of buttermilk, which produced both a lighter texture and a tangier flavor. The sweetener also had an effect on texture; honey and maple syrup added nice flavor accents, but they also added moisture. Granulated and light brown sugars made for a better texture, but the light brown sugar did more to accentuate the corn flavor. Two eggs worked well in this bread, offering structure without cakiness. A modest amount of baking powder boosted by a bit of baking soda (to react with the acidic buttermilk) yielded the best rise.

The fat used in cornbread can vary from bacon drippings to melted butter or vegetable oil. Cooking bacon for this relatively quick recipe seemed an unnecessary step, and butter indisputably added more flavor and color than vegetable oil. Because we were already using the food processor for the corn, we decided to avoid dirtying another bowl and added all of the wet ingredients together. We even added the light brown sugar to the wet mix to eliminate the pesky lumps it had been forming in the flour mixture. Then we noticed that some recipes added the melted butter last. This created subtle streaks of unmixed butter in the batter, but, as the bread baked, the butter rose to the surface and created a more deeply browned top crust and a stronger butter flavor. Now our recipe, too, would add the butter last. For the best flavor and texture, our recipe would also add a lot more butter than many others—a whole stick.

Although the increase in butter and the adjustment to the mixing method improved the browning, the bread was still missing a thick and crunchy crust. Southern cornbreads, which usually showcase such a crust, are baked in fat-coated, piping-hot cast-iron skillets. Because some cooks don't own a cast-iron (or any other ovenproof) skillet, we tried an 8-inch square baking dish. Heating it in the oven or on the stovetop before adding the batter was not only awkward but dangerous (especially with Pyrex, which can shatter if handled this way), so we abandoned this idea. Most recipes that call for a baking dish use a moderate oven temperature of 350 degrees. A hotter oven—the kind used in many Southern recipes with a skillet—was better. Baked at 400 degrees, the crust was both crunchy and full of buttery, toasted corn flavor.

WHAT WE LEARNED: To compensate for the distinct lack of corn flavor from degerminated cornmeal, add pureed corn to the batter. Light brown sugar accentuates the corn flavor while buttermilk adds a pleasant tanginess. For a crisp, browned crust without a cast-iron skillet, add the butter last and bake the cornbread at 400 degrees.

ALL-PURPOSE CORNBREAD

Makes one 8-inch square

Before preparing the baking dish or any of the other ingredients, measure out the frozen corn kernels and let them stand at room temperature until thawed. When corn is in season, fresh cooked kernels can be substituted for the frozen corn. This recipe was developed with Quaker yellow cornmeal; a stone-ground whole-grain cornmeal will work but will yield a drier and less tender cornbread. We prefer a Pyrex glass baking dish because it yields a nice golden-brown crust, but a metal baking dish (nonstick or traditional) will also work. The cornbread is best served warm; leftovers can be wrapped in foil and reheated in a 350-degree oven for 10 to 15 minutes.

1½ cups (7½ ounces) unbleached all-purpose flour
1 cup (5½ ounces) yellow cornmeal (see note)
2 teaspoons baking powder
¾ teaspoon salt
¼ teaspoon baking soda
1 cup buttermilk
¾ cup frozen corn kernels, thawed
¼ cup packed light brown sugar
2 large eggs
8 tablespoons (1 stick) unsalted butter, melted
    and cooled slightly

1. Adjust an oven rack to the middle position; heat the oven to 400 degrees. Spray an 8-inch square baking dish with nonstick cooking spray. Whisk the flour, cornmeal, baking powder, salt, and baking soda in a medium bowl until combined; set aside.

2. In a food processor or blender, process the buttermilk, thawed corn kernels, and brown sugar until combined, about 5 seconds. Add the eggs and process until well combined (the corn lumps will remain), about 5 seconds longer.

3. Using a rubber spatula, make a well in the center of the dry ingredients; pour the wet ingredients into the well. Begin folding the dry ingredients into the wet, giving the mixture only a few turns to barely combine; add the melted butter and continue folding until the dry ingredients are just moistened. Pour the batter into the prepared baking dish; smooth the surface with a rubber spatula. Bake until deep golden brown and a toothpick inserted in the center comes out clean, 25 to 35 minutes. Cool on a wire rack 10 minutes; invert the cornbread onto the wire rack, then turn right-side up and continue to cool until warm, about 10 minutes longer. Cut into pieces and serve.

VARIATION

SPICY JALAPEÑO-CHEDDAR CORNBREAD

Shred 4 ounces sharp cheddar cheese (you should have about 1 cup). Follow the recipe for All-Purpose Cornbread, reducing the salt to ½ teaspoon; add ⅜ teaspoon cayenne, 1 medium jalapeño chile, stemmed, seeded, and chopped fine, and half of the shredded cheddar to the flour mixture in step 1 and toss well to combine. Reduce the sugar to 2 tablespoons and sprinkle the remaining cheddar over the batter in the baking dish just before baking.

GETTING IT RIGHT:
A Corny Solution

Fresh   Canned   Frozen

The secret to cornbread with real corn flavor is pretty simple: Use corn, not just cornmeal. We tried fresh cooked corn (cut right from the cob), rinsed canned corn, and thawed frozen corn. Fresh corn was best, but frozen was nearly as good—and a lot easier to use.

EQUIPMENT CORNER: Plastic Wrap

SARAN, THE MARKETING NAME FOR A MATERIAL CALLED Polyvinylidene Chloride, or PVDC, was developed by Dow Chemicals in the 1930s. It was used originally to coat auto upholstery and to seal WWII planes from the salty sea air; in 1953 it was released as a product for domestic use.

Now, of course, there are dozens of plastic wraps on the market, and we wondered if there were any real differences among them. So we gathered six brands—five from supermarket shelves and one food-service brand, available in warehouse clubs or by mail-order, that came enthusiastically recommended by several test-kitchen colleagues. Our tests focused on four things—ability to keep food fresh, strength, microwave resistance, and sealing ability (on glass, ceramic, metal, and plastic bowls).

To test the ability to keep food fresh, we covered bowls of guacamole by pressing the wrap directly onto the surface of the guacamole. Polyvinylidene Chloride (PVDC), the basis of Saran, is said to be less permeable by oxygen than other plastics, specifically Polyethylene and Polyvinyl Chloride (PVC), which is the basis of other wraps. In our tests, though, each seemed impermeable enough. We checked the guacamole every day for signs of discoloration due to exposure to oxygen, and they all looked fine after 24 hours. It wasn't until 72 hours later that they began to discolor.

To test for strength, we wrapped spice-rubbed racks of ribs with each wrap and handled the ribs as we would in a barbecue recipe. No punctures; all the wraps passed this test. Likewise, none of the wraps melted or burst in the microwave tests, unless they came into contact with hot fat (in which case they melted and/or ripped at the point of contact). So far, the wraps were neck and neck in our tests—this was going to come down to seal.

The real differences came when we tried using these wraps to cover bowls made of glass, metal, and plastic. The Glad Press'n Seal stuck to all three, but only if the bowls were perfectly dry. A glass bowl kept in a refrigerator for a

GETTING IT RIGHT: Troubleshooting Pie Pastry

There are three key steps: cutting the fat into the flour, adding the liquid, and rolling out the dough. Use these tips to troubleshoot each of these steps.

COMBINE THE FLOUR AND FAT. Ideally, small lumps of butter should be evenly distributed throughout the dough. In the oven, these lumps will promote the formation of flaky layers. If the butter pieces are too large, the dough will be difficult to roll out. If the butter pieces are completely incorporated into the flour, the crust will be crumbly and cookie-like. When the butter has been properly incorporated into the flour, the largest pieces will be about the size of a pea.

Butter Is Too Lumpy

Butter Is Just Right

Butter Is Too Small

ADD THE RIGHT AMOUNT OF WATER. Our recipe begins with a minimum of water. You will probably need to add more water, depending on the brand of flour and the humidity level in your kitchen. Take a small handful of dough out of the food processor and pinch it together. If the dough seems at all floury or won't hold together, it needs more water. When the dough is properly hydrated, it will form large clumps and no dry flour will remain. The dough can be tacky but not sticky or gluey.

Needs More Water

Perfectly Moistened

ROLL OUT THE DOUGH. The goal here is to shape a perfect circle and fit it into a pie plate. Here are some key points to keep in mind.

Keep it cold. If the dough is too warm, the butter will melt and cause sticking. Chill the dough thoroughly (at least 1 hour) before attempting to roll it out. If the dough is chilled for several hours (or days) it will become rock hard. Let it warm slightly (until pliable) before attempting to roll it out.

Keep it covered. A floured counter will keep dough from sticking but the extra flour can make the dough tough. We prefer to roll dough between sheets of parchment paper or plastic wrap.

Keep it turning. A misshapen piece of dough is hard to fit into a pie plate and often has thinner edges. For a perfect dough round of even thickness, don't keep rolling over the same spot or in the same direction. Starting at the center of the dough, roll away from yourself two or three times, then rotate the disk one-quarter turn and repeat.

EQUIPMENT CORNER: Rolling Pins

ONCE UPON A TIME, ROLLING PINS FELL INTO TWO BASIC camps: standard wooden pins with dowel-style, ball-bearing handles and French rolling pins (also wooden)—basically, solid cylinders with tapered ends. Not anymore. These days, the old standbys compete for space in the bakeware aisle with newfangled models. Made from fancy materials and boasting souped-up ergonomic designs and "deluxe" features, do these new pins make traditional wooden rolling pins passé? We rolled out pie crust, pizza, and tart dough with 10 different pins to find out.

Testing revealed that heavy, brutish marble smashes, rather than rolls, delicate dough. The solid metal pins we tested were also on the heavy side but we had more difficulty with their slippery high-gloss coatings. A nylon pin (usually reserved for work with fondant) works fine but, at $65, is hardly worth the price. Ironically, handles designed specifically for comfort (molded or vertical, upright extensions) are anything but comfortable. Surprisingly, a glass pin proved to be sturdy, but we don't want to find out what it takes to break one of these in our bare hands.

Small scraps of dough stuck to all of the pins, but not enough to hinder their performance. Sticking is usually blamed on warm dough. Stay-cool rolling pins (ice-filled glass or refrigerated marble and metal) are meant to keep rich, buttery dough from melting too quickly. The test kitchen's infrared thermometer revealed that the difference was only a few degrees, not enough to buy you much extra time.

Gimmick-free wooden pins are durable, dirt-cheap, and will manage any task ably. Tapered (French) rolling pins have an edge in versatility. For example, dough that is still too cold to roll easily can be persuaded by a few wallops. Try that with a glass pin. A 20-inch pin is long enough without feeling awkward. Beware of French pins with a diameter smaller than 1½ inches. These are "all taper" and lack a flat surface to ensure a level roll.

Handled-rolling-pin users quickly adapted to tapered pins, but a few felt that handles enable more force to be applied to resilient dough. A plain-Jane wooden version is just fine, but go for at least 12 inches and the largest diameter you can handle without the pin becoming too heavy (smaller diameters and large hands lead to knuckle-imprinted pie dough).

Rating Rolling Pins

WE BROUGHT NINE DIFFERENT PINS INTO THE KITCHEN AND ASKED A VARIETY OF TESTERS WITH DIFFERENT levels of strength and experience and different-sized hands to roll out delicate pâte sucrée (sweet tart dough), pâte brisée (pie dough), and more elastic, resilient pizza dough. The rolling pins are listed in order of preference. See www.americastestkitchen.com for up-to-date prices and mail-order sources for top-rated products.

RECOMMENDED
Fante's French Rolling Pin with Tapered Ends
$8
We like the extra width and weight of this pin. The subtle taper provides more straight rolling surface at the center of the pin, which our testers appreciated.

RECOMMENDED
Fante's Handled Maple Rolling Pin
$12
The handles on this pin provided extra leverage that smaller testers found useful.

RECOMMENDED WITH RESERVATIONS
Fox Run French-Style Straight Wood Rolling Pin
$8
The largest size in this style suited testers with big hands; it was slightly less maneuverable than the tapered models.

RECOMMENDED WITH RESERVATIONS
Matfer Nylon Rolling Pin
$65
This model is genuinely nonstick and easy to handle, but is it worth $65? No.

RECOMMENDED WITH RESERVATIONS
Oxo Good Grips Rolling Pin
$24.99
This pin has nonstick, contoured handles, weighted so that the handles remain upright while rolling, but several testers found this feature uncomfortable.

NOT RECOMMENDED
Bennington Flameware Glass Rolling Pin
$15
This pin can be filled with cold water and/or ice cubes in order to keep the dough cool, and is strong enough for rolling dough, but don't beat a piece of chilled dough flat with it.

NOT RECOMMENDED
Creative Home Marble Rolling Pin
$10
You can chill this pin before using to keep dough cool. But it's so heavy that it obliterates delicate doughs (pâte brisée), and even some sturdy ones (pizza dough).

NOT RECOMMENDED
The Pin Tapered Solid Aluminum Rolling Pin
$35
This pin is too slippery once your hands get greasy, too narrow and light to be really efficient, and offers minimal cooling advantage.

NOT RECOMMENDED
"Italian" Beechwood Wood Rolling Pin w/ Knob Handles
$9
There is no advantage to the knobs on this pin's handles, which allow fingers to drag in the dough.

TASTING LAB: Premium Butters

THE PRINCIPAL DIFFERENCES BETWEEN "REGULAR" butter and "premium" butter are fat content and price. According to U.S. Department of Agriculture standards, all butter must consist of at least 80 percent milk fat. (The rest is mostly water, with some milk solids, too.) Because fat costs money, regular butters rarely contain more than 80 percent. Premium butters have a milk fat content of 82 to 88 percent, which is typical of European butters. That is why these premium butters are often called "European style."

Traditionally, cream was left to sit for a few days and sour slightly before it was churned, giving the butter a subtly tangy and slightly acidic character. Some present-day butter makers attempt to reproduce this flavor by adding a bacterial culture to the cream before agitating it into butter. We included two of these cultured butters in our lineup, in addition to nine high-fat butters that were not cultured.

As a benchmark, we included regular Land O'Lakes butter. We divided these butters into two categories: salted and unsalted. In a preliminary tasting, we discovered that the differences among various premium butters were subtle and nearly disappeared once you started to bake or cook with them. As a result, we only tasted premium butters straight from the package.

Among the salted butters, Land O'Lakes Ultra Creamy was the winner, followed by regular Land O'Lakes butter, which easily held its own against butters costing twice as much. As for the unsalted butters, Land O'Lakes Ultra Creamy was again the winner, although two French butters were close runners-up. This time the regular Land O'Lakes butter finished in the middle of the pack.

So, yes, the Land O'Lakes Ultra Creamy butter is a winner (especially for spreading on toast, where its rich flavor can be appreciated), but you can save money and be quite happy with the company's regular, cheaper product as well.

Rating Premium Salted Butters

TWENTY MEMBERS OF THE AMERICA'S TEST KITCHEN STAFF SAMPLED SIX SALTED BUTTERS. THE BUTTERS WERE allowed to come to room temperature, and tasters were encouraged to sample the butters plain in order to experience their melting properties directly on the tongue. Tasters also spread the butters on baguette slices, which were offered along with seltzer as a palate cleanser. The butters are listed in order of preference based on their scores in this tasting, but all brands are recommended. All brands are sold in supermarkets and gourmet markets nationwide.

RECOMMENDED

Land O'Lakes Ultra Creamy Salted Butter

$2.89 for 8 ounces

This high-fat butter was lighter tasting than some of the other samples but very pleasantly creamy and smooth. A few tasters picked up a "hint of fruitiness," and it had a good salt punch.

RECOMMENDED

Land O'Lakes Regular Salted Butter

$3.69 for 16 ounces

This "regular" butter was well liked for its clean, rich flavor and noticeably creamy mouthfeel. Most tasters considered it "a little light on flavor" but smooth and pleasant. The salt was pronounced.

RECOMMENDED

Lurpak Slightly Salted Danish Butter

$3.99 for 8 ounces

This Danish butter carried a "subtle, delicate nut flavor" and "slight tang." As one taster noted, the "flavor is rich and sweet and complex, but it doesn't have the staying power of some others."

RECOMMENDED

Le Gall Beurre de Baratte de Bretagne Butter with Fleur de Sel

$6.99 for 8.82 ounces

Dense in texture with unexpected nuggets of sea salt, this French butter had "pretty big flavor" and noticeable tang, but it was "intensely salty."

RECOMMENDED

Vermont Butter & Cheese Company Salted Cultured Butter

$3.29 for 8 ounces

Most tasters welcomed the "nice tangy finish" of this cultured butter. "I'd spend money on this," wrote one fan. Another considered it "so buttery it almost tastes artificial."

RECOMMENDED

Kerrygold Pure Irish Butter

$2.59 for 8 ounces

This vivid yellow Irish butter was described as "very rich" and "savory." More than one taster picked up a "grassy" essence, while a couple thought it tasted somewhat musty.

Rating Premium Unsalted Butters

TWENTY MEMBERS OF THE AMERICA'S TEST KITCHEN STAFF SAMPLED SEVEN UNSALTED BUTTERS. THE BUTTERS WERE allowed to come to room temperature, and tasters were encouraged to sample the butters plain in order to experience their melting properties directly on the tongue. Tasters also spread the butters on baguette slices, which were offered along with seltzer as a palate cleanser. The butters are listed in order of preference based on their scores in this tasting, but all brands are recommended. All brands are sold in supermarkets and gourmet markets nationwide.

RECOMMENDED

Land O'Lakes Ultra Creamy Butter

$2.89 for 8 ounces

This butter was "rich," "lush," and "tangy," with a creamy mouthfeel that coated the tongue nicely. More than one taster picked up on subtle lemony notes. It has a fuller flavor than its salted counterpart.

RECOMMENDED

Président Unsalted Butter

$2.99 for 7 ounces

This French butter was "very rich but not terribly complex." Or, as one taster noted, "It's not like 'wow' in the mouth." It still received reputable scores and was well liked for its simplicity and clean flavor.

RECOMMENDED

Celles sur Belle Premium Churned Unsalted Butter

$5.29 for 8.8 ounces

This French butter was extremely neutral in flavor, with little richness but an overall pleasant, clean taste. It also had a nice, slow melt in the mouth, with a creamy finish.

RECOMMENDED

Land O'Lakes Unsalted Sweet Butter

$3.69 for 16 ounces

This supermarket standard was "bland upfront, with a slight, creamy finish," making it "mediocre" overall. It melted quickly but evenly in the mouth—too quickly for some tasters.

RECOMMENDED

Organic Valley European-Style Cultured Butter

$2.99 for 8 ounces

As one taster noted, the tangy flavor of this cultured American butter "takes getting used to . . . good, just different." This butter had a slightly grassy flavor and was one of the creamiest.

RECOMMENDED

Plugrá European-Style Unsalted Butter

$4.99 for 8 ounces

An American brand popular with chefs, Plugrá was considered "best in show" by a few tasters but unbalanced by others. Although less creamy than other butters, it had "a ton of character."

RECOMMENDED

Jana Valley Imported Sweet Cream Butter

$1.99 for 8.8 ounces

This reasonably priced Czech butter was more milky than creamy, which made it seem a little lean compared to the other butters. "Clean and adequate," said one taster, "but it doesn't feel decadent."

A cookie press is convenient to portion spritz cookies, but a pastry bag, fitted with a star tip, can produce a variety of shapes not found in a press and is the choice of the test kitchen.

COOKIES

CHAPTER 24

There seems to be a cookie to fit any occasion or mood. In this chapter we look at two popular cookies, one from each end of the style spectrum—the homey oatmeal and the dainty spritz.

Oatmeal cookies fit into the category of the fuss-free drop cookie: the sturdy dough is dropped by spoonfuls straight onto the baking sheet. But fuss-free doesn't mean problem-free. Oatmeal cookies can be notoriously dense and dry. We wanted a thick, chewy cookie with nicely crisped edges—the type of cookie that we could dunk in a cold glass of milk. There's also the choice of what to include in this cookie. Dried fruit, nuts, and chocolate—we wanted all these standards, but the question was, what kind and how much?

Spritz cookies, Norwegian in origin, are made by pressing the very soft dough through a cookie press or squeezing it through a pastry bag fitted with a shaped tip. Unlike oatmeal cookies, the ingredient list for spritz cookies is markedly short—the flavor and texture of the dough relies almost exclusively on butter. These cookies should have a melt-in-your-mouth texture, and once baked should retain their hallmark swirled shape. Too often, though, these cookies make a better holiday table decoration than a tasty dessert—when bland and flavorless, they're no better than bad shortbread. We aimed to make an elegant spritz cookie with flavor to match.

IN THIS CHAPTER

THE RECIPES

Chocolate-Chunk Oatmeal Cookies with Pecans and Dried Cherries

Spritz Cookies
Spritz Cookies with Lemon Essence
Almond Spritz Cookies

EQUIPMENT CORNER

Cookie Presses

SCIENCE DESK

Convection Ovens
Why Brown Sugar Makes Chewy Cookies

THE ULTIMATE OATMEAL COOKIE

WHAT WE WANTED: A crispy-edged, chewy-in-the-middle loaded oatmeal cookie.

Oatmeal cookies—graced with earthy oat flavor and hearty, chewy texture—can serve as the perfect vehicle for almost any addition, be it spices, chocolate, nuts, or dried fruit. But many recipe writers in pursuit of the "ultimate" oatmeal cookies lapse into a kitchen-sink mentality, overloading the dough with a crazy jumble of ingredients. Peanut Butter–Chocolate-Coconut-Cinnamon-Raisin–Brazil Nut Oatmeal Cookies are a good example. Rather than create yet another cookie monster, our goal was to edit the ultimate oatmeal cookie—delete the unnecessary ingredients and arrive at a perfect combination of oats, nuts, chocolate, and fruit.

A taste test of overloaded oatmeal cookie recipes revealed another problem: poor texture. In our opinion, the ideal oatmeal cookie is crisp around the edges and chewy in the middle. Initial recipe tests produced dry, tough cookies. In addition to trimming the ingredient list, we would have to take a close look at the formula for the dough itself. The ultimate oatmeal cookie—even with just the right amount of added ingredients—would require an ultimately forgiving cookie dough.

We focused first on ingredient selection, and chocolate was at the top of the list. When we pitted semisweet chips against chopped dark and milk chocolates, the bitter edge of the hand-chopped dark chocolate, as well as its irregular distribution in the cookie, gave it the upper hand.

Nuts and oats are natural complements. After sampling pecans, walnuts, hazelnuts, almonds, and peanuts, tasters professed some distinct preferences. Pecans were first for their sweetness and walnuts second for their meatiness, while hazelnuts were liked for their richness and crunch. Almonds were considered bland when paired with the oats, while peanuts overpowered them. Toasting the nuts first deepened their flavor and added more crunch.

Raisins are a familiar addition to oatmeal cookies, but they seemed too sweet in a cookie loaded with chocolate. Tasters felt the same way about flaked coconut and the rest of the tropical gang, including dried pineapple, mango, and papaya. We had better luck with sour cherries and tart cranberries, which offered an assertive tang that stood out against the other additions.

All of the flavor components we wanted were now in place: sweet, tangy, nutty, and chocolatey. But using equal amounts of each (1 cup) did not translate to equal representation. The strong, rich flavor of the chocolate dominated the cookies. Reducing the amount of chocolate to ¾ cup brought the flavors into balance. In a final adjustment, we opted to omit all ground spices (common to most oatmeal cookies), which paired poorly with the chocolate and dried cherries. Cinnamon, nutmeg, and the like were doing more harm than good, and the cookies had plenty of flavor without them.

Cramming almost 3 cups of filling into the test kitchen's favorite oatmeal cookie recipe was taking its toll. Tasters complained about the dry, doorstop-like texture of the cookies—the same problem we had run into with the test recipes. Reducing the oats was a first step in bringing back the chew; the batter was softer and the cookies less dry.

Still looking to add moisture, we turned to the sweetener. Because brown sugar is more moist than white sugar, we thought it might help (see "Why Brown Sugar Makes Chewy Cookies" on page 318). Our working recipe called for a mixture of light brown and granulated sugars. After testing a half-dozen combinations, we found that all dark brown sugar was best; all light brown was next best. Cookies made with brown sugar were much more moist and chewy than cookies made with granulated, and the brown sugar also gave the cookies a rich, dark color and deep caramel flavor.

Fewer oats and all brown sugar—these changes had altered the texture in our favor. But the next modification sealed the deal. The baking powder that we had been using in the recipe was making the cookies crisp from the inside out, a problem since we wanted a chewy interior and a crisp exterior. When we switched the baking powder to baking soda, the cookies puffed in the oven and then collapsed, losing their shape and yielding not a hint of crispy exterior. Because we wanted a combination of crisp edges and chewy centers, we thought that a combination of baking powder and soda might work. Sure enough, this pairing produced cookies that were light and crisp on the outside but chewy, dense, and soft in the center. Because of all the additional ingredients, these cookies required a lot more leavener than regular oatmeal cookies. In the end, we used ¾ teaspoon baking powder and ½ teaspoon baking soda, about twice the leavening power found in a typical oatmeal cookie recipe.

A couple of finishing touches: First, when we were portioning these cookies, we found out that size does matter. Tasters preferred a larger cookie (more contrast between crisp edges and chewy centers), and a spring-loaded ice cream scoop made quick work of this thick dough. Second, though we are normally loath to rotate trays of cookies during baking and usually opt to bake one tray at a time, waiting 40 minutes to bake two batches of cookies seemed a waste of time. Baking both trays at once and rotating the pans was a small inconvenience, but it also cut our time in the kitchen by 20 minutes.

In the end, a moderate hand with ingredients, fewer oats, brown sugar instead of white, and good amounts of baking powder and soda produced a fully loaded—not overloaded—cookie with good chew. It's the ultimate oatmeal cookie, one that packs lots of flavor but delivers on texture, too.

WHAT WE LEARNED: Don't overload the cookies with ingredients. A careful balance of flavors and textures—and a combination of baking powder and soda—allows the cookies to remain crisp around the edges and chewy inside. Less oats and the use of brown sugar keep the cookies moist and chewy. Toast the nuts for extra crunch and use a tart dried fruit, such as sour cherries, to balance the sweetness of the chocolate.

CHOCOLATE-CHUNK OATMEAL COOKIES WITH PECANS AND DRIED CHERRIES

Makes sixteen 4-inch cookies

We like these cookies made with pecans and dried sour cherries, but walnuts or skinned hazelnuts can be substituted for the pecans, and dried cranberries for the cherries. Quick oats used in place of the old-fashioned oats will yield a cookie with slightly less chewiness. If your baking sheets are smaller than the ones described in the recipe, bake the cookies in three batches instead of two. These cookies keep for 4 to 5 days stored in an airtight container or zipper-lock plastic bag, but they will lose their crisp exterior and become uniformly chewy after a day or so. To recrisp the cookies, place them on a baking sheet into a 425-degree oven for 4 or 5 minutes. Make sure to let the cookies cool on the baking sheet for a few minutes before removing them, and eat them while they're warm.

1¼ cups (6¼ ounces) unbleached all-purpose flour
¾ teaspoon baking powder
½ teaspoon baking soda
½ teaspoon salt
1¼ cups old-fashioned rolled oats
1 cup pecans, toasted and chopped
1 cup dried sour cherries, chopped coarse
4 ounces bittersweet chocolate, chopped into chunks about the size of chocolate chips (about ¾ cup)
12 tablespoons (1½ sticks) unsalted butter, softened but still cool
1½ cups (10½ ounces) packed brown sugar, preferably dark
1 large egg
1 teaspoon vanilla extract

1. Adjust the oven racks to the upper- and lower-middle positions; heat the oven to 350 degrees. Line 2 large (18 by 12-inch) baking sheets with parchment paper.

2. Whisk the flour, baking powder, baking soda, and salt in a medium bowl. In a second medium bowl, stir together the oats, pecans, cherries, and chocolate.

3. In a standing mixer, beat the butter and sugar at medium speed until no sugar lumps remain, about 1 minute. Scrape down the sides of the bowl with a rubber spatula; add the egg and vanilla and beat on medium-low speed until fully incorporated, about 30 seconds. Scrape down the bowl; with the mixer running at low speed, add the flour mixture; mix until just combined, about 30 seconds. With the mixer still running on low, gradually add the oat-nut mixture; mix until just incorporated. Give the dough a final stir with the rubber spatula to ensure that no flour pockets remain and the ingredients are evenly distributed.

4. Divide the dough evenly into 16 portions, each about ¼ cup, then roll between your palms into balls about 2 inches in diameter; stagger 8 balls on each baking sheet, spacing them about 2½ inches apart. Using your hands, gently press each dough ball to 1-inch thickness. Bake the cookies 12 minutes, rotate the sheets front to back and top to bottom, and then continue to bake until the cookies are medium brown and the edges have begun to set but the centers are still soft (the cookies will seem underdone and will appear raw, wet, and shiny in the cracks), 8 to 10 minutes longer. Do not overbake.

5. Cool the cookies on the baking sheets on a wire rack 5 minutes; using a wide metal spatula, transfer the cookies to the wire rack and cool to room temperature.

GETTING IT RIGHT: Loading Up the Flavor

The best oatmeal cookies contain a mix of chocolate, nuts, and fruit. Here's how to make the most of each ingredient and get the right balance of flavors.

Chocolate

Irregular, hand-chopped chunks are better than chips. Use bittersweet chocolate to reduce overall sweetness.

Nuts

Pecans are our top choice, followed by walnuts. Toast the nuts in a 350-degree oven for about 8 minutes to maximize their flavor.

Dried Fruit

Choose something tart, such as cherries or cranberries, and chop it coarse.

SCIENCE DESK: Convection Ovens

IN ADDITION TO THE USUAL BAKE AND BROIL, MANY new ovens now offer convection settings. Wondering when and how to use the convection option, we decided to make a dozen of our recipes in the test kitchen's Wolf and KitchenAid ovens using both the convection setting and the regular bake setting.

How does a convection oven work? A built-in fan circulates the hot air, which helps to maintain a constant temperature and eliminate hot spots. This should translate to even browning and faster cooking because the hot air fully engulfs the food and conveys the heat more efficiently than it does in a standard oven, where the hot air does not circulate.

Most ovens with a convection feature are equipped with at least two convection settings: convect-bake and convect-roast. In the former, a majority of the heat is generated from the lower heating element to mitigate surface browning. In the latter, heat is generated from both the upper and lower heating elements to promote the surface browning desired in most roasted preparations. In our tests,

If you want cookies that are chewy in the middle, take them out of the oven before they look done. Trust us—the cookies will set up as they cool.

Properly Baked
When the cookies are set but the dough in the cracks still looks wet, take them out of the oven. Once cooled, the cookies will bend, not snap.

Baked Too Long
Cookies that look matte (rather than shiny) have been overbaked. Once cooled, their texture will be crumbly and dry.

we used the convection setting appropriate for the preparation and in some cases tested both. Manufacturers recommend reducing the oven temperature by 25 to 50 degrees when using a convection setting, and we incorporated these temperature adjustments into our tests. The following is a review of our findings.

Cakes We found no advantage to baking yellow layer cakes on the convect-bake setting. In the convection mode, the cakes required a 25-degree temperature reduction to prevent the surfaces from becoming dry and leathery. This temperature adjustment slowed baking by several minutes, with no improvement in the cakes.

Cookies With the oven temperature reduced 25 degrees, cookies baked up nicely on the convect-bake setting, but the baking sheets still required top-to-bottom shuffling. (When

we lowered the temperature by 50 degrees and extended the baking time, we found that the cookies browned evenly without switching the position of the baking sheets. We are, however, hesitant to recommend a universal 50-degree temperature reduction when baking cookies on a convection setting. Attempt this at your own risk.) We found that cookies that are better baked one sheet at a time in a standard oven can be baked two sheets at a time on the convect-bake setting.

Roast Chicken Chickens roasted on the convect-roast setting were done 10 to 15 minutes ahead of those roasted in a standard oven, and the skins were darker and more evenly browned. Chickens roasted on the convect-bake setting also cooked faster, but they did not brown any better than in a standard oven. Stick with convect-roast. No temperature adjustment is necessary.

Yeasted Bread When we baked free-form rustic loaves on preheated baking stones, the convect-bake setting yielded a loaf with a slightly thicker, crispier crust. The loaves browned and rose on par with each other, indicating that no time and temperature adjustments are necessary.

Prebaked Tart Shell With the oven temperature reduced 25 degrees, tart shells lined with foil, filled with pie weights, and prebaked on the convect-bake setting browned a bit more quickly than tart shells baked on the standard bake setting. Once the foil and weights were removed and the shells returned to the oven, the bottom of the convection-baked tart shells browned better and more evenly.

To Summarize Convection settings do promote even browning and work well for preparations in which browning and crisp surfaces are desired. Temperature reduction is necessary for delicate and sugary baked goods such as cookies and tart shells but not for sturdier, more savory foods such as roast chicken and yeasted breads.

SCIENCE DESK: Why Brown Sugar Makes Chewy Cookies

WHEN WE SUBSTITUTED BROWN SUGAR FOR GRANULATED sugar in our cookie recipe, we expected a deeper flavor and color, but we were really surprised by the dramatic change in texture. The cookies went from dry and crunchy to soft and chewy. This isn't the first time we noticed this phenomenon in the test kitchen. We wondered why brown sugar is often the secret to chewier cookies.

Clearly, brown sugar contains more moisture than granulated (this is obvious to the touch), but most of this moisture burns off in the oven. We figured that something in the brown sugar itself must be responsible for making chewy cookies. As it turns out, that something is called invert sugar, which is all but absent in granulated sugar.

How does invert sugar work its magic? Invert sugar consists of glucose and fructose, two simple sugars. Invert sugar is especially hygroscopic, meaning that it pulls water from wherever it can be found, the best source being the air. And invert sugar keeps on drawing in moisture even after cookies have been baked, thus helping to keep them chewy as they cool. So when it comes to chew in cookies, regular granulated sugar—with its lack of invert sugar—is simply no competition for brown sugar.

TECHNIQUE: Individually Quick-Frozen Cookies

Freezing cookie dough in logs lets you cut off slices to make freshly baked cookies when the whim strikes, but some cooks find it difficult to slice through the frozen dough and choose instead to freeze the dough as follows.

1. Scoop out or roll individual balls of cookie dough and place them on a baking sheet lined with parchment or waxed paper. Place the cookie sheet in the freezer for an hour or two, until the dough balls are completely frozen.

2. Once the dough balls are frozen hard, transfer them to a zipper-lock bag for storage in the freezer. There is no need to defrost the dough balls before baking them; just increase the baking time by a minute or two.

HOLIDAY SPRITZ COOKIES

WHAT WE WANTED: Spritz cookies that really are as good as they look, rich with butter yet still delicate and crisp.

It's the peak of the festive holiday season, and you find yourself at yet another party, standing next to one more long buffet table. You spy a towering plate of cookies and instinctively reach for the golden-swirled kiss—only to discover a bland, gummy, stick-to-the-roof-of-your-mouth impostor. But this is not the way spritz cookies were meant to be. Scandinavian in origin, they are the most simple of butter cookies, their distinct design created by the pressing, or spritzing, of a very soft dough through a piping bag or a cookie press. Whichever tool is used, the shaping technique allows for an extremely buttery dough (a high-butter dough would be difficult to roll out), which translates into light, crisp cookies.

A victim of vanity to be sure, the spritz cookie has been subject to all manner of insult by recipe writers intent on finding shortcuts to a more shapely cookie. And the worst offenders have produced the most attractive cookies. Their crime? Using vegetable shortening in place of butter, which makes the cookies flavorless and waxy. Recipe writers who do use butter often add so many eggs (to keep the cookies from spreading in the oven) that the cookies bake up soft and chewy rather than light and crisp. Yet another tactic used to guarantee a shapely cookie is to add an excess of confectioners' sugar to the dough. The confectioners' sugar, which is laced with cornstarch, makes the cookies pasty.

The foundation for the spritz cookie is a dough that is soft enough to press or pipe yet sturdy enough to hold its shape in the oven. And it must be made with butter, and lots of it. Starting with a nice even two sticks of butter and ¾ cup granulated sugar, we found that we could add no more than 2 cups of flour before the dough got too stiff. From here, we tested the use of eggs, as many recipes varied in this regard. With no eggs, the cookies were like shortbread—buttery, but too tender and crumbly, with an ill-defined shape. One whole egg resulted in chewy, tough cookies. By adding only yolks, we got more tender cookies that also retained their shape. But even two yolks were too many, resulting in greasy, eggy-tasting cookies; just one yolk made them tender, crisp, and sturdy.

But a mere yolk did not contribute enough liquid to make a smooth, workable dough. Adding more butter didn't solve the problem, so we turned to dairy, trying milk, half-and-half, and heavy cream. Each improved the texture of the dough, but the milk and half-and-half caused the cookies to spread in the oven. The cookies made with heavy cream—just 1 tablespoon—not only held their shape but were also the most flavorful.

Fearing that we might be missing out on some helpful (rather than harmful) innovation happened upon by another baker, we tested some additional ingredients. We added baking powder, presumably for a lighter, airier texture; instead, the dramatic rise and puff in the oven obliterated the precise "spritz" shape we were after. As for flour, the softer, more finely milled cake flour resulted in a cookie that was tender to the point of being pasty. A similar result ensued when we added a small amount of cornstarch to all-purpose flour, a common technique for tenderizing baked goods. Superfine sugar, a finer version of granulated sugar, gave the cookies a tighter crumb, something sought after in cookies that are rolled flat and cut out but not in a spritz cookie. Granulated was still the sugar of choice, but a few tasters complained that the cookies were too sweet. Reducing the sugar to ⅔ cup tamed the sweetness and brought the butter flavor to the foreground. We were now satisfied that these cookies needed no secret ingredient; all they needed were a few simple ingredients gathered in the proper proportions.

The standard technique for mixing this dough involves creaming, or whipping the butter and sugar together until light and fluffy, before adding the other ingredients. The

large, sharp-edged crystals of granulated sugar allow pockets of air to be whipped into the butter, and these pockets expand in the heat of the oven, producing a light, crisp texture. Because these cookies contain no leavener and only one egg yolk, they rely on this action for their ethereal texture. Creaming is also essential for producing a dough light enough to easily press into cookies.

Most home bakers turn to a cookie press to shape spritz cookies. Professionals often use a pastry bag, which can be used for myriad baking and decorating tasks. A test of cookie presses did uncover a winner—the Wilton Comfort Grip Cookie Press (see page 323)—but an all-purpose pastry bag has its advantages. It allows for fancier shapes (stars, rosettes, and S shapes are generally beyond the reach of a press), and the bag also provides more control and freedom of motion. We prefer to use a pastry bag, but we've found that a good cookie press can offer convenience.

Oven temperature had a direct impact on the texture of the cookies. If it was too low, the cookies became dry and crisp all the way through. Too high and the outside crisped while the inside remained soft. Tasters preferred a slight variation in texture, which was perfectly achieved at the moderately high temperature of 375 degrees.

We concluded that great spritz cookies aren't so complicated after all. No shortcuts, no gimmicks—just simple ingredients and the right technique can make holiday dreams come true.

WHAT WE LEARNED: For a light, crisp, buttery cookie, keep the ingredient list simple. Just one egg yolk and a mere tablespoon of heavy cream provide enough liquid to make the dough workable, while reducing the amount of sugar slightly allows the buttery flavor to take center stage.

SPRITZ COOKIES

Makes about 6 dozen 1½-inch cookies

If using a pastry bag, use a star tip to create the various shapes. For stars, a ½- to ⅝-inch tip works best, but for rosettes and S shapes, use a ⅜-inch tip (measure the diameter of the tip at the smallest point). To create stars, hold the bag at a 90-degree angle to the baking sheet and pipe the dough straight down, as shown in illustration 3 on page 321; stars should be about 1 inch in diameter. To create rosettes, pipe the dough while moving the bag in a circular motion, ending at the center of the rosette; rosettes should be about 1¼ inches in diameter. To create S shapes, pipe the dough into compact S's; they should be about 2 inches long and 1 inch wide. If you make an error while piping, the dough can be scraped off the baking sheet and repiped.

We had the best results baking these cookies one sheet at a time. When reusing a baking sheet, make sure that it has completely cooled before forming more cookies on it. Unbaked dough can be refrigerated in an airtight container for up to 4 days; to use, let it stand at room temperature until softened, about 45 minutes. Baked cookies will keep for more than a week if stored in an airtight container or zipper-lock bag.

GETTING IT RIGHT: A Prettier Spritz

| Perfect | Puny |
| From a Pastry Bag | From a Press |

A traditional piping bag gives the baker more control over the size and shape of the cookies, providing for a more attractive result. A cookie press offers less control and makes small, squat cookies.

1	large egg yolk
1	tablespoon heavy cream
1	teaspoon vanilla extract
16	tablespoons (2 sticks) unsalted butter, softened but still cool
⅔	cup (about 4¾ ounces) sugar
¼	teaspoon salt
2	cups (10 ounces) unbleached all-purpose flour

1. Adjust an oven rack to the middle position; heat the oven to 375 degrees. In a small bowl, beat the egg yolk, cream, and vanilla with a fork until combined; set aside.

2. In a standing mixer, cream the butter, sugar, and salt at medium-high speed until light and fluffy, 3 to 4 minutes. Scrape down the bowl with a rubber spatula. With the mixer running at medium speed, add the yolk-cream mixture and beat until incorporated, about 30 seconds. Scrape down the bowl. With the mixer running at low speed, gradually beat in the flour until combined. Scrape down the bowl and give a final stir with the rubber spatula to ensure that no flour pockets remain.

3. If using a cookie press to form the cookies, follow the manufacturer's instructions to fill the press; if using a pastry bag (see note), follow illustrations 1 through 3 (at right) to fill the bag. Press or pipe cookies onto ungreased baking sheets, spacing them about 1½ inches apart. Bake, one sheet at a time, until the cookies are light golden brown, 10 to 12 minutes, rotating the baking sheet halfway through the baking time. Cool the cookies on the baking sheet until just warm, 10 to 15 minutes; using a metal spatula, transfer them to a wire rack and cool to room temperature.

VARIATIONS

SPRITZ COOKIES WITH LEMON ESSENCE

Follow the recipe for Spritz Cookies, adding 1 teaspoon lemon juice to the yolk-cream mixture in step 1 and adding 1 teaspoon finely grated lemon zest to the butter along with the sugar and salt in step 2.

ALMOND SPRITZ COOKIES

Grind ½ cup sliced almonds and 2 tablespoons of the flour called for in Spritz Cookies in a food processor until powdery and evenly fine, about 60 seconds; combine the almond mixture with the remaining flour. Follow the recipe for Spritz Cookies, substituting ¾ teaspoon almond extract for the vanilla.

TECHNIQUE: Filling a Pastry Bag

1. Make a C shape with one hand and hold the piping bag. Fold the bag over that hand about halfway down, insert the tip, and scrape the dough into the bag.

2. When the bag is about half full, pull up the sides, push down the dough, and twist tightly while again pushing down on the dough to squeeze out any air.

3. Grab the bag at the base of the twist. Using the other hand as a guide, hold the top at a 90-degree angle about ½ inch above the baking sheet and squeeze to form the shape.

EQUIPMENT CORNER: Cookie Presses

FOR THOSE OF US LACKING A STEADY HAND OR EXPERIENCE with a pastry bag, a cookie press would seem indispensable for making attractive spritz cookies. These inexpensive tools promise to produce consistently shaped cookies in record time. We tested six models to see if they lived up to their claims.

Old-fashioned cookie presses rely on a screw-driven plunger to press the dough through cut dies, resulting in dozens of possible shapes. In our tests, these presses were awkward to use, especially with buttery hands. The one electric press we tested was even worse. The production of uniform cookies depended on split-second timing; hold down that power button too long or release it too soon—by what seemed like a millisecond—and you ended up with a cookie swollen to unrecognizable proportions or one so puny it was destined to burn.

A third style of cookie press relies on a triggered, ratcheting mechanism. One click of the ratchet yields a perfect cookie every time. Our favorite press of this kind, the Wilton Comfort Grip Cookie Press, was nearly goofproof and allowed us to make dozens of cookies in just minutes. This sort of press does have its limitations, however. Its one-cookie-at-a-time design restricts it to "drop" cookies. It is extremely difficult to produce an elongated cookie, for example, with this sort of press. Even for a novice baker, a pastry bag is better suited for making fancier shapes. But it's hard to argue with the convenience of a good cookie press, especially if volume and uniformity are your main concerns.

Rating Cookie Presses

WE TESTED SIX COOKIE PRESSES FOR CONSISTENCY (ABILITY TO PRODUCE COOKIES OF UNIFORM SIZE), comfort, and efficiency. The presses are listed in order of preference. See www.americastestkitchen.com for up-to-date prices and mail-order sources for top-rated products.

RECOMMENDED

Wilton Comfort Grip Cookie Press 2104-4011 (Trigger)

$12.99

This press was quick, efficient, and easy to use. Also, the least expensive of the bunch. But it can only produce a limited number of shapes.

RECOMMENDED WITH RESERVATIONS

Williams-Sonoma Cookie Press (Trigger)

$24

The trigger action on this press was slightly stiff and the handle less comfortable than other trigger models. Cookies appeared slightly bloated, without crisp definition.

RECOMMENDED WITH RESERVATIONS

Wilton Cookie Max Cookie Press (Pump action)

$14.99

Testers found this pump action press to be awkward to use, in part because it required two hands.

RECOMMENDED WITH RESERVATIONS

Kuhn Rikon Clear Barrel Cookie Press and Decorating Set (Trigger)

$15.99

This press had the stiffest, most slippery trigger of all the trigger models, and cookies were bloated in some shapes.

NOT RECOMMENDED

Mirro Cookie Pastry Set (Twist action plunger)

$21.95

Testers found the twist action plunger on this model especially awkward to use, particularly when hands become slippery or sticky from the buttery dough.

NOT RECOMMENDED

Salton Electric Cookie Press (Electric)

$24.99

The power button on this electric model was overly sensitive. A fraction of a second too little or too long on the button and cookies came out misshapen and mis-sized.

A cake stand makes it easier for Bridget to accurately place the second layer of cake over the filling.

OLD-FASHIONED
CHAPTER 25
birthday cake

IN THIS CHAPTER

THE RECIPES

Classic White Layer Cake with
Butter Frosting and Raspberry-
Almond Filling

EQUIPMENT CORNER

Measuring Spoons

TASTING LAB

Raspberry Preserves

Remember how your birthday cake always brought a smile to your face when you were a kid? An entire dessert was baked, assembled, and frosted in honor of you. If you were lucky, you also had a hand in choosing the flavor of the cake—and the frosting. It might seem a small pleasure, but it was one that could be counted on once a year, every year. But for adults, this tradition seems to have fallen by the wayside, which just doesn't seem right. After all, everyone deserves a cake baked in his or her honor at least once a year.

In this chapter, we aim to resurrect the traditional birthday cake. No tiramisù takeoffs or cupcake shortcuts need apply. We've developed an honest-to-goodness layer cake with an old-fashioned jam filling and real butter frosting—the type of cake guaranteed to put a smile on anyone's face.

OLD-FASHIONED BIRTHDAY CAKE

WHAT WE WANTED: The ultimate birthday dessert—layers of white cake with an exceptionally fine crumb, accented by a not-too-sweet fruit jam filling and old-fashioned butter frosting.

White layer cake has been a classic birthday cake for more than a hundred years. The cake's snowy white interior is stunning against the pale frostings with which it is so often paired. When we think birthday cake, this is it.

White cake is simply a basic butter cake made with egg whites instead of whole eggs. The lack of yolks produces the characteristic color, and they also make the cake soft and fine grained, a bit like pound cake but much lighter and more delicate. Unfortunately, the white cakes we have baked over the years, although good enough, always fell short of our high expectations. They came out a little dry and chewy—one might say cottony—and we noticed that they were riddled with tunnels and small holes. What was going wrong?

Early on, we suspected the mixing method might be to blame. We had always mixed white cakes according to standard cookbook procedure; that is, we had creamed the butter and sugar, added the flour and milk alternately, and finally folded in stiffly beaten egg whites. Because this mixing method brings the flour into direct contact with liquid, it encourages the flour to form the elastic protein gluten. When beaten, gluten forms a stretchy net of rope-like fibers that not only make the cake tough but also press the air cells together into holes and tunnels. Cookbook recipes generally recommend deft, gentle handling of the batter to minimize gluten development, but it seemed that no matter how little we beat or how delicately we folded, the cakes did not improve.

In trying to avoid an "overglutenized" cake batter with other cakes, we ordinarily use the so-called two-stage mixing method. This method entails creaming the flour, butter, and sugar together (rather than just the butter and sugar) before adding the eggs and other liquid ingredients. Because the flour is mixed with butter at the start, it is partially waterproofed and thus less prone to develop gluten. In the case of white cake, however, we could not bring ourselves to try this method because it uses unbeaten eggs, and every traditional recipe for white cake calls for stiffly beaten egg whites folded into the batter at the end. Surely the cake's special texture depended on beating the whites first, we thought. So we stuck with the creaming method and tried to improve the results by fiddling with the proportions. Into the garbage went a dozen cakes.

Luckily, we happened upon a recipe called Old-Fashioned White Cake in the 1943 edition of the *Joy of Cooking* (Scribner). The recipe called for working the butter into the flour with one's fingertips, as when making piecrust, and then whisking in beaten egg whites. We were intrigued—here was a two-stage white cake, but with the beaten egg whites we thought were necessary. Upon testing, the cake indeed proved to be more tender than the others we had made, and it also had a finer crumb. After a few more experiments, we eventually arrived at a white cake that we thought very good but, alas, still not quite perfect. There were still those holes.

We were stumped and might have stayed stumped if we had not been paying particularly close attention one day while we were folding egg whites into a soufflé batter. As the rubber spatula drew the egg whites up from the bottom of the bowl and over the top of the batter, we noticed how coarse and bubbly the whites were, even though they were not overbeaten and had seemed perfectly smooth and thick when taken from the mixer just moments before. Could it be that beaten egg whites, instead of promoting an ethereal texture in white cakes, actually formed large air pockets and caused those unsightly holes?

We tried the "old-fashioned" recipe again, only this time we simply mixed the egg whites with the milk before

beating them into the flour and butter mixture. The results were fantastic. The cake was not only fine-grained and without holes but, to our surprise, also larger and lighter than the ones we'd prepared with beaten whites. And the method couldn't be simpler, quicker, or more nearly failure-proof. The two-stage method had proved, after all, to be the way to go.

Of course, we were curious to know the reason for this surprising outcome, so we did some boning up on egg whites. Apparently, beating has something of the same effect on egg whites that cooking does. Both beating and heating cause some of the individual protein strands to uncoil, whereupon they bump into each other and start linking up into an increasingly tight, dense web. It is this linking process that causes cooked whites to coagulate and beaten whites to stiffen. The problem, then, with putting beaten egg whites into a batter is that the whites have, in this respect, already been partially cooked. Because of this, the whites do not mix well with the rest of the batter and tend instead to create large air pockets when the cake bakes. Unbeaten egg whites, on the other hand, mix easily with the rest of the ingredients. When, during baking, they set and stiffen, they provide the structure necessary to hold the fine air bubbles beaten into the batter by creaming. The result is a wonderfully velvety cake, perfect for that birthday person.

WHAT WE LEARNED: Mix the flour and butter together to minimize gluten development. Mix unbeaten whites into the batter rather than folding in beaten whites; this technique guarantees a fine-grained cake without unsightly holes.

CLASSIC WHITE LAYER CAKE WITH BUTTER FROSTING AND RASPBERRY-ALMOND FILLING

Serves 12

If you have forgotten to bring the milk and egg white mixture to room temperature, set the bottom of the measuring cup containing it in a pan of hot water and stir until the mixture feels cool rather than cold, around 65 degrees. The cake layers can be wrapped in plastic wrap and stored for 1 day; the frosting can be covered with plastic wrap and set aside at room temperature for several hours. Once assembled, the cake should be covered with an inverted bowl or cake cover and refrigerated. Under its coat of frosting, it will remain fresh for up to 3 days. Bring it to room temperature before serving. There will be enough frosting left to pipe a border around the base and top of the cake; to decorate the cake more elaborately, you should make 1½ times the frosting recipe. If desired, finish the sides of the cake with 1 cup of sliced almonds.

classic white cake

2¼	cups (9 ounces) plain cake flour plus more for dusting the pans
1	cup milk, at room temperature
6	large egg whites, at room temperature
2	teaspoons almond extract
1	teaspoon vanilla extract
1¾	cups (12¼ ounces) granulated sugar
4	teaspoons baking powder
1	teaspoon salt
12	tablespoons (1½ sticks) unsalted butter, softened but still cool

butter frosting

16	tablespoons (2 sticks) unsalted butter, softened but still cool
4	cups (1 pound) confectioners' sugar
1	tablespoon vanilla extract
1	tablespoon milk
	Pinch salt

raspberry–almond filling

½   cup blanched slivered almonds, toasted and
    chopped coarse
⅓   cup seedless raspberry jam

1. FOR THE CAKE: Adjust an oven rack to the middle position and heat the oven to 350 degrees. Spray two 9-inch round cake pans with nonstick cooking spray; line the bottoms with parchment or waxed paper rounds. Spray the paper rounds, dust the pans with flour, and knock out the excess.

2. Pour the milk, egg whites, and extracts into a 2-cup liquid measuring cup and mix with a fork until blended.

3. Mix the flour, granulated sugar, baking powder, and salt in the bowl of a standing mixer set at low speed. Add the butter; continue beating at low speed until the mixture resembles moist crumbs, with no powdery streaks remaining.

4. Add all but ½ cup of the milk mixture to the crumbs and beat at medium speed for 1½ minutes. Add the remaining ½ cup of the milk mixture and beat 30 seconds more. Stop the mixer and scrape the sides of the bowl with a rubber spatula. Return the mixer to medium (or high) speed and beat 20 seconds longer.

5. Divide the batter evenly between the prepared cake pans; using a rubber spatula, spread the batter to the pan walls and smooth the tops. Place the pans 3 inches from the oven walls and 3 inches apart. (If your oven is small, place the pans on separate racks in staggered fashion to allow for air circulation.) Bake until a toothpick or thin skewer inserted in the center of the cakes comes out clean, 23 to 25 minutes.

6. Let the cakes rest in the pans for 3 minutes. Loosen from the sides of the pans with a knife, if necessary, and invert onto wire racks. Reinvert onto additional wire racks. Let cool completely, about 1½ hours.

7. FOR THE FROSTING: Beat the butter, confectioners' sugar, vanilla, milk, and salt in the bowl of a standing mixer at low speed until the sugar is moistened. Increase the speed to medium-high; beat, stopping twice to scrape down the bowl, until creamy and fluffy, about 1½ minutes. Avoid overbeating or the frosting will be too soft to pipe.

8. FOR THE FILLING: Before assembling the cake, set aside ¾ cup of the frosting for decoration. Spread a small dab of frosting in the center of the cake plate to anchor the cake and set down one cake layer. Combine ½ cup of the remaining frosting with the almonds in a small bowl and spread over the first layer. Carefully spread the jam on top, then cover with the second cake layer. Spread the frosting over the top and sides of the cake. Pipe the reserved frosting around the perimeter of the cake at the base and the top. Cut the cake into slices and serve.

EQUIPMENT CORNER: Measuring Spoons

EVEN COOKS WHO CAN'T BE BOTHERED TO PULL OUT a measuring spoon for stovetop recipes know that such cavalier imprecision (read: eyeballing) won't cut it when baking. But which brand is best? We brought seven different models of spoons into the kitchen to find out.

The first factor to consider was accuracy. According to the National Institute of Standards and Technology's Office of Weights and Measures, one teaspoon of water should weigh exactly 14.742 grams. After filling seven spoons to level, then carefully weighing the contents, we concluded that every brand was sufficiently accurate (within a gram or two).

We decided that design would have to be the primary factor in determining a winner. Is the handle easy to hold? Is the bowl deep enough to accommodate liquids with minimal chance of spilling? We knew from plenty of kitchen experience to avoid the really shallow, old-fashioned spoons, like our grandmothers had. (Shallow spoons pose a higher risk of spillage than deep spoons.)

Is the shape such that it can be dipped into short jars as well as tall, narrow spice jars to scoop up contents? We measured dry ingredients by scooping a heaping spoonful, then sweeping it to level (a method we call "dip and sweep"). This was easy enough if the bowl and handle met in a smooth joint; less so if the bowl had a raised lip. Fat spoons, spoons with short handles, overly bulky spoons, and spoons with raised handles also made this task difficult.

So where did we end up? The sturdy Cuisipro spoons feature an elongated, oval shape that proved optimal for scooping ingredients from narrow jars. In addition, the ends of the handles curl down, putting them level with the spoon's base and thereby allowing a full measure to be set down on the counter with no tipping and no mess. Perfection is in the details.

Rating Measuring Spoons

WE TESTED SEVEN TYPES OF MEASURING SPOONS AND rated them for accuracy, design, and bowl shape. The spoons are listed in order of preference. See www.americastestkitchen.com for up-to-date prices and mail-order sources for top-rated products.

HIGHLY RECOMMENDED
Cuisipro Measuring Spoons $10.95
Has all the right features. The oval shape makes for easy scooping from tall, narrow jars, the bowls are nice and deep, and the clever design—a bend at the end of the handle—allows the spoon to sit upright on its own. They also come in a set of odd sizes.

RECOMMENDED WITH RESERVATIONS
Oxo Good Grips Stainless Steel Measuring Spoons $9.99
Neon markings are easy to read, but the set fails to include a ⅛ teaspoon measure.

RECOMMENDED WITH RESERVATIONS
Amco Spice Spoons "Rectangle Spoons" $9.99
Testers were not fond of the shallow bowls. The name implies that these spoons will fit into spice jars, but the tablespoon does not fit into a short spice jar.

NOT RECOMMENDED
Amco Basic Ingredients $4.99
The raised handle on these spoons complicates a clean sweep.

NOT RECOMMENDED
KitchenArt Adjust-A-Spoon $5.99
This spoon is too bulky to fit in many containers, and the adjustable slide gets in the way of a clean sweep.

NOT RECOMMENDED
Oggi Corporation Spoons $14.99
These spoons have a strange design with difficult-to-grasp stubby handles.

NOT RECOMMENDED
Pyrex Accessories Measuring Spoons $2.99
The thick, blunt edges of these spoons made it difficult to scoop up some ingredients in our tests.

TECHNIQUE: Keeping Track of Bakeware Sizes

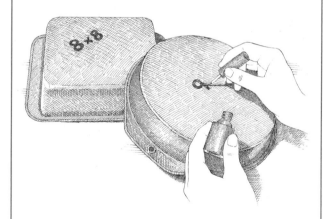

With manufacturers' indication of size on baking pans being either illegible or nonexistent, it's helpful to take matters into your own hands and use ovensafe metal paint (available at hardware stores) to mark pan bottoms, noting dimensions or capacity.

JELLIES, JAMS, PRESERVES, AND FRUIT SPREADS TAKE UP the majority of a supermarket aisle, and there is probably a jar in the door of your fridge. Does it matter what kind of raspberry preserves you buy? Jam or fruit spread? Seedless? We gathered nine brands to find out.

In supermarkets, raspberry jelly has been almost completely replaced by fruit spreads (made with juice concentrates, usually pear and white grape). These lack strong, recognizable raspberry flavor and are one-dimensionally sweet. Based on our tasting, only jam or preserves will do. The difference between these two is small; preserves contain large fruit chunks while the fruit in jam should be formless. Both are great for our layer cake (or toast) and survive the oven well. The flavor should be undeniably raspberry without too much acidic tartness or cloying sweetness. Seedless versions came across as artificial and overprocessed.

So what did our tasters like? Smucker's Red Raspberry Preserves fit the bill on all accounts, with the more viscous and seedier Trappist Red Raspberry Jam a close second.

Rating Raspberry Preserves

FIFTEEN MEMBERS OF THE AMERICA'S TEST KITCHEN STAFF TASTED NINE PRESERVES STRAIGHT FROM THEIR JARS. The preserves are listed in order of preference based on their scores in this tasting. All brands are available in supermarkets nationwide.

RECOMMENDED
Smucker's Red Raspberry Preserves
$2.99 for 18 ounces

The best of the bunch was preferred in raspberry bars and on toast. "Classic, clean" flavor with an appropriate amount of seeds is, as one taster noted, "exactly what this should be."

RECOMMENDED
Trappist Red Raspberry Jam
$3.49 for 12 ounces

Flavor-wise, this jam was very similar to our favorite, but a few "too thick" or "too seedy" comments knocked it down from a first-place tie.

RECOMMENDED WITH RESERVATIONS
American Spoon Foods Red Raspberry Preserves
$6.95 for 9.5 ounces

These very thick, reduced preserves are on the tart side, and tasters loved or hated the flavor, calling it either "deep and complex" or "burnt." All agreed the "seedy" texture is a problem. Not kid friendly.

RECOMMENDED WITH RESERVATIONS
Bonne Maman Raspberry Preserves
$3.29 for 13 ounces

For those with a sweet tooth. Tasters deemed this entry "more spreadable" (not as thick) than higher-rated preserves, but some felt that the "tooth-achingly sweet" flavor hid the raspberries.

RECOMMENDED WITH RESERVATIONS
Smucker's Seedless Red Raspberry Jam
$2.69 for 18 ounces

The favorite seedless option is a smoother, sweeter version of our winner. But even self-proclaimed "seed haters" wanted a few seeds to "add authenticity."

NOT RECOMMENDED
American Spoon Foods Red Raspberry Spoon Fruit
$6.95 for 9 ounces

No added sugar (just white grape juice concentrate) made for a very tart spread that seemed "healthy" and "natural." But the fruit-butter-like spread was too thick for many tasters and had enough seeds and fiber to warrant a "can I have some jam with my seeds?" comment.

NOT RECOMMENDED
Dickinson's Pure Seedless Cascade Mountain Red Raspberry Preserves
$4.29 for 10 ounces

Tasters like a few seeds and a good hit of raspberry; this had neither. Its smooth texture and "generic berry flavor" didn't do much for us.

NOT RECOMMENDED
Polaner Raspberry All-Fruit Spreadable Fruit
$1.79 for 10 ounces

This entry reminded tasters of apples, strawberries, and grapes, but not raspberry (the first ingredients are pear and grape juice concentrates). Its "Jell-O-like texture" didn't help.

NOT RECOMMENDED
Cascadian Farm Organic Raspberry Fruit Spread
$3.99 for 17 ounces

This spread's bright red color is attractive, but its texture is "weepy" and watery. A dead ringer for strawberry-flavored jam. "Someone forgot the raspberries?"

Fish *(cont.)*

   flipping, 166

   halibut steaks

      Pan-Roasted, 156–57, *233*

      serving, 158

      trimming cartilage from, 156

      types of, 157

   Meunière with Browned Butter and
      Lemon, *128,* 164–66

      with Capers, 167

      with Toasted Slivered Almonds,
         167

   tuna steaks

      cooking and slicing, 150

      Pan-Seared Pepper-Crusted, 150

      Pan-Seared Sesame-Crusted,
         131, 148–50

      pan-searing, best varieties for, 151

      shapes of, 150

Flavor injectors, 116

Flours, types of, 228

Fontina

   Broccoli Rabe, and Sun-Dried
      Tomatoes, Frittata with, 7

   Grilled Tomato and Cheese Pizzas
      for a Charcoal Grill, 222–26, *229*

   Grilled Tomato and Cheese Pizzas
      for a Gas Grill, 226

**Food processors, mini, ratings of,
   198–99**

Food processors, ratings of, 293–95

Food storage bags, ratings of, 81–83

Fraisage, effect of, 291

Frittatas, 4–7

   Asparagus, Ham, and Gruyère, 5–6,
      118

   Bacon, Potato, and Cheddar, 6–7

   with Broccoli Rabe, Sun-Dried
      Tomatoes, and Fontina, 7

   Leek, Prosciutto, and Goat Cheese,
      6

Fruit

   dried, for oatmeal cookies, 316

   Sangria, 218–19

   Summer, Tart, Free-Form, *243,*
      289–92

   Summer, Tartlets, Free-Form, 292–93

   see also specific fruits

Fryers, electric, ratings of, 205–6

G

Garlic

   Garlicky Lime Sauce with Cilantro,
      145

   Oil, Spicy, 226

   -Rosemary Smashed Potatoes, 93

   Toasted, and Parmesan, Pan-
      Roasted Asparagus with, 104, *234*

Gas grills, indirect cooking on, 263

Giblet Pan Gravy for a Crowd, 110–11

**Gingered Biscuits, Blueberry Cobbler
   with, 288**

Ginger-Soy Sauce with Scallions, 150

Goat cheese

   Leek, and Prosciutto Frittata, 6

   and Leek Quiche, 11

Graters, nutmeg, ratings of, 43

Gravy, Giblet Pan, for a Crowd, 110–11

Grilled dishes

   barbecued pulled chicken

      for a Charcoal Grill, *120,*
         274–77

      for a Crowd, 278

      for a Gas Grill, 278

   barbecued pulled pork

      on a Charcoal Grill, 260–63

      on a Gas Grill, 263

      with Mojo Sauce, Cuban-Style,
         264

   grilled tomato and cheese pizzas

      for a Charcoal Grill, 222–26,
         229

      for a Gas Grill, 226

   grill-roasted pork loin

      for a Charcoal Grill, *244,*
         246–48

      for a Gas Grill, 249

Grills, charcoal

   best charcoal for, 278–79

   indirect cooking on, 262

   lighting, 248, 249

Grills, gas, indirect cooking on, 263

Gruyère

   Asparagus, and Ham Frittata, 5–6,
      118

   Cubano Quesadillas, 20

   and Hard Salami, French Potato
      Salad with, 254

   Quiche Lorraine, 11

H

Halibut steaks

   Pan-Roasted, 156–57, *233*

   serving, 158

   trimming cartilage from, 156

   types of, 157

Ham

   Asparagus, and Gruyère Frittata,
      5–6, *118*

   and Asparagus Quiche, 11

   Cubano Quesadillas, 20

   Leek, Prosciutto, and Goat Cheese
      Frittata, 6

I

Ingredients

   beans, 32

   beef brisket, 87, 89–90

   beef chuck roasts, 183

   chicken legs, 276

   comal-roasted chiles, 37

   corn, for cornbread, 270

   corn tortillas, 34

   Cotija cheese, 37

   crema Mexicana, 37

   epazote, 37

   flatfish fillets, 167

   flour types, 228

   halibut steaks, 157

   jalapeño chiles, 18

   mustard, 254

   for oatmeal cookies, 316

   pork chops, 136, 137

   tuna steaks, 151

   see also Tastings; Techniques

J

Jalapeño(s)

   -Cheddar Cornbread, Spicy, 270

   Green Curry Paste, 193–94

   heat levels in, 18

   Red Curry Paste, 195–96

Jambalaya, Skillet, 67–68

K

Kitchen twine, ratings of, 250–51

Knives
chef's, ratings of, 32–33
electric, ratings of, 90

L

Lamb
Indian Curry, 186–88
resting before carving, 145
Lasagna, Skillet, 62–63, *119*
with Sausage and Peppers, 63
Leek(s)
and Chives, Buttermilk Mashed
Potatoes with, 57
cleaning, 57
and Goat Cheese Quiche, 11
Prosciutto, and Goat Cheese
Frittata, 6
and Tarragon, Chicken and
Dumplings with, 74
Lemon Essence, Spritz Cookies with,
321
Lemon grass, mincing, 194
Lifting racks, 116
Lime Sauce, Garlicky, with Cilantro,
145
Liquid measuring cups, ratings of,
265–67

M

Macadamia, Banana, and Coconut
Filling, German Chocolate Cake
with, 337
Main dishes
Asparagus, Ham, and Gruyère
Frittata, 4–6
Bacon, Potato, and Cheddar, 6–7
with Broccoli Rabe, Sun-Dried
Tomatoes, and Fontina, 7
Leek, Prosciutto, and Goat
Cheese, 6
barbecued pulled chicken
for a Charcoal Grill, *120,* 274–77
for a Crowd, 278
for a Gas Grill, 278
barbecued pulled pork
on a Charcoal Grill, 260–63
on a Gas Grill, 263

Main dishes *(cont.)*
with Mojo Sauce, Cuban-Style,
264
Beef Braised in Barolo, *127,* 180–82
Beef Tacos, 22–25, *231*
Butternut Squash Risotto, 44–47,
124
with Spinach and Toasted Pine
Nuts, 47
Chicken and Dumplings, 72–74
with Leeks and Tarragon, 74
Chicken Teriyaki, *125,* 207–9
Crisp-Skin High-Roast Butterflied
Chicken with Potatoes, 96–98
curry
Beef, with Crushed Spices and
Channa Dal, 189
Indian, 186–88
Thai Green, with Chicken,
Broccoli, and Mushrooms,
190–93
Thai Red, with Shrimp,
Pineapple, and Peanuts,
194–95
Fettuccine Alfredo, *121,* 176–77
Fish Meunière with Browned
Butter and Lemon, *128,* 164–66
with Capers, 167
with Toasted Slivered Almonds,
167
grilled tomato and cheese pizzas
for a Charcoal Grill, 222–26,
229
for a Gas Grill, 226
grill-roasted pork loin
for a Charcoal Grill, *244,* 246–48
for a Gas Grill, 249
Onion-Braised Beef Brisket, 86–89,
232
Orange-Flavored Chicken, *126,*
202–4
Paella, *122,* 212–15
in a Paella Pan, 216
Pan-Roasted Halibut Steaks,
156–57, *233*
Pan-Seared Inexpensive Steak,
50–53, *130*
Pan-Seared Oven-Roasted Pork
Tenderloins, *123,* 142–44

Main dishes *(cont.)*
Pan-Seared Scallops with Wilted
Spinach, Watercress, and Orange
Salad, 170–72
Pan-Seared Sesame-Crusted Tuna
Steaks, *131,* 148–50
Pepper-Crusted, 150
Pork Chops with Vinegar and
Sweet Peppers, *132,* 134–37
with Balsamic Vinegar, 137
Quesadillas, 19–21
Cheddar, Bacon, and Scallion, 20
Corn and Black Bean, with
Pepper Jack Cheese, 21
Cubano, 20
with Queso Fresco and
Roasted Peppers, 20
Quiche Lorraine, 10–11
Crabmeat, 11
Ham and Asparagus, 11
Leek and Goat Cheese, 11
Roast Turkey for a Crowd, 108–10,
117
Skillet Jambalaya, 67–68
Skillet Lasagna, 62–63, *119*
with Sausage and Peppers, 63
Marshmallow Topping, Toasted,
Candied Sweet Potato Casserole
with, 115
Measuring cups, liquid, ratings of,
265–67
Measuring spoons, ratings of, 329
Meat
resting before carving, 145
see also Beef; Lamb; Pork; Veal
Mitts, oven, ratings of, 158–61
Mojo Sauce, 264
Mushrooms, Chicken, and Broccoli,
Thai Green Curry with, 190–93
Mussels
Paella, *122,* 212–15
Paella in a Paella Pan, 216
Mustard
-Chili Spice Rub, 249
-Cream Pan Sauce, 54
Dijon, taste tests on, 255–57
fresh, buying, 254
-Garlic Butter with Thyme, 99
Sauce, Mid–South Carolina, 264

N

Nutmeg graters, ratings of, 43

Nuts
best, for oatmeal cookies, 316
French Potato Salad with Arugula, Roquefort, and Walnuts, 253
German Chocolate Cake with Banana, Macadamia, and Coconut Filling, 337
German Chocolate Cake with Coffee, Cashew, and Coconut Filling, 337
Pine, Toasted, and Spinach, Butternut Squash Risotto with, 47
Thai Red Curry with Shrimp, Pineapple, and Peanuts, 194–95
see also Almond(s); Pecan(s)

O

Oatmeal cookies
best flavorings for, 316
Chocolate-Chunk, with Pecans and Dried Cranberries, 239, 314–16
ensuring chewy texture, 317

Oil, frying, disposing of, 205

Olive oil
Spicy Garlic Oil, 226
taste tests on, 217

Onion-Braised Beef Brisket, 86–89, 232

Orange(s)
-Almond Vinaigrette, Warm, Pan-Roasted Asparagus with, 104
-Avocado Salsa, 150
cutting, 173
-Flavored Chicken, 126, 202–4
Mojo Sauce, 264
Sangria, 218–19
Wilted Spinach, and Watercress Salad, Pan-Seared Scallops with, 170–72

Oven mitts, ratings of, 158–61

P

Paella, 122, 212–15
in a Paella Pan, 216
pans, ratings of, 216

Pans
bottoms of, marking sizes of, 330

Pans (cont.)
cake, ratings of, 342–43
paella, ratings of, 216
roasting, 116

Parmesan
Fettuccine Alfredo, 121, 176–77
grilled tomato and cheese pizzas
for a Charcoal Grill, 222–26, 229
for a Gas Grill, 226
taste tests on, 178–79

Pasta
Fettuccine Alfredo, 121, 176–77
Skillet Lasagna, 62–63, 119
with Sausage and Peppers, 63

Pastry bags
filling, 321
shaping cookies with, 320

Pastry dough
Foolproof All-Butter Pie Pastry, 302–5
Pie Dough for Prebaked Pie Shell, 12–13
rolling and fitting, 12
smearing (fraisage), effect of, 291

Peanut Dressing, Spicy, Confetti Cabbage Salad with, 281–82

Peanuts, Pineapple, and Shrimp, Thai Red Curry with, 194–95

Pecan(s)
Candied Sweet Potato Casserole, 114–15
-Coconut Filling, German Chocolate Cake with, 240, 334–37
and Dried Cranberries, Chocolate-Chunk Oatmeal Cookies with, 239, 314–16
Sausage, and Apricots, Bread Stuffing with, 112

Peels, baking, ratings of, 227

Pepper-Crusted Tuna Steaks, Pan-Seared, 150

Pepper(s)
Red, and Cabbage Salad with Lime-Cumin Vinaigrette, 282–83
Roasted, and Queso Fresco, Quesadillas with, 20
and Sausage, Skillet Lasagna with, 63
Sweet, and Balsamic Vinegar, Pork Chops with, 137

Pepper(s) (cont.)
Sweet, and Vinegar, Pork Chops with, 132, 134–37
see also Chiles

Pie Dough
Foolproof All-Butter Pie Pastry, 302–5
for Prebaked Pie Shell, 12–13
rolling and fitting, 12

Pie(s)
apple
best apple types for, 300
Deep-Dish, 241, 298–301
decorative edges for, 13
double-crust, assembling, 304
pie weights, pennies used as, 13
see also Pie Dough; Quiche

Pineapple, Shrimp, and Peanuts, Thai Red Curry with, 194–95

Pine Nuts, Toasted, and Spinach, Butternut Squash Risotto with, 47

Pizzas
baking peels for, ratings of, 227
dough, judging rise in, 226
grilled
Tomato and Cheese, for a Charcoal Grill, 222–26, 229
Tomato and Cheese, for a Gas Grill, 226
troubleshooting, 225

Plastic wrap, ratings of, 270–71

Pork
barbecued pulled
on a Charcoal Grill, 260–63
on a Gas Grill, 263
key steps to, 261
with Mojo Sauce, Cuban-Style, 264
chops
with Balsamic Vinegar and Sweet Peppers, 137
browning, 138
buying, 136
cuts of, 137
with Vinegar and Sweet Peppers, 132, 134–37
loin
Grill-Roasted, for a Charcoal Grill, 244, 246–48

Pork (cont.)

    Grill-Roasted, for a Gas Grill,
       249

  resting before carving, 145

  Skillet Lasagna, 62–63, *119*

  tenderloins

    Pan-Seared Oven-Roasted,
      123, 142–44

    removing silver skin from,
      144

  see also Bacon; Ham; Sausage(s)

Potato(es)

  Bacon, and Cheddar Frittata, 6–7

  Crisp-Skin High-Roast Butterflied
    Chicken with, 96–98

  Mashed, Buttermilk, 55–57, *232*

    keeping warm, 92

    with Leeks and Chives, 57

    Ranch, 57

  Salad, French, 252–53

    with Arugula, Roquefort, and
      Walnuts, 253

    with Hard Salami and Gruyère,
      254

    with Radishes, Cornichons, and
      Capers, *235,* 254

  Smashed, 91–93, *123*

    with Bacon and Parsley, 93

    Garlic-Rosemary, 93

    keeping warm, 92

  Sweet, Casserole, Candied, 114–15

    with Toasted Marshmallow
      Topping, 115

Poultry. *See* Chicken; Turkey

Prosciutto, Leek, and Goat Cheese
  Frittata, 6

Q

Quesadillas, 19–21

  Cheddar, Bacon, and Scallion, 20

  Corn and Black Bean, with Pepper
    Jack Cheese, 21

  Cubano, 20

  quesadilla makers, ratings of, 21

  with Queso Fresco and Roasted
    Peppers, 20

Queso Fresco and Roasted Peppers,
  Quesadillas with, 20

Quiche Lorraine, 10–11

  Crabmeat, 11

  Ham and Asparagus, 11

  Leek and Goat Cheese, 11

R

Racks, lifting, 116

Racks, roasting (V-racks), 116

Radishes, Cornichons, and Capers,
  French Potato Salad with, *235,* 254

Raspberry

  -Almond Filling, Classic White
    Layer Cake with Butter Frosting
    and, 326–28

  preserves, taste tests on, 330–31

Rice

  Butternut Squash Risotto, 44–47,
    124

    with Spinach and Toasted Pine
      Nuts, 47

  Paella, *122,* 212–15

    in a Paella Pan, 216

  Skillet Jambalaya, 67–68

Risotto, Butternut Squash, 44–47, *124*

  with Spinach and Toasted Pine
    Nuts, 47

Roasting bags, 116

Roasting pans, 116

Roasting racks, grilling with, 278

Rolling pins, ratings of, 306–7

Roquefort, Arugula, and Walnuts,
  French Potato Salad with, 253

S

Salad

  cabbage

    Confetti, with Spicy Peanut
      Dressing, 281–82

    and Red Pepper, with Lime-
      Cumin Vinaigrette, 282–83

    Sweet-and-Sour, with Apple
      and Fennel, 283

  Potato, French, 252–53

    with Arugula, Roquefort, and
      Walnuts, 253

    with Hard Salami and Gruyère,
      254

Salad (cont.)

    with Radishes, Cornichons, and
      Capers, *235,* 254

  Wilted Spinach, Watercress, and
    Orange, Pan-Seared Scallops
    with, 170–72

Salami, Hard, and Gruyère, French
  Potato Salad with, 254

Salsas

  Avocado-Orange, 150

  Tomato, Fresh, 16–17

Sangria, 218–19

Sauces

  barbecue

    Eastern North Carolina, 263–64

    Mustard, Mid–South Carolina,
      264

    taste tests on, 279–80

  Chunky Cherry Tomato–Basil
    Vinaigrette, 158

  Ginger-Soy, with Scallions, 150

  Mojo, 264

  pan

    Banana-Date Chutney, 144–45

    Dried Cherry–Port, with
      Onions and Marmalade, 144

    Garlicky Lime, with Cilantro,
      145

    Giblet, Gravy for a Crowd,
      110–11

    Mustard-Cream, 54

    Tomato-Caper, 54

  salsa

    Avocado-Orange, 150

    Fresh Tomato, 16–17

  see also Butter(s)

Sauciers, ratings of, 57–59

Sausage(s)

  French Potato Salad with Hard
    Salami and Gruyère, 254

  Paella, *122,* 212–15

    in a Paella Pan, 216

  Pecans, and Apricots, Bread Stuffing
    with, 112

  and Peppers, Skillet Lasagna with, 63

  Skillet Jambalaya, 67–68

Scallops, Pan-Seared, with Wilted
  Spinach, Watercress, and Orange
  Salad, 170–72

Science desk
    beans, digestive effects of, 32
    brisket, cooking until tender, 89–90
    chewy cookies, best sugar for, 318
    convection ovens, 316–17
    grills, best charcoal for, 278–79
    jalapeños, heat levels in, 18
    meat, resting before carving, 145
Seafood. *See* Fish; Shellfish
Sesame-Crusted Tuna Steaks,
    Pan-Seared, *131,* 148–50
Shellfish
    Crabmeat Quiche, 11
    Indian Curry, 186–88
    Paella, *122,* 212–15
        in a Paella Pan, 216
    Pan-Seared Scallops with Wilted
        Spinach, Watercress, and Orange
        Salad, 170–72
    shrimp, deveining, 215
    Skillet Jambalaya, 67–68
    Thai Red Curry with Shrimp,
        Pineapple, and Peanuts, 194–95
Shrimp
    deveining, 215
    Indian Curry, 186–88
    Paella, *122,* 212–15
        in a Paella Pan, 216
    Pineapple, and Peanuts, Thai Red
        Curry with, 194–95
    Skillet Jambalaya, 67–68
Side dishes
    All-Purpose Cornbread, *237,*
        268–70
        Spicy Jalapeño-Cheddar, 270
    Boston Baked Beans, 79–81, *236*
    Buttermilk Mashed Potatoes, 55–57,
        232
        with Leeks and Chives, 57
        Ranch, 57
    cabbage salad
        Confetti, with Spicy Peanut
            Dressing, 281–82
        and Red Pepper, with Lime-
            Cumin Vinaigrette, 282–83
        Sweet-and-Sour, with Apple
            and Fennel, 283
    Candied Sweet Potato Casserole,
        114–15

Side dishes *(cont.)*
        with Toasted Marshmallow
            Topping, 115
    Classic Bread Stuffing with Sage
        and Thyme, 111–12
        with Bacon and Apples, 112
        with Sausage, Pecans, and
            Apricots, 112
    French Potato Salad, 252–53
        with Arugula, Roquefort, and
            Walnuts, 253
        with Hard Salami and Gruyère,
            254
        with Radishes, Cornichons, and
            Capers, *235,* 254
    Pan-Roasted Asparagus, 103–4
        with Toasted Garlic and
            Parmesan, 104, *234*
        with Warm Orange-Almond
            Vinaigrette, 104
    Smashed Potatoes, 91–93, *123*
        with Bacon and Parsley, 93
        Garlic-Rosemary, 93
Skillets, celebrity, ratings of, 69
Soup
    Black Bean, 28–31
        with Chipotle Chiles, 31
    Butternut Squash, 40–42
        with Cinnamon-Sugar
            Croutons, 42
        Curried, 42
    Tortilla, 34–37, *129*
Soy sauce
    Ginger-Soy Sauce with Scallions, 150
    taste tests on, 152–54
Spice(s)
    Dry Rub for Barbecue, 265
    Rub, Chili-Mustard, 249
    Rub, Sweet and Savory, 250
    storing, 31
Spinach
    and Toasted Pine Nuts, Butternut
        Squash Risotto with, 47
    Wilted, Watercress, and Orange Salad,
        Pan-Seared Scallops with, 170–72
Spritz Cookies, *238,* 319–21
    Almond, 321
    with Lemon Essence, 321
    shaping, with pastry bag, 320

Squash, butternut
    cutting up, 40
    dicing, 46
    Risotto, 44–47, *124*
        with Spinach and Toasted Pine
            Nuts, 47
    Soup, 40–42
        with Cinnamon-Sugar
            Croutons, 42
        Curried, 42
Stuffing, bread. *See* **Bread stuffing**
Sugar, brown, storing and measuring,
337
Sweet Potato Casserole, Candied,
114–15
    with Toasted Marshmallow Topping,
        115

T

Tacos, Beef, 22–25, *231*
Taco shells
    Home-Fried, 25
    preparing, 24
    store-bought, taste tests on, 25
Tarts
    dough for
        fraisage, effect of, 291
        mixing, 292
    Free-Form Summer Fruit, *243,*
        289–92
    Free-Form Summer Fruit Tartlets,
        292–93
Tastings
    bacon, supermarket, 7–9
    barbecue sauce, 279–80
    Barolo wine substitutes, 183
    beef steaks, inexpensive, 52
    butter alternatives, 167–69
    butters, premium, 308–10
    chicken, whole, 100–102
    chicken broths, supermarket, 76–78
    cocoa powders, 338–41
    coconut milk, 196–97
    cumin, 31
    Dijon mustard, 255–57
    olive oil, 217
    Parmesan cheese, 178–79
    raspberry preserves, 330–31

Tastings *(cont.)*

soy sauce, 152–54

stuffing, packaged, 112–13

taco shells, store-bought, 25

teriyaki sauce, store-bought, 209

tomatoes, canned diced, 64–66

tortillas, flour, 21

white wine vinegar, gourmet, 138

white wine vinegar, supermarket, 139–41

Techniques

avocado, pitting and dicing, 151

beef steaks, testing for doneness, 51

brown sugar, storing and measuring, 337

butternut squash, cutting up, 40

butternut squash, dicing, 46

cabbage, shredding, 281

charcoal grills, indirect cooking on, 262

chicken, butterflying, 99

chicken, shredding, 68

chicken breasts, cutting into strips, 193

chicken thighs, preparing, 208

cookie dough balls, freezing, 318

cutting boards, stabilizing, 100

double-crust pies, assembling, 304

dough rise, judging, 226

fennel, preparing, 283

fish fillets, flipping, 166

frying oil, disposing of, 205

gas grill, indirect cooking on, 263

halibut steaks, serving, 158

halibut steaks, trimming cartilage from, 156

leeks, cleaning, 57

lemon grass, mincing, 194

mashed potatoes, keeping warm, 92

oranges, cutting, 173

pan bottoms, marking sizes of, 330

pastry bags, filling, 321

pie crusts, decorative edges for, 13

pie dough, rolling and fitting, 12

Techniques *(cont.)*

pie weights, pennies used as, 13

pork silver skin, removing, 144

pulled pork, preparing, 261

shrimp, deveining, 215

spices, storing, 31

taco shells, preparing, 24

tomatoes, cutting for salsa, 18

Teriyaki sauce, taste tests on, 209

Thermometers

easy-read, about, 116

instant-read, about, 116

remote, ratings of, 105

Tomato(es)

canned diced, taste tests on, 64–66

-Caper Pan Sauce, 54

and cheese pizzas, grilled

for a Charcoal Grill, 222–26, *229*

for a Gas Grill, 226

Cherry, –Basil Vinaigrette, Chunky, 158

cutting, for salsa, 18

Salsa, Fresh, 16–17

Skillet Lasagna, 62–63, *119*

with Sausage and Peppers, 63

Sun-Dried, Broccoli Rabe, and Fontina, Frittata with, 7

Tortilla(s)

Beef Tacos, 22–25, *231*

corn, buying, 34

flour, taste tests on, 21

Quesadillas, 19–21

Soup, 34–37, *129*

Taco Shells, Home-Fried, 25

taco shells, preparing, 24

Tuna steaks

cooking and slicing, 150

Pan-Seared Pepper-Crusted, 150

Pan-Seared Sesame-Crusted, *131*, 148–50

pan-searing, best varieties for, 151

shapes of, 150

Turkey

gadgets, ratings of, 115–16

Giblet Pan Gravy for a Crowd, 110–11

Roast, for a Crowd, 108–10, *117*

Turkey forks, 116

Twine, kitchen, ratings of, 250–51

V

Veal

resting before carving, 145

Skillet Lasagna, 62–63, *119*

Vegetables

Indian Curry, 186–88

see also specific vegetables

Vinaigrette, Chunky Cherry Tomato–Basil, 158

Vinegar, white wine

gourmet, taste tests on, 138

supermarket, taste tests on, 139–41

V-racks, 116

W

Walnuts, Arugula, and Roquefort, French Potato Salad with, 253

Watercress, Spinach, and Orange Salad, Wilted, Pan-Seared Scallops with, 170–72

Wine

Barolo, substitutes for, 183

Beef Braised in Barolo, *127*, 180–82

Sangria, 218–19

wine saver devices, ratings of, 173

Z

Zipper-lock bags, ratings of, 81–83